Reinforcement Learning with TensorFlow

A beginner's guide to designing self-learning systems with TensorFlow and OpenAI Gym

Sayon Dutta

BIRMINGHAM - MUMBAI

Reinforcement Learning with TensorFlow

Commissioning Editor: Amey Varangaonkar
Acquisition Editor: Viraj Madhav
Content Development Editor: Aaryaman Singh, Varun Sony
Technical Editor: Dharmendra Yadav
Copy Editors: Safis Editing
Project Coordinator: Manthan Patel
Proofreader: Safis Editing
Indexer: Tejal Daruwale Soni
Graphics: Tania Dutta
Production Coordinator: Shantanu Zagade

First published: April 2018

Production reference: 1200418

Published by Packt Publishing Ltd.
Livery Place
35 Livery Street
Birmingham
B3 2PB, UK.

ISBN 978-1-78883-572-5

www.packtpub.com

`mapt.io`

Mapt is an online digital library that gives you full access to over 5,000 books and videos, as well as industry leading tools to help you plan your personal development and advance your career. For more information, please visit our website.

Why subscribe?

- Spend less time learning and more time coding with practical eBooks and Videos from over 4,000 industry professionals

- Improve your learning with Skill Plans built especially for you

- Get a free eBook or video every month

- Mapt is fully searchable

- Copy and paste, print, and bookmark content

PacktPub.com

Did you know that Packt offers eBook versions of every book published, with PDF and ePub files available? You can upgrade to the eBook version at `www.PacktPub.com` and as a print book customer, you are entitled to a discount on the eBook copy. Get in touch with us at `service@packtpub.com` for more details.

At `www.PacktPub.com`, you can also read a collection of free technical articles, sign up for a range of free newsletters, and receive exclusive discounts and offers on Packt books and eBooks.

Contributors

About the author

Sayon Dutta is an Artificial Intelligence researcher and developer. A graduate from IIT Kharagpur, he owns the software copyright for Mobile Irrigation Scheduler. At present, he is an AI engineer at Wissen Technology. He co-founded an AI startup Marax AI Inc., focused on AI-powered customer churn prediction. With over 2.5 years of experience in AI, he invests most of his time implementing AI research papers for industrial use cases, and weightlifting.

I would extend my gratitude to Maa and Baba for everything, especially for teaching me that life is all about hustle and the key to enjoyment is getting used to it; my brothers Arnav, Kedia, Rawat, Abhishek Singh, and Garg for helping me in my lowest times. Thanks to the Packt team, especially Viraj for reaching out, and Aaryaman and Varun for guiding me throughout. Thanks to the AI community and my readers.

About the reviewer

Narotam Singh has been in Indian Meteorological Department, Ministry of Earth Sciences, India, since 1996. He has been actively involved with various technical programs and training of officers of GoI in IT and communication. He did his PG in electronics in 1996, and Diploma and PG diploma in computer engineering in 1994 and 1997 respectively. He is working in the enigmatic field of neural networks, deep learning, and machine learning app development in iOS with Core ML.

Packt is searching for authors like you

If you're interested in becoming an author for Packt, please visit `authors.packtpub.com` and apply today. We have worked with thousands of developers and tech professionals, just like you, to help them share their insight with the global tech community. You can make a general application, apply for a specific hot topic that we are recruiting an author for, or submit your own idea.

Table of Contents

Preface

Reinforcement learning (RL) allows you to develop smart, quick, and self-learning systems in your business surroundings. It is an effective method to train your learning agents and solve a variety of problems in artificial intelligence—from games, self-driving cars, and robots to enterprise applications that range from data center energy saving (cooling data centers) to smart warehousing solutions.

The book covers the major advancements and successes achieved in deep reinforcement learning by synergizing deep neural network architectures with reinforcement learning. The book also introduces readers to the concept of Reinforcement Learning, its advantages and why it's gaining so much popularity. It discusses MDPs, Monte Carlo tree searches, policy and value iteration, temporal difference learning such as Q-learning, and SARSA. You will use TensorFlow and OpenAI Gym to build simple neural network models that learn from their own actions. You will also see how reinforcement learning algorithms play a role in games, image processing, and NLP.

By the end of this book, you will have a firm understanding of what reinforcement learning is and how to put your knowledge to practical use by leveraging the power of TensorFlow and OpenAI Gym.

Who this book is for

If you want to get started with reinforcement learning using TensorFlow in the most practical way, this book will be a useful resource. The book assumes prior knowledge of traditional machine learning and linear algebra, as well as some understanding of the TensorFlow framework. No previous experience of reinforcement learning and deep neural networks is required.

What this book covers

Chapter 1, *Deep Reinforcement – Architectures and Frameworks*, covers the relevant and common deep learning architectures, basics of logistic regression, neural networks, RNN, LSTMs, and CNNs. We also cover an overview of reinforcement learning, the various technologies, frameworks, tools, and techniques, along with what has been achieved so far, the future, and various interesting applications.

Chapter 2, *Training Reinforcement Learning Agents Using OpenAI Gym*, explains that OpenAI Gym is a toolkit for developing and comparing reinforcement learning algorithms. It supports teaching agents everything from walking to playing games such as Pong or Breakout. In this chapter, we learn how to use the OpenAI Gym framework to program interesting RL applications.

Chapter 3, *Markov Decision Process*, discusses the fundamental concepts behind reinforcement learning such as MDP, Bellman Value functions, POMDP, concepts of value iteration, reward's sequence, and training a reinforcement learning agent using value iteration in an MDP environment from OpenAI Gym.

Chapter 4, *Policy Gradients*, shows a way of implementing reinforcement learning systems by directly deriving the policies. Policy gradients are faster and can work in continuous state-action spaces. We cover the basics of policy gradient such as policy objective functions, temporal difference rule, policy gradients, and actor-critic algorithms. We learn to apply a policy gradient algorithm to train an agent to play the game of Pong.

Chapter 5, *Q-Learning and Deep Q-Networks*, explains that algorithms such as **State-Action-Reward-State-Action (SARSA)**, MCTS, and DQN have enabled a new era of RL, including AlphaGo. In this chapter, we take a look at the building blocks of Q-Learning and applying deep neural networks (such as CNNs) to create DQN. We also implement SARSA, Q-learning, and DQN to create agents to play the games of Mountain Car, Cartpole, and Atari Breakout.

Chapter 6, *Asynchronous Methods*, teaches asynchronous methods: asynchronous one-step Q-learning, asynchronous one-step SARSA, asynchronous n-step Q-learning, and **asynchronous advantage actor-critic (A3C)**. A3C is a state-of-the-art deep reinforcement learning framework. We also implement A3C to create a reinforcement learning agent.

Chapter 7, *Robo Everything – Real Strategy Gaming*, brings together the RL foundations, technologies, and frameworks together to develop RL pipelines and systems. We will also discuss the system-level strategies to make reinforcement learning problems easier to solve (shaping, curriculum learning, apprenticeship learning, building blocks, and multiconcepts).

Chapter 8, *AlphaGo – Reinforcement Learning at Its Best*, covers one of the most successful stories: the success of AI in playing and winning the game of Go against the world champion. In this chapter, we look at the algorithms, architectures, pipelines, hardware, training methodologies, and game strategies employed by AlphaGo.

Chapter 9, *Reinforcement Learning in Autonomous Driving*, illustrates one of the most interesting applications of RL, that is, autonomous driving. There are many use cases such as multi-lane merging and driving policies for negotiating roundabouts. We cover the challenges in autonomous driving and discuss proposed research-based solutions. We also introduce the famous MIT Deep Traffic simulator to test our reinforcement learning framework.

Chapter 10, *Financial Portfolio Management*, covers the application of RL techniques in the financial world. Many predict that AI will be the norm in asset management, trading desks, and portfolio management.

Chapter 11, *Reinforcement Learning in Robotics*, shows another interesting domain in which RL has found a lot of applications—robotics. The challenges of implementing RL in robotics and the probable solutions are covered.

Chapter 12, *Deep Reinforcement Learning in Ad Tech*, covers topics such as computational advertising challenges, bidding strategies, and real-time bidding by reinforcement learning in display advertising.

Chapter 13, *Reinforcement Learning in Image Processing*, is about the most famous domain in computer vision—object detection—and how reinforcement learning is trying to solve it.

Chapter 14, *Deep Reinforcement Learning in NLP* , illustrates the use of reinforcement learning in text summarization and question answering, which will give you a basic idea of how researchers are reaping the benefits of reinforcement learning in these domains.

Appendix A, *Further topics in Reinforcement Learning*, has an introductory overview of some of the topics that were out of the scope of this book. But we mention them in brief and end these topics with external links for you to explore them further.

To get the most out of this book

The following are the requirements to get the most out of this book:

- Python and TensorFlow
- Linear algebra as a prerequisite for neural networks
- Installation bundle: Python, TensorFlow, and OpenAI gym (shown in Chapter 1, *Deep Learning – Architectures and Frameworks* and Chapter 2, *Training Reinforcement Learning Agents Using OpenAI Gym*)

Download the example code files

You can download the example code files for this book from your account at
`www.packtpub.com`. If you purchased this book elsewhere, you can visit
`www.packtpub.com/support` and register to have the files emailed directly to you.

You can download the code files by following these steps:

1. Log in or register at `www.packtpub.com`.
2. Select the **SUPPORT** tab.
3. Click on **Code Downloads & Errata**.
4. Enter the name of the book in the **Search** box and follow the onscreen
   instructions.

Once the file is downloaded, please make sure that you unzip or extract the folder using the
latest version of:

- WinRAR/7-Zip for Windows
- Zipeg/iZip/UnRarX for Mac
- 7-Zip/PeaZip for Linux

The code bundle for the book is also hosted on GitHub at `https://github.com/
PacktPublishing/Reinforcement-Learning-with-TensorFlow`. In case there's an update to
the code, it will be updated on the existing GitHub repository.

We also have other code bundles from our rich catalog of books and videos available
at `https://github.com/PacktPublishing/`. Check them out!

Download the color images

We also provide a PDF file that has color images of the screenshots/diagrams used in this
book. You can download it here: `http://www.packtpub.com/sites/default/files/
downloads/ReinforcementLearningwithTensorFlow_ColorImages.pdf`.

Conventions used

There are a number of text conventions used throughout this book.

`CodeInText`: Indicates code words in text, database table names, folder names, filenames, file extensions, pathnames, dummy URLs, user input, and Twitter handles. Here is an example: "The `sigmoid(x)` and `relu(x)` refer to the functions performing sigmoid and ReLU activation calculations respectively."

A block of code is set as follows:

```
def discretization(env, obs):
    env_low = env.observation_space.low
    env_high = env.observation_space.high
```

Any command-line input or output is written as follows:

```
Episode 1 completed with total reward 8433.30289388 in 26839 steps
Episode 2 completed with total reward 3072.93369963 in 8811 steps
Episode 3 completed with total reward 1230.81734028 in 4395 steps
Episode 4 completed with total reward 2182.31111239 in 6629 steps
```

Bold: Indicates a new term, an important word, or words that you see onscreen. For example, words in menus or dialog boxes appear in the text like this. Here is an example: "Select **System info** from the **Administration** panel."

Warnings or important notes appear like this.

Tips and tricks appear like this.

Get in touch

Feedback from our readers is always welcome.

General feedback: Email `feedback@packtpub.com` and mention the book title in the subject of your message. If you have questions about any aspect of this book, please email us at `questions@packtpub.com`.

Errata: Although we have taken every care to ensure the accuracy of our content, mistakes do happen. If you have found a mistake in this book, we would be grateful if you would report this to us. Please visit `www.packtpub.com/submit-errata`, selecting your book, clicking on the Errata Submission Form link, and entering the details.

Piracy: If you come across any illegal copies of our works in any form on the Internet, we would be grateful if you would provide us with the location address or website name. Please contact us at `copyright@packtpub.com` with a link to the material.

If you are interested in becoming an author: If there is a topic that you have expertise in and you are interested in either writing or contributing to a book, please visit `authors.packtpub.com`.

Reviews

Please leave a review. Once you have read and used this book, why not leave a review on the site that you purchased it from? Potential readers can then see and use your unbiased opinion to make purchase decisions, we at Packt can understand what you think about our products, and our authors can see your feedback on their book. Thank you!

For more information about Packt, please visit `packtpub.com`.

Deep Learning – Architectures and Frameworks

Artificial neural networks are computational systems that provide us with important tools to solve challenging machine learning tasks, ranging from image recognition to speech translation. Recent breakthroughs, such as Google DeepMind's AlphaGo defeating the best Go players or Carnegie Mellon University's Libratus defeating the world's best professional poker players, have demonstrated the advancement in the algorithms; these algorithms learn a narrow intelligence like a human would and achieve superhuman-level performance. In plain speech, artificial neural networks are a loose representation of the human brain that we can program in a computer; to be precise, it's an approach inspired by our knowledge of the functions of the human brain. A key concept of neural networks is to create a representation space of the input data and then solve the problem in that space; that is, warping the data from its current state in such a way that it can be represented in a different state where it can solve the concerned problem statement (say, a classification or regression). Deep learning means multiple hidden representations, that is, a neural network with many layers to create more effective representations of the data. Each layer refines the information received from the previous one.

Reinforcement learning, on the other hand, is another wing of machine learning, which is a technique to learn any kind of activity that follows a sequence of actions. A reinforcement learning agent gathers the information from the environment and creates a representation of the states; it then performs an action that results in a new state and a reward (that is, quantifiable feedback from the environment telling us whether the action was good or bad). This phenomenon continues until the agent is able to improve the performance beyond a certain threshold, that is, maximizing the expected value of the rewards. At each step, these actions can be chosen randomly, can be fixed, or can be supervised using a neural network. The supervision of predicting action using a deep neural network opens a new domain, called **deep reinforcement learning**. This forms the base of AlphaGo, Libratus, and many other breakthrough research in the field of artificial intelligence.

We will cover the following topics in this chapter:

- Deep learning
- Reinforcement learning
- Introduction to TensorFlow and OpenAI Gym
- The influential researchers and projects in reinforcement learning

Deep learning

Deep learning refers to training large neural networks. Let's first discuss some basic use cases of neural networks and why deep learning is creating such a furore even though these neural networks have been here for decades.

Following are the examples of supervised learning in neural networks:

Inputs(x)	Output(y)	Application domain	Suggested neural network approach
House features	Price of the house	Real estate	Standard neural network with rectified linear unit in the output layer
Ad and user info Click on ad ?	Yes(1) or No(0)	Online advertising	Standard neural network with binary classification
Image object	Classifying from 100 different objects, that is (1,2,.....,100)	Photo tagging	Convolutional neural network (since image, that is, spatial data)
Audio	Text transcript	Speech recognition	Recurrent neural network (since both input-output are sequential data)
English	Chinese	Machine translation	Recurrent neural network (since the input is a sequential data)
Image, radar information	Position of other cars	Autonomous driving	Customized hybrid/complex neural network

We will go into the details of the previously-mentioned neural networks in the coming sections of this chapter, but first we must understand that different types of neural networks are used based on the objective of the problem statement.

Supervised learning is an approach in machine learning where an agent is trained using pairs of input features and their corresponding output/target values (also called labels).

Traditional machine learning algorithms worked very well for the structured data, where most of the input features were very well defined. This is not the case with the unstructured data, such as audio, image, and text, where the data is a signal, pixels, and letters, respectively. It's harder for the computers to make sense of the unstructured data than the structured data. The neural network's ability to make predictions based on this unstructured data is the key reason behind their popularity and generate economic value.

First, it's the scale at the present moment, that is the scale of data, computational power and new algorithms, which is driving the progress in deep learning. It's been over four decades of internet, resulting in an enormous amount of digital footprints accumulating and growing. During that period, research and technological development helped to expand the storage and processing ability of computational systems. Currently, owing to these heavy computational systems and massive amounts of data, we are able to verify discoveries in the field of artificial intelligence done over the past three decades.

Now, what do we need to implement deep learning?

First, we need a large amount of data.

Second, we need to train a reasonably large neural network.

So, why not train a large neural network on small amounts of data?

Think back to your data structure lessons, where the utility of the structure is to sufficiently handle a particular type of value. For example, you will not store a scalar value in a variable that has the tensor data type. Similarly, these large neural networks create distinct representations and develop comprehending patterns given the high volume of data, as shown in the following graph:

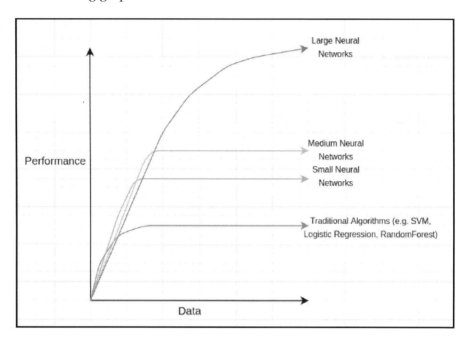

Please refer to the preceding graphical representation of data versus performance of different machine learning algorithms for the following inferences:

1. We see that the performance of traditional machine learning algorithms converges after a certain time as they are not able to absorb distinct representations with data volume beyond a threshold.

2. Check the bottom left part of the graph, near the origin. This is the region where the relative ordering of the algorithms is not well defined. Due to the small data size, the inner representations are not that distinct. As a result, the performance metrics of all the algorithms coincide. At this level, performance is directly proportional to better feature engineering. But these hand engineered features fail with the increase in data size. That's where deep neural networks come in as they are able to capture better representations from large amounts of data.

Therefore, we can conclude that one shouldn't fit a deep learning architecture in to any encountered data. The volume and variety of the data obtained indicate which algorithm to apply. Sometimes small data works better with traditional machine learning algorithms rather than deep neural networks.

Deep learning problem statements and algorithms can be further segregated into four different segments based on their area of research and application:

- **General deep learning**: Densely-connected layers or fully-connected networks

- **Sequence models**: Recurrent neural networks, Long Short Term Memory Networks, Gated Recurrent Units, and so on

- **Spatial data models** (images, for example): Convolutional neural networks, Generative Adversarial Networks

- **Others**: Unsupervised learning, reinforcement learning, sparse encoding, and so on

Presently, the industry is mostly driven by the first three segments, but the future of Artificial Intelligence rests on the advancements in the fourth segment. Walking down the journey of advancements in machine learning, we can see that until now, these learning models were giving real numbers as output, for example, movie reviews (sentiment score) and image classification (class object). But now, as well as, other type of outputs are being generated, for example, image captioning (input: image, output: text), machine translation (input: text, output: text), and speech recognition (input: audio, output: text).

Human-level performance is necessary and being commonly applied in deep learning. Human-level accuracy becomes constant after some time converging to the highest possible point. This point is called the Optimal Error Rate (also known as the Bayes Error Rate, that is, the lowest possible error rate for any classifier of a random outcome).

The reason behind this is that a lot of problems have a theoretical limit in performance owing to the noise in the data. Therefore, human-level accuracy is a good approach to improving your models by doing error analysis. This is done by incorporating human-level error, training set error, and validation set error to estimate bias variance effects, that is, the underfitting and overfitting conditions.

The scale of data, type of algorithm, and performance metrics are a set of approaches that help us to benchmark the level of improvements with respect to different machine learning algorithms. Thereby, governing the crucial decision of whether to invest in deep learning or go with the traditional machine learning approaches.

A basic perceptron with some input features (three, here in the following diagram) looks as follows:

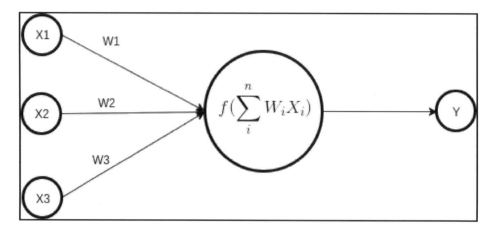

The preceding diagram sets the basic approach of what a neural network looks like if we have input in the first layer and output in the next. Let's try to interpret it a bit. Here:

- X1, X2, and X3 are input feature variables, that is, the dimension of input here is 3 (considering there's no bias variable).

- W1, W2, and W3 are the corresponding weights associated with feature variables. When we talk about the training of neural networks, we mean to say the training of weights. Thus, these form the parameters of our small neural network.

- The function in the output layer is an activation function applied over the aggregation of the information received from the previous layer. This function creates a representation state that corresponds to the actual output. The series of processes from the input layer to the output layer resulting into a predicted output is called forward propagation.

- The error value between the output from the activation function and actual output is minimized through multiple iterations.

- Minimization of the error only happens if we change the value of the weights (going from the output layer toward the input layer) in the direction that can minimize our error function. This process is termed backpropagation, as we are moving in the opposite direction.

Now, keeping these basics in mind, let's go into demystifying the neural networks further using logistic regression as a neural network and try to create a neural network with one hidden layer.

Activation functions for deep learning

Activation functions are the integral units of artificial neural networks. They decide whether a particular neuron is activated or not, that is, whether the information received by the neuron is relevant or not. The activation function performs nonlinear transformation on the receiving signal (data).

We will discuss some of the popular activation functions in the following sections.

The sigmoid function

Sigmoid is a smooth and continuously differentiable function. It results in nonlinear output. The sigmoid function is represented here:

$$\sigma(x) = \frac{1}{1+e^{-x}}$$

Please, look at the observations in the following graph of the sigmoid function. The function ranges from 0 to 1. Observing the curve of the function, we see that the gradient is very high when x values between -3 and 3, but becomes flat beyond that. Thus, we can say that small changes in x near these points will bring large changes in the value of the sigmoid function. Therefore, the function goals in pushing the values of the sigmoid function towards the extremes.

Therefore, it's being used in classification problems:

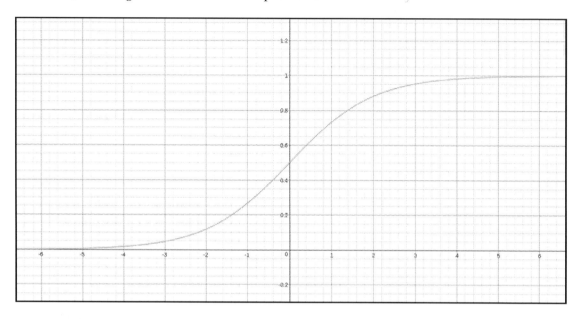

Looking at the gradient of the following sigmoid function, we observe a smooth curve dependent on x. Since the gradient curve is continuous, it's easy to backpropagate the error and update the parameters, that is, W and b:

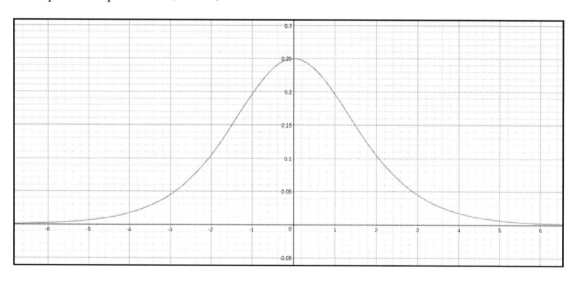

Sigmoids are widely used but its disadvantage is that the function goes flat beyond +3 and -3. Thus, whenever the function falls in that region, the gradients tends to approach zero and the learning of our neural network comes to a halt.

Since the sigmoid function outputs values from 0 to 1, that is, all positive, it's non symmetrical around the origin and all output signals are positive, that is, of the same sign. To tackle this, the sigmoid function has been scaled to the tanh function, which we will study next. Moreover, since the gradient results in a very small value, it's susceptible to the vanishing gradient problem (which we will discuss later in this chapter).

The tanh function

Tanh is a continuous function symmetric around the origin; it ranges from -1 to 1. The tanh function is represented as follows:

$$\tanh(x) = \frac{e^x - e^{-x}}{e^x + e^{-x}}$$

Thus the output signals will be both positive and negative thereby, adding to the segregation of the signals around the origin. As mentioned earlier, it is continuous and also non linear plus differentiable at all points. We can observe these properties in the graph of the tanh function in the following diagram. Though symmetrical, it becomes flat beyond -2 and 2:

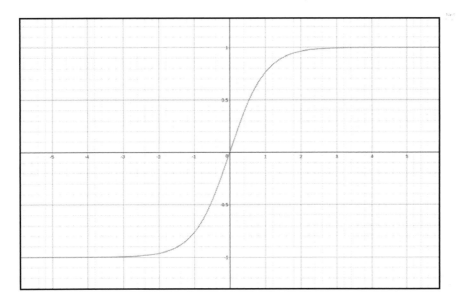

Now looking at the gradient curve of the following tanh function, we observe it being steeper than the sigmoid function. The tanh function also has the vanishing gradient problem:

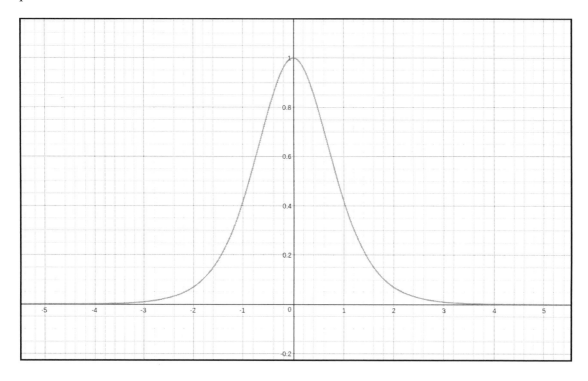

The softmax function

The softmax function is mainly used to handle classification problems and preferably used in the output layer, outputting the probabilities of the output classes. As seen earlier, while solving the binary logistic regression, we witnessed that the sigmoid function was able to handle only two classes. In order to handle multi-class we need a function that can generate values for all the classes and those values follow the rules of probability. This objective is fulfilled by the softmax function, which shrinks the outputs for each class between 0 and 1 and divides them by the sum of the outputs for all the classes:

$$softmax(x_i) = \frac{e^{x_i}}{\sum\limits_{i}^{c} e^{x_j}}$$

For examples, $x \in \{1,2,3,4\}$, where x refers to four classes.

Then, the softmax function will gives results (rounded to three decimal places) as:

$$softmax(x_1) = \frac{e^1}{\sum_i^4 e^x} = \frac{e^1}{e^1 + e^2 + e^3 + e^4} = 0.032$$

$$softmax(x_2) = \frac{e^2}{\sum_i^4 e^x} = \frac{e^2}{e^1 + e^2 + e^3 + e^4} = 0.088$$

$$softmax(x_3) = \frac{e^3}{\sum_i^4 e^x} = \frac{e^3}{e^1 + e^2 + e^3 + e^4} = 0.240$$

$$softmax(x_4) = \frac{e^4}{\sum_i^4 e^x} = \frac{e^4}{e^1 + e^2 + e^3 + e^4} = 0.640$$

Thus, we see the probabilities of all the classes. Since the output of every classifier demands probabilistic values for all the classes, the softmax function becomes the best candidate for the outer layer activation function of the classifier.

The rectified linear unit function

The **rectified linear unit**, better known as **ReLU**, is the most widely used activation function:

$$f(x) = max(0, x)$$

The ReLU function has the advantage of being non linear. Thus, backpropagation is easy and can therefore stack multiple hidden layers activated by the ReLU function, where for x<=0, the function *f(x) = 0* and *for x>0, f(x)=x.*

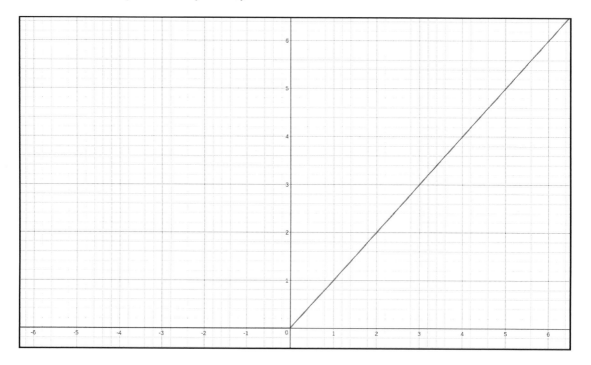

The main advantage of the ReLU function over other activation functions is that it does not activate all the neurons at the same time. This can be observed from the preceding graph of the ReLU function, where we see that if the input is negative it outputs zero and the neuron does not activate. This results in a sparse network, and fast and easy computation.

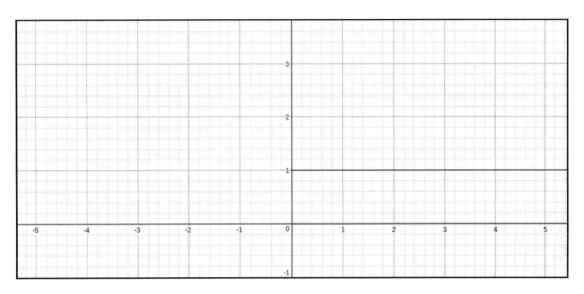

Derivative graph of ReLU, shows f'(x) = 0 for x<=0 and f'(x) = 1 for x>0

Looking at the preceding gradients graph of ReLU preceding, we can see the negative side of the graph shows a constant zero. Therefore, activations falling in that region will have zero gradients and therefore, weights will not get updated. This leads to inactivity of the nodes/neurons as they will not learn. To overcome this problem, we have Leaky ReLUs, which modify the function as:

$$f(x) = ax, x \geq 0$$

$$x, x \geq 0$$

This prevents the gradient from becoming zero in the negative side and the weight training continues, but slowly, owing to the low value of a.

How to choose the right activation function

The activation function is decided depending upon the objective of the problem statement and the concerned properties. Some of the inferences are as follows:

- Sigmoid functions work very well in the case of shallow networks and binary classifiers. Deeper networks may lead to vanishing gradients.

- The ReLU function is the most widely used, and try using Leaky ReLU to avoid the case of dead neurons. Thus, start with ReLU, then move to another activation function if ReLU doesn't provide good results.

- Use softmax in the outer layer for the multi-class classification.

- Avoid using ReLU in the outer layer.

Logistic regression as a neural network

Logistic regression is a classifier algorithm. Here, we try to predict the probability of the output classes. The class with the highest probability becomes the predicted output. The error between the actual and predicted output is calculated using cross-entropy and minimized through backpropagation. Check the following diagram for binary logistic regression and multi-class logistic regression. The difference is based on the problem statement. If the unique number of output classes is two then it's called **binary classification**, if it's more than two then it's called multi-class classification. If there are no hidden layers, we use the sigmoid function for the binary classification and we get the architecture for binary logistic regression. Similarly, if there are no hidden layers and we use use the softmax function for the multi-class classification, we get the architecture for multi-class logistic regression.

Now a question arises, why not use the sigmoid function for multi-class logistic regression ?

The answer, which is true for all predicted output layers of any neural network, is that the predicted outputs should follow a probability distribution. In normal terms, say the output has N classes. This will result in N probabilities for an input data having, say, d dimensions. Thus, the sum of the N probabilities for this one input data should be 1 and each of those probabilities should be between 0 and 1 inclusive.

On the one hand, the summation of the sigmoid function for N different classes may not be 1 in the majority of cases. Therefore, in case of binary, the sigmoid function is applied to obtain the probability of one class, that is, $p(y = 1|x)$, and for the other class the probability, that is, $p(y = 0|x) = 1 - p(y = 1|x)$. On the other hand, the output of a softmax function is values satisfying the probability distribution properties. In the diagram, σ refers to the sigmoid function:

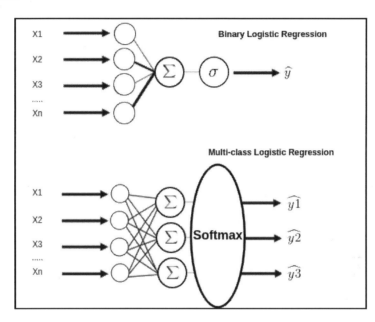

A follow-up question might also arise: what if we use softmax in binary logistic regression?

As mentioned previously, as long as your predicted output follows the rules of probability distribution, everything is fine. Later, we will discuss cross entropy and the importance of probability distribution as a building block for any machine learning problem especially dealing with classification tasks.

A probability distribution is valid if the probabilities of all the values in the distribution are between 0 and 1, inclusive, and the sum of those probabilities must be 1.

Logistic regression can be viewed in a very small neural network. Let's try to go through a step-by-step process to implement a binary logistic regression, as shown here:

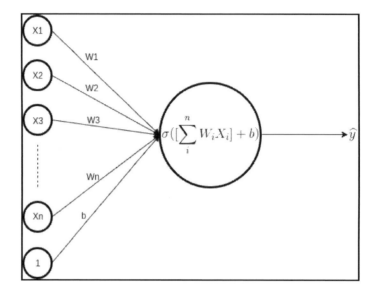

Notation

Let the data be of the form $(x_{(i)}, y_{(i)})$, where:

- $x_{(i)} \in R$, $y_{(i)} \in \{0,1\}$ (number of classes = 2 because it's a binary classification)

- $x_{(i)}$ is 'n' dimensional, that is, $x_{(i)} = \{X_{(i)}1, X_{(i)}2, X_{(i)}3, \ldots\ldots, X_{(i)}n\}$ (refers to the preceding diagram)

- The number of training examples is m. Thus the training set looks as follows:

  - $\{(x_{(1)}, y_{(1)}), (x_{(2)}, y_{(2)}), \ldots, (x_{(m)}, y_{(m)})\}$.

  - m = size of training dataset.

  - And, since $x = [x_{(1)}, x_{(2)}, \ldots, x_{(m)}]$, where, each $x_{(i)} = \{X_{(i)}1, X_{(i)}2, X_{(i)}3, \ldots, X_{(i)}n\}$.

  - Therefore, X is a matrix of size $n * m$, that is, number of features * number of training examples.

  - $Y = [y_{(1)}, y_{(2)}, \ldots, y_{(m)}]$, a vector of m outputs, where, each $y_{(i)} \in \{0,1\}$.

  - Parameters : Weights $W \in R$, and bias $b \in R$, $W = \{W1, W2, W3, \ldots, Wn\}$ where Wi and b is a scalar value.

Objective

The objective of any supervised classification learning algorithm is to predict the correct class with higher probability. Therefore, for each given $x_{(i)}$, we have to calculate the predicted output, that is, the probability $\hat{y}_{(i)} = P(y_{(i)} = 1 | x_{(i)})$. Therefore, $\hat{y}_{(i)} \in [0,1]$.

Referring to binary logistic regression in the preceding diagram:

- Predicted output, that is, $\hat{y}_{(i)} = \sigma(W x_{(i)} + b)$. Here, the sigmoid function shrinks the value of $W x_{(i)} + b$ between 0 and 1.

- This means, when $W x_{(i)} + b \to +\infty$, the sigmoid function of this, that is $\sigma(W x_{(i)} + b) \to 1$.

- When $W x_{(i)} + b \to -\infty$, the sigmoid function of this, that is, $\sigma(W x_{(i)} + b) \to 0$.

Once we have calculated $\hat{y}$, that is, the predicted output, we are done with our forward propagation task. Now, we will calculate the error value using the cost function and try to backpropagate to minimize our error value by changing the values of our parameters, W and b, through gradient descent.

The cost function

The cost function is a metric that determines how well or poorly a machine learning algorithm performed with regards to the actual training output and the predicted output. If you remember linear regression, where the sum of squares of errors was used as the loss function, that is, $L(y_{(i)}, \hat{y}_{(i)}) = \frac{1}{2} \times (y_{(i)} - \hat{y}_{(i)})^2$. This works better in a convex curve, but in the case of classification, the curve is non convex; as a result, the gradient descent doesn't work well and doesn't tend to global optimum. Therefore, we use cross-entropy loss which fits better in classification tasks as the cost function.

Cross entropy as loss function (for i^{th} input data), that is,

$$L_i = -\sum_{c=1}^{C} y_{(c)} log(\hat{y}_c)$$

, where C refers to different output classes.

Thus, cost function = Average cross entropy loss (for the whole dataset), that is,

$$J = \frac{1}{m} \sum_{i=1}^{m} L_i = \frac{1}{m} \sum_{i=1}^{m} [-\sum_{c=1}^{C} y_{(c)} log(\hat{y}_c)]_i$$

.

In case of binary logistic regression, output classes are only two, that is, 0 and 1, since the sum of class values will always be 1. Therefore (for i^{th} input data), if one class is $y_{(i)}$, the other will be $1-y_{(i)}$. Similarly, since the probability of class $y_{(i)}$ is $\hat{y}_{(i)}$ (prediction), then the probability of the other class, that is, $1-y_{(i)}$, will be $1-\hat{y}_{(i)}$.

Therefore, the loss function modifies to $L(y_{(i)}, \hat{y}_{(i)}) = -[y_{(i)} log \hat{y}_{(i)} + (1-y_{(i)}) log(1-\hat{y}_{(i)})]$, where:

- If $y_{(i)}=1$, that is, $L(y_{(i)}, \hat{y}_{(i)}) = -log \hat{y}_{(i)}$. Therefore, to minimize L, $\hat{y}_{(i)}$ should be large, that is, closer to 1.

- If $y_{(i)}=0$, that is, $L(y_{(i)}, \hat{y}_{(i)}) = -log(1-\hat{y}_{(i)})$. Therefore, to minimize L, $\hat{y}_{(i)}$ should be small, that is, closer to 0.

Loss function applies to a single example whereas cost function applies on the whole training lot. Thus, the cost function for this case will be:

$$J(W,b) = \frac{-1}{m} \sum_{i=1}^{m} [y_{(i)} \log \hat{y}_{(i)} + (1 - y_{(i)}) \log(1 - \hat{y}_{(i)})]$$

The gradient descent algorithm

The gradient descent algorithm is an optimization algorithm to find the minimum of the function using first order derivatives, that is, we differentiate functions with respect to their parameters to first order only. Here, the objective of the gradient descent algorithm would be to minimize the cost function $J(W,b)$ with regards to W and b.

This approach includes following steps for numerous iterations to minimize $J(W,b)$:

- $$W - \alpha \times \frac{\partial J(W,b)}{\partial W} \to W$$

- $$b - \alpha \times \frac{\partial J(W,b)}{\partial b} \to b$$

α used in the above equations refers to the learning rate. The learning rate is the speed at which the learning agent adapts to new knowledge. Thus, α, that is, the learning rate is a hyperparameter that needs to be assigned as a scalar value or as a function of time. In this way, in every iteration, the values of W and b are updated as mentioned in the preceding formula until the value of the cost function reaches an acceptable minimum value.

The gradient descent algorithm means moving down the slope. The slope of the the curve is represented by the cost function J with regards to the parameters. The gradient, that is, the slope, gives the direction of increasing slope if it's positive, and decreasing if it's negative. Thus, we use a negative sign to multiply with our slope since we have to go opposite to the direction of the increasing slope and toward the direction of the decreasing.

Using the optimum learning rate, α, the descent is controlled and we don't overshoot the local minimum. If the learning rate, α, is very small, then convergence will take more time, while if it's very high then it might overshoot and miss the minimum and diverge owing to the large number of iterations:

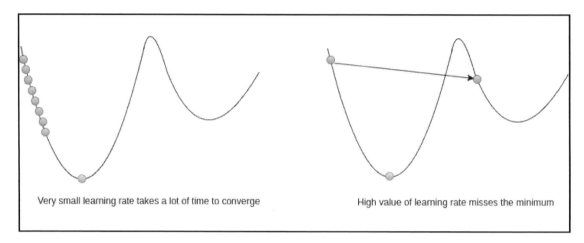

Very small learning rate takes a lot of time to converge

High value of learning rate misses the minimum

The computational graph

A basic neural network consists of forward propagation followed by a backward propagation. As a result, it consists of a series of steps that includes the values of different nodes, weights, and biases, as well as derivatives of cost function with regards to all the weights and biases. In order to keep track of these processes, the **computational graph** comes into the picture. The computational graph also keeps track of chain rule differentiation irrespective of the depth of the neural network.

Steps to solve logistic regression using gradient descent

Putting together all the building blocks we've just covered, let's try to solve a binary logistic regression with two input features.

The basic steps to compute are:

1. Calculate $Z_{(i)} = W x_{(i)} + b, \forall i$

2. Calculate $\widehat{y}_{(i)} = \sigma(Z_{(i)}), \forall i$, the predicted output

3. Calculate the cost function: $J(W,b) = \dfrac{-1}{m} \sum_{i}^{m} [y_{(i)} \log \widehat{y}_{(i)} + (1 - y_{(i)}) \log (1 - \widehat{y}_{(i)})]$

Say we have two input features, that is, two dimensions and *m* samples dataset. Therefore, the following would be the case:

1. $x = \{X1, X2\}$

2. Weights $W = \{W1, W2\}$ and bias b

3. Therefore, $Z_{(i)} = W1 X_{(i)}1 + W2 X_{(i)}2 + b$, and, $\widehat{y}_{(i)} = \sigma(Z_{(i)})$

4. Calculate $J(W,b)$ (average loss over all the examples)

5. Calculating the derivative with regards to *W1*, *W2* and b that is $\dfrac{\partial J(W,b)}{\partial W_1}$, $\dfrac{\partial J(W,b)}{\partial W_2}$ and $\dfrac{\partial J(W,b)}{\partial b}$, respectively

6. Modify $W1, W2$ and b as mentioned in the preceding gradient descent section

The pseudo code of the preceding *m* samples dataset are:

1. Initialize the value of the learning rate, α, and the number of epochs, *e*
2. Loop over many number of epochs *e'* (where each time a full dataset will pass in batches)
3. Initialize *J* (cost function) and *b* (bias) as 0, and for *W1* and *W2*, you can go for random normal or **xavier initialization** (explained in the next section)

Here, a is $\hat{y}$, dw1 is $\frac{\partial J}{\partial w_1}$, dw2 is $\frac{\partial J}{\partial w_2}$ and db is $\frac{\partial J}{\partial b}$. Each iteration contains a loop iterating over m examples.

The pseudo code for the same is given here:

```
w1 = xavier initialization, w2 = xavier initialization, e = 100, α = 0.0001
for j → 1 to e :
    J = 0, dw1 = 0, dw2 = 0, db = 0
    for i → 1 to m :
        z = w1x1[i] + w2x2[i] + b
        a = σ(z)
        J = J - [ y[i] log a + (1-y) log (1-a) ]
        dw1 = dw1 + (a-y[i]) * x1[i]
        dw2 = dw2 + (a-y[i]) * x2[i]
        db = db + (a-y[i])
    J = J / m
    dw1 = dw1 / m
    dw2 = dw2 / m
    db = db / m
    w1 = w1 - α * dw1
    w2 = w2 - α * dw2
```

What is xavier initialization?

Xavier Initialization is the initialization of weights in the neural networks, as a random variable following the Gaussian distribution where the variance $var(W)$ being given by

$$var(W) = \frac{2}{n_i + n_{out}}$$

Where, n_i is the number of units in the current layer, that is, the incoming signal units, and n_{out} is the number of units in the next layer, that is, the outgoing resulting signal units. In short, $n_i \times n_{out}$ is the shape of W.

Why do we use xavier initialization?

The following factors call for the application of xavier initialization:

- If the weights in a network start very small, most of the signals will shrink and become dormant at the activation function in the later layers

- If the weights start very large, most of the signals will massively grow and pass through the activation functions in the later layers

Thus, xavier initialization helps in generating optimal weights, such that the signals are within optimal range, thereby minimizing the chances of the signals getting neither too small nor too large.

The derivation of the preceding formula is beyond the scope of this book. Feel free to search here (`http://andyljones.tumblr.com/post/110998971763/an-explanation-of-xavier-initialization`) and go through the derivation for a better understanding.

The neural network model

A neural network model is similar to the preceding logistic regression model. The only difference is the addition of hidden layers between the input and output layers. Let's consider a single hidden layer neural network for classification to understand the process as shown in the following diagram:

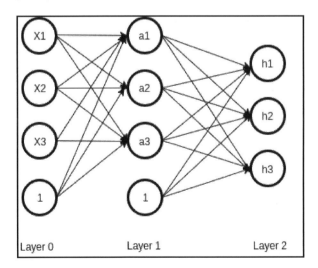

Here, **Layer 0** is the input layer, **Layer 1** is the hidden layer, and **Layer 2** is the output layer. This is also known as **two layered neural networks**, owing to the fact that when we count the number of layers in a neural network, we don't consider input layer as the first layer. Thus, input layer is considered as **Layer 0** and then successive layers get the notation of **Layer 1**, **Layer 2**, and so on.

Now, a basic question which comes to mind: why the layers between the input and output layer termed as hidden layers ?

This is because the values of the nodes in the hidden layers are not present in the training set. As we have seen, at every node two calculations happen. These are:

- Aggregation of the input signals from previous layers

- Subjecting the aggregated signal to an activation to create deeper inner representations, which in turn are the values of the corresponding hidden nodes

Referring to the preceding diagram, we have three input features, $x1, x2$, and $x3$. The node showing value 1 is regarded as the bias unit. Each layer, except the output, generally has a bias unit. Bias units can be regarded as an intercept term and play an important role in shifting the activation function left or right. Remember, the number of hidden layers and nodes in them are hyperparameters that we define at the start. Here, we have defined the number of hidden layers to be one and the number of hidden nodes to be three, $a1, a2$, and $a3$. Thus, we can say we have three input units, three hidden units, and three output units ($h1, h2$, and $h3$, since we have out of three classes to predict). This will give us the shape of weights and biases associated with the layers. For example, **Layer 0** has 3 units and **Layer 1** has 3. The shape of the weight matrix and bias vector associated with Layer i is given by:

$$shape\ of\ W_{(i,i+1)} = current\ layer\ number\ of\ units \times next\ layer\ number\ of\ units$$

$$i.e., Layer_i\ number\ of\ units \times Layer_{i+1}\ number\ of\ units$$

$$shape\ of\ b_{(i,i+1)} = next\ layer\ number\ of\ units$$

$$i.e., Layer_{i+1}\ number\ of\ units$$

Therefore, the shapes of :

- $W_{(0,1)}$ will be 3×3 and $b_{(0,1)}$ will be 3

- $W_{(1,2)}$ will be 3×1 and $b_{(1,2)}$ will be 1

Now, let's understand the following notation:

- $W_{a(i)}^{d(i+1)}$: Here, it refers to the value of weight connecting node a in Layer i to node d in Layer i+1

- $b_{(i,i+1)}^{d}$: Here, it refers to the value of the bias connecting the bias unit node in Layer i to node d in Layer i+1

Therefore, the nodes in the hidden layers can be calculated in the following way:

$$a1 = f\left(W_{1(0)}^{1(1)} \times X1 + W_{2(0)}^{1(1)} \times X2 + W_{3(0)}^{1(1)} \times X3 + b_{(0,1)}^{1} \times 1\right)$$

$$a2 = f\left(W_{1(0)}^{2(1)} \times X1 + W_{2(0)}^{2(1)} \times X2 + W_{3(0)}^{2(1)} \times X3 + b_{(0,1)}^{2} \times 1\right)$$

$$a3 = f\left(W_{1(0)}^{3(1)} \times X1 + W_{2(0)}^{3(1)} \times X2 + W_{3(0)}^{3(1)} \times X3 + b_{(0,1)}^{3} \times 1\right)$$

Where, the f function refers to the activation function. Remember the logistic regression where we used sigmoid and softmax a the activation function for binary and multi-class logistic regression respectively.

Similarly, we can calculate the output unit, as so:

$$h1 = f\left(W_{1(1)}^{1(2)} \times a1 + W_{2(1)}^{1(2)} \times a2 + W_{3(1)}^{1(2)} \times a3 + b_{(1,2)}^{1} \times 1\right)$$

$$h2 = f\left(W_{1(1)}^{2(2)} \times a1 + W_{2(1)}^{2(2)} \times a2 + W_{3(1)}^{2(2)} \times a3 + b_{(1,2)}^{2} \times 1\right)$$

$$h3 = f\left(W_{1(1)}^{3(2)} \times a1 + W_{2(1)}^{3(2)} \times a2 + W_{3(1)}^{3(2)} \times a3 + b_{(1,2)}^{3} \times 1\right)$$

This brings us to an end of the forward propagation process. Our next task is to train the neural network (that is, train the weights and biases parameters) through backpropagation.

Let the actual output classes be $Y1, Y2$ and $Y3$.

Recalling the cost function section in linear regression, we used cross entropy to formulate our cost function. Since, the cost function is defined by,

$$J = \frac{1}{m} \sum_{i=1}^{m} L_i = \frac{1}{m} \sum_{i=1}^{m} \left[- \sum_{c=1}^{C} y_{(c)} log(\hat{y}_c) \right]_i$$

where, $C = 3$, $y_c = Yc$, $\hat{y}_c = hc$ and m = number of examples

Since this is a classification problem, for each example the output will have only one output class as 1 and the rest would be zero. For example, for i, it would be:

$$\left[- \sum_{c=1}^{C} y_{(c)} log(\hat{y}_c) \right]_i = \left[-y log(\hat{y}) \right]_i$$

Thus, cost function $J = \frac{1}{m} \sum_{i=1}^{m} \left[-y log(\hat{y}) \right]_i$

Now, our goal is to minimize the cost function J with regards to W and b. In order to train our given neural network, first randomly initialize W and b. Then we will try to optimize J through gradient descent where we will update W and b accordingly at the learning rate, α, in the following manner:

- $$W_{a(i)}^{d(i+1)} - \alpha \times \frac{\partial J}{\partial W_{a(i)}^{d(i+1)}} \rightarrow W_{a(i)}^{d(i+1)}$$

- $$b_{(i,i+1)}^{d} - \alpha \times \frac{\partial J}{\partial b_{(i,i+1)}^{d}} \rightarrow b_{(i,i+1)}^{d}$$

After setting up this structure, we have to perform these optimization steps (of updating W and b) repeatedly for numerous iterations to train our neural network.

This brings us to the end of the basic of neural networks, which forms the basic building block of any neural network, shallow or deep. Our next frontier will be to understand some of the famous deep neural network architectures, such as **recurrent neural networks (RNNs)** and **convolutional neural networks (CNNs)**. Apart from that, we will also have a look at the benchmarked deep neural network architectures such as AlexNet, VGG-net, and Inception.

Recurrent neural networks

Recurrent neural networks, abbreviated as RNNs, is used in cases of sequential data, whether as an input, output, or both. The reason RNNs became so effective is because of their architecture to aggregate the learning from the past datasets and use that along with the new data to enhance the learning. This way, it captures the sequence of events, which wasn't possible in a feed forward neural network nor in earlier approaches of statistical time series analysis.

Consider time series data such as stock market, audio, or video datasets, where the sequence of events matters a lot. Thus, in this case, apart from the collective learning from the whole data, the order of learning from the data encountered over time matters. This will help to capture the underlying trend.

The ability to perform sequence based learning is what makes RNNs highly effective. Let's take a step back and try to understand the problem. Consider the following data diagram:

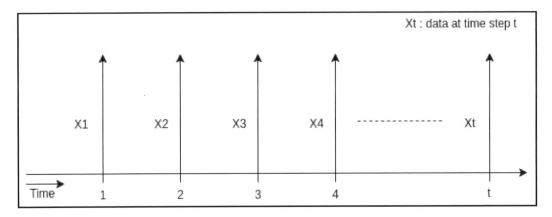

Imagine you have a sequence of events similar to the ones in the diagram, and at each point in time you want to make decisions as per the sequence of events. Now, if your sequence is reasonably stationary, you can use a classifier with similar weights for any time step but here's the glitch. If you run the same classifier separately at different time step data, it will not train to similar weights for different time steps. If you run a single classifier on the whole dataset containing the data of all the time step then the weights will be same but the sequence based learning is hampered. For our solution, we want to share weights over different time steps and utilize what we have learned till the last time step, as shown in the following diagram:

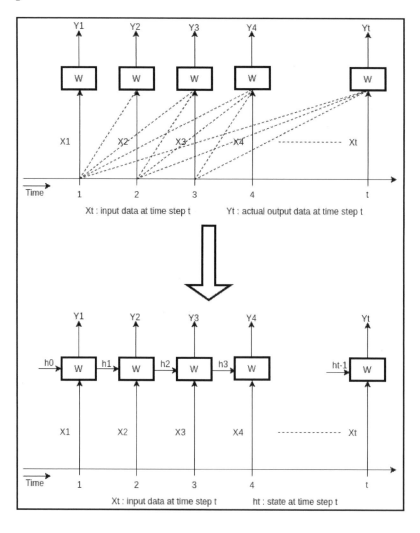

As per the problem, we have understood that our neural network should be able to consider the learnings from the past. This notion can be seen in the preceding diagrammatic representation, where in the first part it shows that at each time step, the network training the weights should consider the data learning from the past, and the second part gives the solution to that. We use a state representation of the classifier output from the previous time step as an input, along with the new time step data to learn the current state representation. This state representation can be defined as the collective learning (or summary) of what happened till last time step, recursively. The state is not the predicted output from the classifier. Instead, when it is subjected to a softmax activation function, it will yield the predicted output.

In order to remember further back, a deeper neural network would be required. Instead, we will go for a single model summarizing the past and provide that information, along with the new information, to our classifier.

Thus, at any time step, t, in a recurrent neural network, the following calculations occur :

- $h_t = f(W_h[h_{t-1}; X_t] + b_h)$.

- W_h and b_h are weights and biases shared over time.

- $\tanh$ is the activation function f .

- $[h_{t-1}; X_t]$ refers to the concatenation of these two information. Say, your input, X_t, is of shape $n \times d$, that is, n samples/rows and d dimensions/columns and h_{t-1} is $n \times l$. Then, your concatenation would result a matrix of shape $n \times (d+l)$.

Since, the shape of any hidden state, h_i, is $n \times l$. Therefore, the shape of W_h is $(d+l) \times l$ and b_h is l.

Since,

$\quad$ shape of $W_{(i, i+1)}$ = current layer number of units × next layer number of units

$\quad$ i.e., Layer$_i$ number of units × Layer$_{i+1}$ number of units

$\quad$ shape of $b_{(i, i+1)}$ = next layer number of units

$\quad$ i.e., Layer$_{i+1}$ number of units

These operations in a given time step, t, constitute an RNN cell unit. Let's visualize the RNN cell at time step t, as shown here:

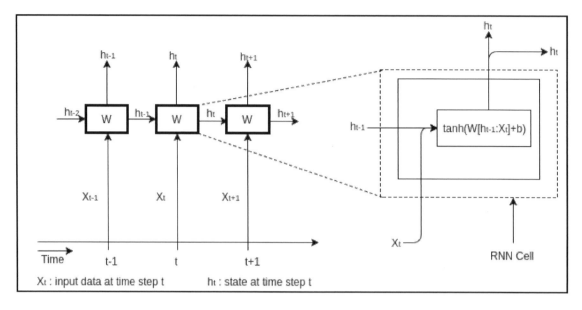

Once we are done with the calculations till the final time step, our forward propagation task is done. The next task would be to minimize the overall loss by backpropagating through time to train our recurrent neural network. The total loss of one such sequence is the summation of loss across all time steps, that is, if the given sequence of X values and their corresponding output sequence of Y values, the loss is given by:

$$L = \sum_{i=1}^{t} L_i = \sum_{i=1}^{t} [-ylog(\hat{y})]_i$$

Thus, the cost function of the whole dataset containing 'm' examples would be (where k refers to the kth example):

$$J = \frac{1}{m} \sum_{m=1}^{k} [\sum_{i=1}^{t} [-ylog(\hat{y})]_i]_k$$

Since the RNNs incorporate the sequential data, backpropagation is extended to backpropagation through time. Here, time is a series of ordered time steps connecting one to the other, which allows backpropagation through different time steps.

Long Short Term Memory Networks

RNNs practically fail to handle **long term dependencies**. As the gap between the output data point in the output sequence and the input data point in the input sequence increases, RNNs fail in connecting the information between the two. This usually happens in text-based tasks such as machine translation, audio to text, and many more where the length of sequences are long.

Long Short Term Memory Networks, also knows as **LSTMs** (introduced by Hochreiter and Schmidhuber), are capable of handling these long-term dependencies. Take a look at the image given here:

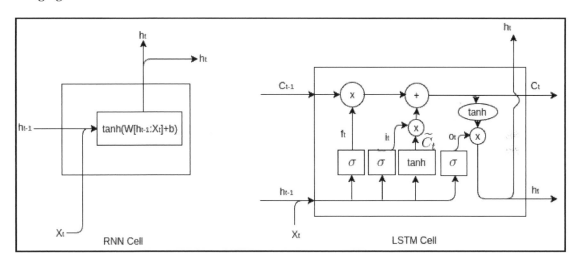

The key feature of LSTM is the cell state C_t. This helps the information to flow unchanged. We will start with the forget gate layer, f_t which takes the concatenation of of last hidden state, h_{t-1} and x_t as the input and trains a neural network that results a number between 0 and 1 for each number in the last cell state C_{t-1}, where 1 means to keep the value and 0 means to forget the value. Thus, this layer is to identify what information to forget from the past and results what information to retain.

$$f_t = \sigma\left(W_f[h_{t-1}; x_t] + b_f\right)$$

Next we come to the input gate layer i_t and tanh layer $\tilde{C}_t$ whose task is to identify what new information to add in to one received from the past to update our information, that is, the cell state. The tanh layer creates vectors of new values, while the input gate layer identifies which of those values to use for the information update. Combining this new information with information retained by using the the forget gate layer, f_t, to update our information, that is, cell state C_t :

$$i_t = \sigma(W_i[h_{t-1}; x_t] + b_i)$$

$$\tilde{C}_t = \tanh(W_C[h_{t-1}; x_t] + b_C)$$

Thus, the new cell state C_t is:

$$C_t = f_t \times C_{t-1} + i_t \times \tilde{C}_t$$

Finally, a neural network is trained at the output gate layer, o_t, returning which values of cell state C_t to output as the hidden state, h_t :

$$o_t = \sigma(W_o[h_{t-1}; x_t] + b_o)$$

$$h_t = o_t \times \tanh(C_t)$$

Thus, an LSTM Cell incorporates the last cell state C_{t-1}, last hidden state h_{t-1} and current time step input x_t, and outputs the updated cell state C_t and the current hidden state h_t .

 LSTMs were a breakthrough as people were able to benchmark remarkable outcomes with RNNs by incorporating them as the cell unit. This was a great step towards the solution for issues concerned with long term dependencies.

Convolutional neural networks

Convolutional neural networks or ConvNets, are deep neural networks that have provided successful results in computer vision. They were inspired by the organization and signal processing of neurons in the visual cortex of animals, that is, individual cortical neurons respond to the stimuli in their concerned small region (of the visual field), called the **receptive field**, and these receptive fields of different neurons overlap altogether covering the whole visual field.

When the input in an input space contains the same kind of information, then we share the weights and train those weights jointly for those input. For spatial data, such as images, this weight-sharing leads to CNNs. Similarly, for a sequential data, such as text, we witnessed this weight-sharing in RNNs.

CNNs have wide applications in the field of computer vision and natural language processing. As far as the industry is concerned, Facebook uses it in their automated image-tagging algorithms, Google in their image search, Amazon in their product recommendation systems, Pinterest to personalize the home feeds, and Instagram for image search and recommendations.

Just like a neuron (or node) in a neural network receives the weighted aggregation of the signals say input from the last layer which then subjected to an activation function leading to an output. Then we backpropagate to minimize our loss function. This is the basic operation that is applied to any kind of neural network, so it will work for CNNs.

Unlike neural networks, where an input is in the form of a vector, CNNs have images as input that are multi-channeled, that is, RGB (three channels: red, green, and blue). Say there's an image of pixel size $a \times b$, then the actual tensor representation would be of an $a \times b \times 3$ shape.

Let's say you have an image similar to the one shown here:

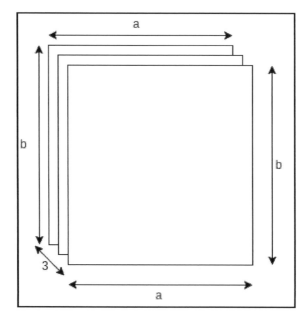

It can be represented as a flat plate that has width, height, and because of the RGB channel, it has a depth of three. Now, take a small patch of this image, say 2 × 2, and run a tiny neural network on it with an output depth of, say, *k*. This will result in a representation patch of shape *1× 1 × k* . Now, slide this neural network horizontally and vertically over the whole image without changing the weights results in another image of different width, height, and depth k (that is, now we have k channels).

This integration task is collectively termed as convolution. Generally, ReLUs are used as the activation function in these neural networks:

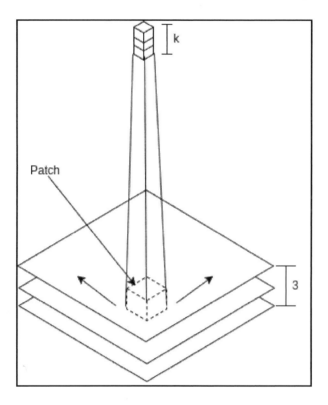

Here, we are mapping 3-feature maps (that is, RGB channels) to k feature maps

The sliding motion of the patch over the image is called striding, and the number of pixels you shift each time, whether horizontally or vertically, is called a **stride**. Striding if the patch doesn't go outside the image space it is regarded as a **valid padding**. On the other hand, if the patch goes outside the image space in order to map the patch size the pixels of the patch which are off the space are padded with zeros. This is called **same padding**.

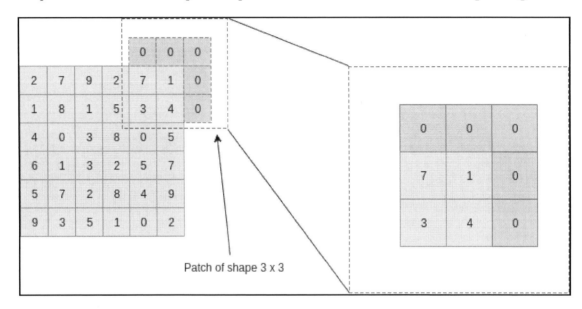

Patch of shape 3 x 3

CNN architecture consists of a series of these convolutional layers. The striding value in these convolutional layers if greater than 1 causes spatial reduction. Thus, stride, patch size, and the activation function become the hyperparameters. Along with convolutional layers, one important layer is sometimes added, it is called the **pooling layer**. This takes all the convolutions in a neighborhood and combines them. One form of pooling is called **max pooling**.

In max pooling, the feature map looks around all the values in the patch and returns the maximum among them. Thus, pooling size (that is, pooling patch/window size) and pooling stride are the hyperparameters. The following image depicts the concept of max pooling:

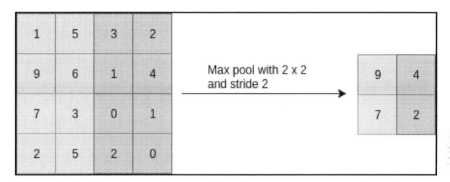

Max pooling often yields more accurate results. Similarly, we have **average pooling**, where instead of maximum value we take the average of the values in the pooling window providing a low resolution view of the feature map.

Manipulating the hyperparameters and ordering of the convolutional layers, by pooling and fully connected layers, many different variants of CNNs have been created which are being used in research and industrial domains. Some of the famous ones among them are the LeNet-5, Alexnet, VGG-Net, and Inception model.

The LeNet-5 convolutional neural network

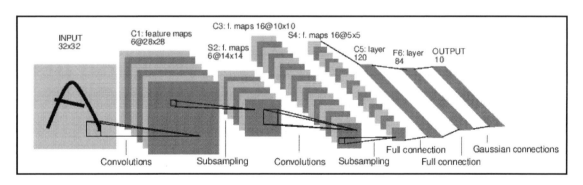

Architecture of LeNet-5, from Gradient-based Learning Applied to Document Recognition by LeCunn et al.(http://yann.lecun.com/exdb/publis/pdf/lecun-98.pdf)

LeNet-5 is a seven-level convolutional neural network, published by the team comprising of Yann LeCunn, Yoshua Bengio, Leon Bottou and Patrick Haffner in 1998 to classify digits, which was used by banks to recognize handwritten numbers on checks. The layers are ordered as:

- Input image | Convolutional Layer 1(ReLU) | Pooling 1 |Convolutional Layer 2(ReLU) |Pooling 2 |Fully Connected (ReLU) 1 | Fully Connected 2 | Output
- LeNet-5 had remarkable results, but the ability to process higher-resolution images required more convolutional layers, such as in AlexNet, VGG-Net, and Inception models.

The AlexNet model

AlexNet, a modification of LeNet, was designed by the group named SuperVision, which was composed of Alex Krizhevsky, Geoffrey Hinton, and Ilya Sutskever. AlexNet made history by achieving the top-5 error percentage of 15.3%, which was 10 points more than the runner-up, in the ImageNet Large Scale Visual Recognition Challenge in 2012.

The architecture uses five convolutional layers, three max pool layers, and three fully connected layers at the end, as shown in the following diagram. There were a total of 60 million parameters in the model trained on 1.2 million images, which took about five to six days on two NVIDIA GTX 580 3GB GPUs. The following image shows the AlexNet model:

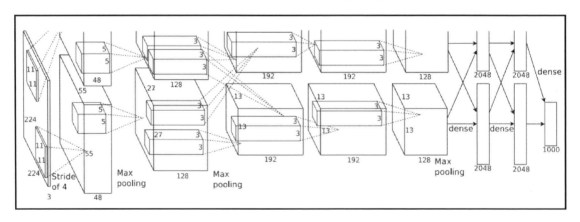

Architecture of AlexNet from ImageNet classification with deep convolutional neural networks by Hinton et al.
(https://papers.nips.cc/paper/4824-imagenet-classification-with-deep-convolutional-neural-networks.pdf)

Convolutional Layer 1 | Max Pool Layer 1 | Normalization Layer 1| Convolutional Layer 2 | Max Pool Layer 2 |Normalization Layer 2 |Convolutional Layer 3 |Convolutional layer 4 | Convolutional Layer 5 | Max Pool Layer 3 |Fully Connected 6 |Fully Connected 7 |Fully Connected 8 | Output

The VGG-Net model

VGG-Net was introduced by Karen Simonyan and Andrew Zisserman from **Visual Geometry Group (VGG)** of the University of Oxford. They used small convolutional filters of size 3 x 3 to train a network of depth 16 and 19. Their team secured first and second place in the localization and classification tasks, respectively, of ImageNet Challenge 2014.

The idea to design a deeper neural network by adding more non-linearity to the model led to incorporate smaller filters to make sure the network didn't have too many parameters. While training, it was difficult to converge the model, so first a pre-trained simpler neural net model was used to initialize the weights of the deeper architecture. However, now we can directly use the xavier initialization method instead of training a neural network to initialize the weights. Due the depth of the model, it's very slow to train.

The Inception model

Inception was created by the team at Google in 2014. The main idea was to create deeper and wider networks while limiting the number of parameters and avoiding overfitting. The following image shows the full Inception module:

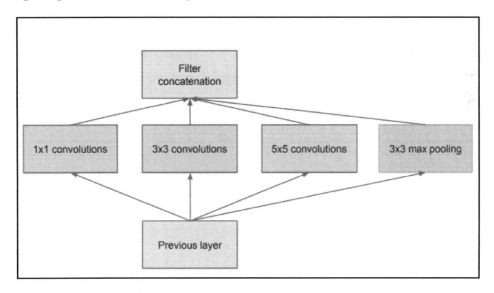

Architecture of Inception model (naive version), from going deeper with convolutions by Szegedy et al.(https://arxiv.org/pdf/1409.4842.pdf)

It applies multiple convolutional layers for a single input and outputs the stacked output of each convolution. The size of convolutions used are mainly 1x1, 3x3, and 5x5. This kind of architecture allows you to extract multi-level features from the same-sized input. An earlier version was also called GoogLeNet, which won the ImageNet challenge in 2014.

Limitations of deep learning

Deep neural networks are black boxes of weights and biases trained over a large amount of data to find hidden patterns through inner representations; it would be impossible for humans, and even if it were possible, then scalability would be an issue. Every neural probably has a different weight. Thus, they will have different gradients.

Training happens during backpropagation. Thus, the direction of training is always from the later layers (output/right side) to the early layers (input/left side). This results in later layers learning very well as compared to the early layers. The deeper the network gets, the more the condition deteriorates. This give rise to two possible problems associated with deep learning, which are:

- The vanishing gradient problem
- The exploding gradient problem

The vanishing gradient problem

The vanishing gradient problem is one of the problems associated with the training of artificial neural networks when the neurons present in the early layers are not able to learn because the gradients that train the weights shrink down to zero. This happens due to the greater depth of neural network, along with activation functions with derivatives resulting in low value.

Try the following steps:

1. Create one hidden layer neural network
2. Add more hidden layers, one by one

We observe the gradient with regards to all the nodes, and find that the gradient values get relatively smaller when we move from the later layers to the early layers. This condition worsens with the further addition of layers. This shows that the early layer neurons are learning slowly compared to the later layer neurons. This condition is called the **vanishing gradient problem**.

The exploding gradient problem

The exploding gradient problem is another problem associated with the training of artificial neural networks when the learning of the neurons present in the early layers diverge because the gradients become too large to cause severe changes in weights avoiding convergence. This generally happens if weights are not assigned properly.

While following the steps mentioned for the vanishing gradient problem, we observe that the gradients explode in the early layers, that is, they become larger. The phenomenon of the early layers diverging is called the **exploding gradient problem**.

Overcoming the limitations of deep learning

These two possible problems can be overcome by:

- Minimizing the use of the sigmoid and tanh activation functions
- Using a momentum-based stochastic gradient descent
- Proper initialization of weights and biases, such as xavier initialization
- Regularization (add regularization loss along with data loss and minimize that)

 For more detail, along with mathematical representations of the vanishing and exploding gradient, you can read this article: Intelligent Signals : Unstable Deep Learning. Why and How to solve them ?

Reinforcement learning

Reinforcement learning is a branch of artificial intelligence that deals with an agent that perceives the information of the environment in the form of state spaces and action spaces, and acts on the environment thereby resulting in a new state and receiving a reward as feedback for that action. This received reward is assigned to the new state. Just like when we had to minimize the cost function in order to train our neural network, here the reinforcement learning agent has to maximize the overall reward to find the the optimal policy to solve a particular task.

How this is different from supervised and unsupervised learning?

In supervised learning, the training dataset has input features, X, and their corresponding output labels, Y. A model is trained on this training dataset, to which test cases having input features, X', are given as the input and the model predicts Y'.

In unsupervised learning, input features, X, of the training set are given for the training purpose. There are no associated Y values. The goal is to create a model that learns to segregate the data into different clusters by understanding the underlying pattern and thereby, classifying them to find some utility. This model is then further used for the input features X' to predict their similarity to one of the clusters.

Reinforcement learning is different from both supervised and unsupervised. Reinforcement learning can guide an agent on how to act in the real world. The interface is broader than the training vectors, like in supervised or unsupervised learning. Here is the entire environment, which can be real or a simulated world. Agents are trained in a different way, where the objective is to reach a goal state, unlike the case of supervised learning where the objective is to maximize the likelihood or minimize cost.

Reinforcement learning agents automatically receive the feedback, that is, rewards from the environment, unlike in supervised learning where labeling requires time-consuming human effort. One of the bigger advantage of reinforcement learning is that phrasing any task's objective in the form of a goal helps in solving a wide variety of problems. For example, the goal of a video game agent would be to win the game by achieving the highest score. This also helps in discovering new approaches to achieving the goal. For example, when AlphaGo became the world champion in Go, it found new, unique ways of winning.

A reinforcement learning agent is like a human. Humans evolved very slowly; an agent reinforces, but it can do that very fast. As far as sensing the environment is concerned, neither humans nor and artificial intelligence agents can sense the entire world at once. The perceived environment creates a state in which agents perform actions and land in a new state, that is, a newly-perceived environment different from the earlier one. This creates a state space that can be finite as well as infinite.

The largest sector interested in this technology is defense. Can reinforcement learning agents replace soldiers that not only walk, but fight, and make important decisions?

Basic terminologies and conventions

The following are the basic terminologies associated with reinforcement learning:

- **Agent**: This we create by programming such that it is able to sense the environment, perform actions, receive feedback, and try to maximize rewards.
- **Environment**: The world where the agent resides. It can be real or simulated.
- **State**: The perception or configuration of the environment that the agent senses. State spaces can be finite or infinite.
- **Rewards**: Feedback the agent receives after any action it has taken. The goal of the agent is to maximize the overall reward, that is, the immediate and the future reward. Rewards are defined in advance. Therefore, they must be created properly to achieve the goal efficiently.
- **Actions**: Anything that the agent is capable of doing in the given environment. Action space can be finite or infinite.
- **SAR triple**: (state, action, reward) is referred as the SAR triple, represented as (s, a, r).
- **Episode**: Represents one complete run of the whole task.

Let's deduce the convention shown in the following diagram:

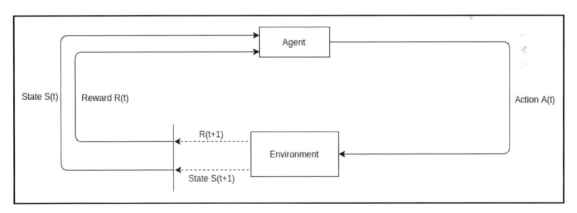

Every task is a sequence of SAR triples. We start from state S(t), perform action A(t) and thereby, receive a reward R(t+1), and land on a new state *S(t+1)*. The current state and action pair gives rewards for the next step. Since, *S(t)* and *A(t)* results in *S(t+1)*, we have a new triple of (current state, action, new state), that is, *[S(t),A(t),S(t+1)] or (s,a,s')*.

Optimality criteria

The optimality criteria are a measure of goodness of fit of the model created over the data. For example, in supervised classification learning algorithms, we have maximum likelihood as the optimality criteria. Thus, on the basis of the problem statement and objective optimality criteria differs. In reinforcement learning, our major goal is to maximize the future rewards. Therefore, we have two different optimality criteria, which are:

- **Value function**: To quantify a state on the basis of future probable rewards
- **Policy**: To guide an agent on what action to take in a given state

We will discuss both of them in detail in the coming topics.

The value function for optimality

Agents should be able to think about both immediate and future rewards. Therefore, a value is assigned to each encountered state that reflects this future information too. This is called value function. Here comes the concept of delayed rewards, where being at present what actions taken now will lead to potential rewards in future.

V(s), that is, value of the state is defined as the expected value of rewards to be received in future for all the actions taken from this state to subsequent states until the agent reaches the goal state. Basically, value functions tell us how good it is to be in this state. The higher the value, the better the state.

Rewards assigned to each (s,a,s') triple is fixed. This is not the case with the value of the state; it is subjected to change with every action in the episode and with different episodes too.

One solution comes in mind, instead of the value function, why don't we store the knowledge of every possible state?

The answer is simple: it's time-consuming and expensive, and this cost grows exponentially. Therefore, it's better to store the knowledge of the current state, that is, V(s):

$$V(s) = E[all\ future\ rewards\ discounted\ |\ S(t)=s]$$

More details on the value function will be covered in `Chapter 3`, *The Markov Decision Process and Partially Observable MDP*.

The policy model for optimality

Policy is defined as the model that guides the agent with action selection in different states. Policy is denoted as Π. Π is basically the probability of a certain action given a particular state:

$$\pi(a, s) = p(A(t) = a | S(t) = s)$$

Thus, a policy map will provide the set of probabilities of different actions given a particular state. The policy along with the value function create a solution that helps in agent navigation as per the policy and the calculated value of the state.

The Q-learning approach to reinforcement learning

Q-learning is an attempt to learn the value $Q(s,a)$ of a specific action given to the agent in a particular state. Consider a table where the number of rows represent the number of states, and the number of columns represent the number of actions. This is called a Q-table. Thus, we have to learn the value to find which action is the best for the agent in a given state.

Steps involved in Q-learning:

1. Initialize the table of $Q(s,a)$ with uniform values (say, all zeros).

2. Observe the current state, s

3. Choose an action, a, by epsilon greedy or any other action selection policies, and take the action

4. As a result, a reward, r, is received and a new state, s', is perceived

5. Update the Q value of the (s,a) pair in the table by using the following Bellman equation:

$$Q(s,a) = r + \gamma(max(Q(s',a')))$$, where γ is the discounting factor

6. Then, set the value of current state as a new state and repeat the process to complete one episode, that is, reaches the terminal state

7. Run multiple episodes to train the agent

To simplify, we can say that the Q-value for a given state, *s*, and action, *a*, is updated by the sum of current reward, *r*, and the discounted (γ) maximum *Q* value for the new state among all its actions. The discount factor delays the reward from the future compared to the present rewards. For example, a reward of 100 today will be worth more than 100 in the future. Similarly, a reward of 100 in the future must be worth less than 100 today. Therefore, we will discount the future rewards. Repeating this update process continuously results in Q-table values converging to accurate measures of the expected future reward for a given action in a given state.

When the volume of the state and action spaces increase, maintaining a Q-table is difficult. In the real world, the state spaces are infinitely large. Thus, there's a requirement of another approach that can produce *Q(s,a)* without a Q-table. One solution is to replace the Q-table with a function. This function will take the state as the input in the form of a vector, and output the vector of Q-values for all the actions in the given state. This function approximator can be represented by a neural network to predict the Q-values. Thus, we can add more layers and fit in a deep neural network for better prediction of Q-values when the state and action space becomes large, which seemed impossible with a Q-table. This gives rise to the Q-network and if a deeper neural network, such as a convolutional neural network, is used then it results in a **deep Q-network (DQN)**.

More details on Q-learning and deep Q-networks will be covered in `Chapter 5`, *Q-Learning and Deep Q-Networks*.

Asynchronous advantage actor-critic

The A3C algorithm was published in June 2016 by the combined team of Google DeepMind and MILA. It is simpler and has a lighter framework that used the asynchronous gradient descent to optimize the deep neural network. It was faster and was able to show good results on the multi-core CPU instead of GPU. One of A3C's big advantages is that it can work on continuous as well as discrete action spaces. As a result, it has opened the gateway for many new challenging problems that have complex state and action spaces.

We will discuss it at a high note here, but we will dig deeper in Chapter 6, *Asynchronous Methods*. Let's start with the name, that is, **asynchronous advantage actor-critic (A3C)** algorithm and unpack it to get the basic overview of the algorithm:

- **Asynchronous**: In DQN, you remember we used a neural network with our agent to predict actions. This means there is one agent and it's interacting with one environment. What A3C does is create multiple copies of the agent-environment to make the agent learn more efficiently. A3C has a global network, and multiple worker agents, where each agent has its own set of network parameters and each of them interact with their copy of the environment simultaneously without interacting with another agent's environment. The reason this works better than a single agent is that the experience of each agent is independent of the experience of the other agents. Thus, the overall experience from all the worker agents results in diverse training.

- **Actor-critic**: Actor-critic combines the benefits of both value iteration and policy iteration. Thus, the network will estimate both a value function, V(s), and a policy, π(s), for a given state, **s**. There will be two separate fully-connected layers at the top of the function approximator neural network that will output the value and policy of the state, respectively. The agent uses the value, which acts as a critic to update the policy, that is, the intelligent actor.

- **Advantage**: Policy gradients used discounted returns telling the agent whether the action was good or bad. Replacing that with Advantage not only quantifies the the good or bad status of the action but helps in encouraging and discouraging actions better(we will discuss this in Chapter 4, *Policy Gradients*).

Introduction to TensorFlow and OpenAI Gym

TensorFlow is the mathematical library created by the team of Google Brain at Google. Thanks to its dataflow programming, it's being heaving used as a deep learning library both in research and development sectors. Since its inception in 2015, TensorFlow has grown a very big community.

OpenAI Gym is a reinforcement learning playground created by the team at OpenAI with an aim to provide a simple interface, since creating an environment is itself a tedious task in reinforcement learning. It provides a good list of environments to test your reinforcement learning algorithms in so that you can benchmark them.

Basic computations in TensorFlow

The base of TensorFlow is the **computational graph**, which we discussed earlier in this chapter, and **tensors**. A tensor is an n-dimensional vector. Thus, a scalar and a matrix variable is also a tensor. Here, we will try some of the basic computations to start with TensorFlow. Please try to implement this section in a python IDE such as Jupyter Notebook.

For the TensorFlow installation and dependencies please refer to the following link:

```
https://www.tensorflow.org/install/
```

Import `tensorflow` by the following command:

```
import tensorflow as tf
```

`tf.zeros()` and `tf.ones()` are some of the functions that instantiate basic tensors. The `tf.zeros()` takes a tensor shape (that is, a tuple) and returns a tensor of that shape with all the values being zero. Similarly, `tf.ones()` takes a tensor shape but returns a tensor of that shape containing only ones. Try the following commands in python shell to create a tensor:

```
>>> tf.zeros(3)

<tf.Tensor 'zeros:0' shape=(3,) dtype=float32>

>>>tf.ones(3)

<tf.Tensor 'ones:0' shape=(3,) dtype=float32>
```

As you can see, TensorFlow returns a reference to the tensor and not the value of the tensor. In order to get the value, we can use `eval()` or `run()`, a function of tensor objects by running a session as follows:

```
>>> a = tf.zeros(3)
>>> with tf.Session() as sess:
        sess.run(a)
        a.eval()

array([0., 0.,0.], dtype=float32)

array([0., 0.,0.], dtype=float32)
```

Next come the `tf.fill()` and `tf.constant()` methods to create a tensor of a certain shape and value:

```
>>> a = tf.fill((2,2),value=4.)
>>> b = tf.constant(4.,shape=(2,2))
>>> with tf.Session() as sess:
        sess.run(a)
        sess.run(b)

array([[ 4., 4.],
[ 4., 4.]], dtype=float32)

array([[ 4., 4.],
[ 4., 4.]], dtype=float32)
```

Next, we have functions that can randomly initialize a tensor. Among them, the most frequently used ones are:

- `tf.random_normal`: Samples random values from the Normal distribution of specified mean and standard deviation
- `tf.random_uniform()`: Samples random values from the Uniform distribution of a specified range

```
>>> a = tf.random_normal((2,2),mean=0,stddev=1)
>>> b = tf.random_uniform((2,2),minval=-3,maxval=3)
>>> with tf.Session() as sess:
        sess.run(a)
        sess.run(b)

array([[-0.31790468, 1.30740941],
[-0.52323157, -0.2980336 ]], dtype=float32)

array([[ 1.38419437, -2.91128755],
[-0.80171156, -0.84285879]], dtype=float32)
```

Variables in TensorFlow are holders for tensors and are defined by the function `tf.Variable()`:

```
>>> a = tf.Variable(tf.ones((2,2)))
>>> a

<tf.Variable 'Variable:0' shape=(2, 2) dtype=float32_ref>
```

The evaluation fails in case of variables because they have to be explicitly initialized by using `tf.global_variables_initializer` within a session:

```
>>> a = tf.Variable(tf.ones((2,2)))
>>> with tf.Session() as sess:
        sess.run(tf.global_variables_initializer())
        a.eval()

array([[ 1.,  1.],
 [ 1.,  1.]], dtype=float32)
```

Next in the queue, we have matrices. Identity matrices are square matrices with ones in the diagonal and zeros elsewhere. This can be done with the function `tf.eye()`:

```
>>> id = tf.eye(4) #size of the square matrix = 4
>>> with tf.Session() as sess:
        sess.run(id)

array([[ 1.,  0.,  0.,  0.],
 [ 0.,  1.,  0.,  0.],
 [ 0.,  0.,  1.,  0.],
 [ 0.,  0.,  0.,  1.]], dtype=float32)
```

Similarly, there are diagonal matrices, which have values in the diagonal and zeros elsewhere, as shown here:

```
>>> a = tf.range(1,5,1)
>>> md = tf.diag(a)
>>> mdn = tf.diag([1,2,5,3,2])
>>> with tf.Session() as sess:
        sess.run(md)
        sess.run(mdn)

array([[1, 0, 0, 0],
[0, 2, 0, 0],
[0, 0, 3, 0],
[0, 0, 0, 4]], dtype=int32)

array([[1, 0, 0, 0, 0],
[0, 2, 0, 0, 0],
[0, 0, 5, 0, 0],
[0, 0, 0, 3, 0],
[0, 0, 0, 0, 2]], dtype=int32)
```

We use the `tf.matrix_transpose()` function to transpose the given matrix, as shown here:

```
>>> a = tf.ones((2,3))
>>> b = tf.transpose(a)
>>> with tf.Session() as sess:
        sess.run(a)
        sess.run(b)

array([[ 1., 1., 1.],
[ 1., 1., 1.]], dtype=float32)

array([[ 1., 1.],
[ 1., 1.],
[ 1., 1.]], dtype=float32)
```

The next matrix operation is the matrix multiplication function as shown here. This is done by the function `tf.matmul()`:

```
>>> a = tf.ones((3,2))
>>> b = tf.ones((2,4))
>>> c = tf.matmul(a,b)
>>> with tf.Session() as sess:
        sess.run(a)
        sess.run(b)
        sess.run(c)

array([[ 1., 1.],
[ 1., 1.],
[ 1., 1.]], dtype=float32)

array([[ 1., 1., 1., 1.],
[ 1., 1., 1., 1.]], dtype=float32)

array([[ 2., 2., 2., 2.],
[ 2., 2., 2., 2.],
[ 2., 2., 2., 2.]], dtype=float32)
```

Reshaping of tensors from one to another is done by using the `tf.reshape()` function, as shown here:

```
>>> a = tf.ones((2,4)) #initial shape is (2,4)
>>> b = tf.reshape(a,(8,)) # reshaping it to a vector of size 8. Thus shape
is (8,)
>>> c = tf.reshape(a,(2,2,2)) #reshaping tensor a to shape (2,2,2)
>>> d = tf.reshape(b,(2,2,2)) #reshaping tensor b to shape (2,2,2)
#####Thus, tensor 'c' and 'd' will be similar
```

```
>>> with tf.Session() as sess:
        sess.run(a)
        sess.run(b)
        sess.run(c)
        sess.run(d)

array([[ 1., 1., 1., 1.],
[ 1., 1., 1., 1.]], dtype=float32)

array([ 1., 1., 1., 1., 1., 1., 1., 1.], dtype=float32)

array([[[ 1., 1.],
[ 1., 1.]],
[[ 1., 1.],
[ 1., 1.]]], dtype=float32)
&gt;
array([[[ 1., 1.],
[ 1., 1.]],
[[ 1., 1.],
[ 1., 1.]]], dtype=float32)
```

The flow of computation in TensorFlow is represented as a computational graph, which is as instance of `tf.Graph`. The graph contains tensors and operation objects, and keeps track of a series of operations and tensors involved. The default instance of the graph can be fetched by `tf.get_default_graph()`:

```
>>> tf.get_default_graph()

<tensorflow.python.framework.ops.Graph object at 0x7fa3e139b550>
```

We will explore complex operations, the creation of neural networks, and much more in TensorFlow in the coming chapters.

An introduction to OpenAI Gym

The OpenAI Gym, created by the team at OpenAI is a playground of different environments where you can develop and compare your reinforcement learning algorithms. It is compatible with deep learning libraries such as TensorFlow and Theano.

OpenAI Gym consists of two parts:

- **The gym open-source library**: This consists of many environments for different test problems where you can test your reinforcement learning algorithms. This suffices with the information of state and action spaces.
- **The OpenAI Gym service**: This allows you to compare the performance of your agent with other trained agents.

For the installation and dependencies, please refer to the following link:

```
https://gym.openai.com/docs/
```

With the basics covered, now we can start with the implementation of reinforcement learning using the OpenAI Gym from next `Chapter 2`, *Training Reinforcement Learning Agents using OpenAI Gym.*

The pioneers and breakthroughs in reinforcement learning

Before going on floor with all the coding, let's shed some light on some of the pioneers, industrial leaders, and research breakthroughs in the field of deep reinforcement learning.

David Silver

Dr. David Silver, with an h-index of 30, heads the research team of reinforcement learning at Google DeepMind and is the lead researcher on AlphaGo. David co-founded Elixir Studios and then completed his PhD in reinforcement learning from the University of Alberta, where he co-introduced the algorithms used in the first master-level 9x9 Go programs. After this, he became a lecturer at University College London. He used to consult for DeepMind before joining full-time in 2013. David lead the AlphaGo project, which became the first program to defeat a top professional player in the game of Go.

Pieter Abbeel

Pieter Abbeel is a professor at UC Berkeley and was a Research Scientist at OpenAI. Pieter completed his PhD in Computer Science under Andrew Ng. His current research focuses on robotics and machine learning, with a particular focus on deep reinforcement learning, deep imitation learning, deep unsupervised learning, meta-learning, learning-to-learn, and AI safety. Pieter also won the NIPS 2016 Best Paper Award.

Google DeepMind

Google DeepMind is a British artificial intelligence company founded in September 2010 and acquired by Google in 2014. They are an industrial leader in the domains of deep reinforcement learning and a neural turing machine. They made news in 2016 when the AlphaGo program defeated Lee Sedol, 9th dan Go player. Google DeepMind has channelized its focus on two big sectors: energy and healthcare.

Here are some of its projects:

- In July 2016, Google DeepMind and Moorfields Eye Hospital announced their collaboration to use eye scans to research early signs of diseases leading to blindness
- In August 2016, Google DeepMind announced its collaboration with University College London Hospital to research and develop an algorithm to automatically differentiate between healthy and cancerous tissues in head and neck areas
- Google DeepMind AI reduced the Google's data center cooling bill by 40%

The AlphaGo program

As mentioned previously in Google DeepMind, AlphaGo is a computer program that first defeated Lee Sedol and then Ke Jie, who at the time was the world No. 1 in Go. In 2017 an improved version, AlphaGo zero was launched that defeated AlphaGo 100 games to 0.

Libratus

Libratus is an artificial intelligence computer program designed by the team led by Professor Tuomas Sandholm at Carnegie Mellon University to play Poker. Libratus and its predecessor, Claudico, share the same meaning, balanced.

In January 2017, it made history by defeating four of the world's best professional poker players in a marathon 20-day poker competition.

Though Libratus focuses on playing poker, its designers mentioned its ability to learn any game that has incomplete information and where opponents are engaging in deception. As a result, they have proposed that the system can be applied to problems in cybersecurity, business negotiations, or medical planning domains.

Summary

In this chapter, we covered the building blocks, such as shallow and deep neural networks that included logistic regression, single hidden layer neural network, RNNs, LSTMs, CNNs, and their other variations. Catering to the these topics, we also covered multiple activation functions, how forward and backward propagation works, and the problems associated with the training of deep neural networks, such as vanishing and exploding gradients.

Then, we covered the very basic terminologies in reinforcement learning that we will explore in detail in the coming chapters. These were the optimality criteria, which are value function and policy. We also gained an understanding of some reinforcement learning algorithms, such as Q-learning and A3C algorithms. Then, we covered some basic computations in the TensorFlow framework, an introduction to OpenAI Gym, and also discussed some of the influential pioneers and research breakthroughs in the field of reinforcement learning.

In the following chapter, we will implement a basic reinforcement learning algorithm to a couple of OpenAI Gym framework environments and get a better understanding of OpenAI Gym.

2
Training Reinforcement Learning Agents Using OpenAI Gym

The OpenAI Gym provides a lot of virtual environments to train your reinforcement learning agents. In reinforcement learning, the most difficult task is to create the environment. This is where OpenAI Gym comes to the rescue, by providing a lot of toy game environments to provide users with a platform to train and benchmark their reinforcement learning agents.

In other words, it provides a playground for the reinforcement learning agent to learn and benchmark their performance, where the agent has to learn to navigate from the start state to the goal state without undergoing any mishaps.

Thus, in this chapter, we will be learning to understand and use environments from OpenAI Gym and trying to implement basic Q-learning and the Q-network for our agents to learn.

OpenAI Gym provides different types of environments. They are as follows:

- Classic control
- Algorithmic
- Atari
- Board games
- Box2D
- Parameter tuning
- MuJoCo
- Toy text
- Safety

- Minecraft
- PyGame learning environment
- Soccer
- Doom

For the details of these broad environment categories and their environmental playground, go to `https://Gym.openai.com/envs/`.

We will cover the following topics in this chapter:

- The OpenAI Gym environment
- Programming an agent using an OpenAI Gym environment
- Using the Q-Network for real-world applications

The OpenAI Gym

In order to download and install OpenAI Gym, you can use any of the following options:

```
$ git clone https://github.com/openai/gym
$ cd gym
$ sudo pip install -e . # minimal install
```

This will do the minimum install. You can later run the following to do a full install:

```
$ sudo pip install -e .[all]
```

You can also fetch Gym as a package for different Python versions as follows:

For Python 2.7, you can use the following options:

```
$ sudo pip install gym              # minimal install
$ sudo pip install gym[all]         # full install
$ sudo pip install gym[atari]       #for Atari specific environment
installation
```

For Python 3.5, you can use the following options:

```
$ sudo pip3 install gym              # minimal install
$ sudo pip3 install gym[all]         # full install
$ sudo pip install gym[atari]        #for Atari specific environment
installation
```

Understanding an OpenAI Gym environment

To understand the basics of importing Gym packages, loading an environment, and other important functions associated with OpenAI Gym, here's an example of a **Frozen Lake** environment.

Load the Frozen Lake environment in the following way:

```
import Gym
env = Gym.make ('FrozenLake-v0')     #make function of Gym loads the specified
environment
```

Next, we come to resetting the environment. While performing a reinforcement learning task, an agent undergoes learning through multiple episodes. As a result, at the start of each episode, the environment needs to be reset so that it comes to its initial situation and the agent begins from the start state. The following code shows the process for resetting an environment:

```
import Gym
env = Gym.make ('FrozenLake-v0')
s = env.reset ()  # resets the environment and returns the start state as a
value
print (s)

-----------
0                 #initial state is 0
```

After taking each action, there might be a requirement to show the status of the agent in the environment. Visualizing that status is done by:

```
env.render ()

-----------
SFFF
FHFH
FFFH
HFFG
```

The preceding output shows that this is an environment with *4 x 4* grids, that is, 16 states arranged in the preceding manner where S, H, F, and G represents different forms of a state where:

- **S**: Start block
- **F**: Frozen block

- **H**: Block has hole
- **G**: Goal block

In newer versions of the Gym, the environment features can't be modified directly. This is done by unwrapping the environment parameters with:

```
env = env.unwrapped
```

Each environment is defined by the state spaces and action spaces for the agent to perform. The type (discrete or continuous) and size of state spaces and action spaces is very important to know in order to build a reinforcement learning agent:

```
print(env.action_space)
print(env.action_space.n)


----------------
Discrete(4)
4
```

The `Discrete(4)` output means that the action space of the Frozen Lake environment is a discrete set of values and has four distinct actions that can be performed by the agent.

```
print(env.observation_space)
print(env.observation_space.n)


----------------
Discrete(16)
16
```

The `Discrete(16)` output means that the observation (state) space of the Frozen Lake environment is a discrete set of values and has 16 different states to be explored by the agent.

Programming an agent using an OpenAI Gym environment

The environment considered for this section is the **Frozen Lake v0**. The actual documentation of the concerned environment can be found at `https://gym.openai.com/envs/FrozenLake-v0/`.

This environment consists of *4 x 4* grids representing a lake. Thus, we have 16 grid blocks, where each block can be a start block(S), frozen block(F), goal block(G), or a hole block(H). Thus, the objective of the agent is to learn to navigate from start to goal without falling in the hole:

```
import Gym
env = Gym.make('FrozenLake-v0')        #loads the environment FrozenLake-v0
env.render()                           # will output the environment and
position of the agent


--------------------

SFFF
FHFH
FFFH
HFFG
```

At any given state, an agent has four actions to perform, which are up, down, left, and right. The reward at each step is 0 except the one leading to the goal state, then the reward would be 1. We start from the S state and our goal is to reach the G state without landing up in the H state in the most optimized path through the F states.

Q-Learning

Now, let's try to program a reinforcement learning agent using Q-learning. Q-learning consists of a Q-table that contains Q-values for each state-action pair. The number of rows in the table is equal to the number of states in the environment and the number of columns equals the number of actions. Since the number of states is 16 and the number of actions is 4, the Q-table for this environment consists of 16 rows and 4 columns. The code for it is given here:

```
print("Number of actions : ",env.action_space.n)
print("Number of states : ",env.observation_space.n)


----------------------

Number of actions : 4
Number of states : 16
```

The steps involved in Q-learning are as follows:

1. Initialize the Q-table with zeros (eventually, updating will happen with a reward received for each action taken during learning).

2. Updating of a Q value for a state-action pair, that is, Q(s, a) is given by:

$$Q(s,a) \; <= \; Q(s,a) + \alpha[r + \gamma \; max_{a'} \; Q(s',a') - Q(s,a)]$$

In this formula:

- s = current state
- a = action taken (choosing new action through epsilon-greedy approach)
- s' = resulted new state
- a' = action for the new state
- r = reward received for the action a
- α = learning rate, that is, the rate at which the learning of the agent converges towards minimized error
- γ = discount factor, that is, discounts the future reward to get an idea of how important that future reward is with regards to the current reward

3. By updating the Q-values as per the formula mentioned in step 2, the table converges to obtain accurate values for an action in a given state.

The Epsilon-Greedy approach

The Epsilon-Greedy is a widely used solution to the explore-exploit dilemma. Exploration is all about searching and exploring new options through experimentation and research to generate new values, while exploitation is all about refining existing options by repeating those options and improving their values.

The Epsilon-Greedy approach is very simple to understand and easy to implement:

```
epsilon(€) = 0.05 or 0.1 #any small value between 0 to 1
#epsilon(€) is the probability of exploration

p = random number between 0 and 1

if p ≤ epsilon(€) :
    pull a random action
else:
    pull current best action
```

Eventually, after several iterations, we discover the best actions among all at each state because it gets the option to explore new random actions as well as exploit the existing actions and refine them.

Let's try to implement a basic Q-learning algorithm to make an agent learn how to navigate across this frozen lake of 16 grids, from the start to the goal without falling into the hole:

```python
# importing dependency libraries
from __future__ import print_function
import Gym
import numpy as np
import time


#Load the environment

env = Gym.make('FrozenLake-v0')

s = env.reset()
print("initial state : ",s)
print()

env.render()
print()

print(env.action_space) #number of actions
print(env.observation_space) #number of states
print()

print("Number of actions : ",env.action_space.n)
print("Number of states : ",env.observation_space.n)
print()

#Epsilon-Greedy approach for Exploration and Exploitation of the state-
action spaces
def epsilon_greedy(Q,s,na):
    epsilon = 0.3
    p = np.random.uniform(low=0,high=1)
    #print(p)
    if p > epsilon:
        return np.argmax(Q[s,:])#say here,initial policy = for each state
consider the action having highest Q-value
    else:
        return env.action_space.sample()


# Q-Learning Implementation

#Initializing Q-table with zeros
```

```
Q = np.zeros([env.observation_space.n,env.action_space.n])

#set hyperparameters
lr = 0.5 #learning rate
y = 0.9 #discount factor lambda
eps = 100000 #total episodes being 100000


for i in range(eps):
    s = env.reset()
    t = False
    while(True):
        a = epsilon_greedy(Q,s,env.action_space.n)
        s_,r,t,_ = env.step(a)
        if (r==0):
            if t==True:
                r = -5 #to give negative rewards when holes turn up
                Q[s_] = np.ones(env.action_space.n)*r #in terminal state Q
value equals the reward
            else:
                r = -1 #to give negative rewards to avoid long routes
        if (r==1):
                r = 100
                Q[s_] = np.ones(env.action_space.n)*r #in terminal state Q
value equals the reward
        Q[s,a] = Q[s,a] + lr * (r + y*np.max(Q[s_,a]) - Q[s,a])
        s = s_
        if (t == True) :
            break

print("Q-table")
print(Q)
print()

print("Output after learning")
print()
#learning ends with the end of the above loop of several episodes above
#let's check how much our agent has learned
s = env.reset()
env.render()
while(True):
    a = np.argmax(Q[s])
    s_,r,t,_ = env.step(a)
    print("===============")
    env.render()
    s = s_
    if(t==True) :
        break
```

```
----------------------------------------------------------------------------
---------------------
<<OUTPUT>>

initial state : 0

SFFF
FHFH
FFFH
HFFG

Discrete(4)
Discrete(16)

Number of actions : 4
Number of states : 16

Q-table
[[  -9.85448046   -7.4657981    -9.59584501  -10.          ]
 [  -9.53200011   -9.54250775   -9.10115662  -10.          ]
 [  -9.65308982   -9.51359977   -7.52052469  -10.          ]
 [  -9.69762313   -9.5540111    -9.56571455  -10.          ]
 [  -9.82319854   -4.83823005   -9.56441915   -9.74234959]
 [  -5.           -5.           -5.           -5.          ]
 [  -9.6554905    -9.44717167   -7.35077759   -9.77885057]
 [  -5.           -5.           -5.           -5.          ]
 [  -9.66012445   -4.28223592   -9.48312882   -9.76812285]
 [  -9.59664264    9.60799515   -4.48137699   -9.61956668]
 [  -9.71057124   -5.6863911    -2.04563412   -9.75341962]
 [  -5.           -5.           -5.           -5.          ]
 [  -5.           -5.           -5.           -5.          ]
 [  -9.54737964   22.84803205   18.17841481   -9.45516929]
 [  -9.69494035   34.16859049   72.04055782   40.62254838]
 [ 100.          100.          100.          100.          ]]

Output after learning

SFFF
FHFH
FFFH
HFFG
===============
  (Down)
SFFF
FHFH
FFFH
HFFG
===============
```

```
   (Down)
SFFF
FHFH
FFFH
HFFG
==============
   (Right)
SFFF
FHFH
FFFH
HFFG
==============
   (Right)
SFFF
FHFH
FFFH
HFFG
==============
   (Right)
SFFF
FHFH
FFFH
HFFG
==============
   (Right)
SFFF
FHFH
FFFH
HFFG
==============
   (Right)
SFFF
FHFH
FFFH
HFFG
==============
   (Right)
SFFF
FHFH
FFFH
HFFG
==============
   (Right)
SFFF
FHFH
FFFH
HFFG
==============
```

```
    (Right)
SFFF
FHFH
FFFH
HFFG
===============
    (Right)
SFFF
FHFH
FFFH
HFFG
===============
    (Right)
SFFF
FHFH
FFFH
HFFG
```

Using the Q-Network for real-world applications

Maintaining a table for a small number of states is possible but in the real world, states become infinite. Thus, there is a need for a solution that incorporates the state information and outputs the Q-values for the actions without using the Q-table. This is where neural network acts a function approximator, which is trained over data of different state information and their corresponding Q-values for all actions, thereby, they are able to predict Q-values for any new state information input. The neural network used to predict Q-values instead of using a Q-table is called Q-network.

Here for the `FrozenLake-v0` environment, let's use a single neural network that takes state information as input, where state information is represented as a one hot encoded vector of the **1 x number of states** shape (here, 1 x 16) and outputs a vector of the **1 x number of actions** shape (here, 1 x 4). The output is the Q-values for all the actions:

```
# considering there are 16 states numbered from state 0 to state 15, then
state number 4 will be # represented in one hot encoded vector as
input_state = [0,0,0,0,1,0,0,0,0,0,0,0,0,0,0,0]
```

With the options of adding more hidden layers and different activation functions, a Q-network definitely has many advantages over a Q-table. Unlike a Q-table, in a Q-network, the Q-values are updated by minimizing the loss through backpropagation. The loss function is given by:

$$Loss = \sum (Q_{target} - Q_{predicted})^2$$

$$Q(s, a)_{target} = r + \gamma\, max_{a'}\, Q(s', a')$$

Let's try to implement this in Python and learn how to implement a basic Q-Network algorithm to make an agent learn to navigate across this frozen lake of 16 grids from the start to the goal without falling into the hole:

```python
# importing dependency libraries
from __future__ import print_function
import Gym
import numpy as np
import tensorflow as tf
import random

# Load the Environment
env = Gym.make('FrozenLake-v0')


# Q - Network Implementation

## Creating Neural Network

tf.reset_default_graph()
# tensors for inputs, weights, biases, Qtarget
inputs =
tf.placeholder(shape=[None,env.observation_space.n],dtype=tf.float32)
W =
tf.get_variable(name="W",dtype=tf.float32,shape=[env.observation_space.n,en
v.action_space.n],initializer=tf.contrib.layers.xavier_initializer())
b = tf.Variable(tf.zeros(shape=[env.action_space.n]),dtype=tf.float32)

qpred = tf.add(tf.matmul(inputs,W),b)
apred = tf.argmax(qpred,1)

qtar = tf.placeholder(shape=[1,env.action_space.n],dtype=tf.float32)
loss = tf.reduce_sum(tf.square(qtar-qpred))

train = tf.train.AdamOptimizer(learning_rate=0.001)
minimizer = train.minimize(loss)
```

```
## Training the neural network

init = tf.global_variables_initializer() #initializing tensor variables
#initializing parameters
y = 0.5 #discount factor
e = 0.3 #epsilon value for epsilon-greedy task
episodes = 10000 #total number of episodes

with tf.Session() as sess:
    sess.run(init)
    for i in range(episodes):
        s = env.reset() #resetting the environment at the start of each
episode
        r_total = 0 #to calculate the sum of rewards in the current episode
        while(True):
            #running the Q-network created above
            a_pred,q_pred =
sess.run([apred,qpred],feed_dict={inputs:np.identity(env.observation_space.
n)[s:s+1]})
            #a_pred is the action prediction by the neural network
            #q_pred contains q_values of the actions at current state 's'
            if np.random.uniform(low=0,high=1) < e: #performing epsilon-
greedy here
                a_pred[0] = env.action_space.sample()
                #exploring different action by randomly assigning them as
the next action
            s_,r,t,_ = env.step(a_pred[0]) #action taken and new state 's_'
is encountered with a feedback reward 'r'
            if r==0:
                if t==True:
                    r=-5 #if hole make the reward more negative
                else:
                    r=-1 #if block is fine/frozen then give slight negative
reward to optimize the path
            if r==1:
                r=5 #good positive goat state reward
            q_pred_new =
sess.run(qpred,feed_dict={inputs:np.identity(env.observation_space.n)[s_:s_
+1]})
            #q_pred_new contains q_values of the actions at the new state
            #update the Q-target value for action taken
            targetQ = q_pred
            max_qpredn = np.max(q_pred_new)
            targetQ[0,a_pred[0]] = r + y*max_qpredn
            #this gives our targetQ
            #train the neural network to minimize the loss
            _ =
sess.run(minimizer,feed_dict={inputs:np.identity(env.observation_space.n)[s
```

```
:s+1],qtar:targetQ})
            s=s_
            if t==True:
                break
    #learning ends with the end of the above loop of several episodes above
    #let's check how much our agent has learned
    print("Output after learning")
    print()
    s = env.reset()
    env.render()
    while(True):
        a =
sess.run(apred,feed_dict={inputs:np.identity(env.observation_space.n)[s:s+1
]})
        s_,r,t,_ = env.step(a[0])
        print("===============")
        env.render()
        s = s_
        if t==True:
            break
```


<<OUTPUT>>

Output after learning

SFFF
FHFH
FFFH
HFFG
===============
   (Down)
SFFF
FHFH
FFFH
HFFG
===============
   (Left)
SFFF
FHFH
FFFH
HFFG
===============
   (Up)
SFFF
FHFH
FFFH
HFFG

```
================
   (Down)
SFFF
FHFH
FFFH
HFFG
================
  (Right)
SFFF
FHFH
FFFH
HFFG
================
  (Right)
SFFF
FHFH
FFFH
HFFG
================
   (Up)
SFFF
FHFH
FFFH
HFFG
```

There is a cost of stability associated with both Q-learning and Q-networks. There will be cases when with the given set of hyperparameters of the Q-values are not converge, but with the same hyperparameters, sometimes converging is witnessed. This is because of the instability of these learning approaches. In order to tackle this, a better initial policy should be defined (here, the maximum Q-value of a given state) if the state space is small. Moreover, hyperparameters, especially learning rate, discount factors, and epsilon value, play an important role. Therefore, these values must be initialized properly.

Q-networks provide more flexibility compared to Q-learning, owing to increasing state spaces. A deep neural network in a Q-network might lead to better learning and performance. As far as playing Atari using Deep Q-Networks, there are many tweaks, which we will discuss in the coming chapters.

Summary

In this chapter, we learned about OpenAI Gym, including the installation of different important functions to load, render, and understand the environment state-action spaces. We learned about the Epsilon-Greedy approach as a solution to the exploration-exploitation dilemma, and tried to implement a basic Q-learning and Q-network algorithm to train a reinforcement-learning agent to navigate an environment from OpenAI Gym.

In the next chapter, we will cover the most fundamental concepts in Reinforcement Learning, which include **Markov Decision Processes (MDPs)**, Bellman Equation, and Markov Chain Monte Carlo.

3
Markov Decision Process

The **Markov decision process**, better known as **MDP**, is an approach in reinforcement learning to take decisions in a gridworld environment. A gridworld environment consists of states in the form of grids, such as the one in the FrozenLake-v0 environment from OpenAI gym, which we tried to examine and solve in the last chapter.

The MDP tries to capture a world in the form of a grid by dividing it into states, actions, models/transition models, and rewards. The solution to an MDP is called a policy and the objective is to find the optimal policy for that MDP task.

Thus, any reinforcement learning task composed of a set of states, actions, and rewards that follows the Markov property would be considered an MDP.

In this chapter, we will dig deep into MDPs, states, actions, rewards, policies, and how to solve them using Bellman equations. Moreover, we will cover the basics of Partially Observable MDP and their complexity in solving. We will also cover the exploration-exploitation dilemma and the famous E3 (explicit, explore, or exploit) algorithm. Then we will come to the fascinating part, where we will program an agent to learn and play pong using the principles of MDP.

We will cover the following topics in this chapter:

- Markov decision processes
- Partially observable Markov decision processes
- Training the FrozenLake-v0 environment using MDP

Markov decision processes

As already mentioned, an MDP is a reinforcement learning approach in a gridworld environment containing sets of states, actions, and rewards, following the Markov property to obtain an optimal policy. MDP is defined as the collection of the following:

- **States**: S
- **Actions**: A(s), A
- **Transition model**: T(s,a,s') ~ P(s'|s,a)
- **Rewards**: R(s), R(s,a), R(s,a,s')
- **Policy**: $\pi(s) \rightarrow a_{\pi^*}$ is the optimal policy

In the case of an MDP, the environment is fully observable, that is, whatever observation the agent makes at any point in time is enough to make an optimal decision. In case of a partially observable environment, the agent needs a memory to store the past observations to make the best possible decisions.

Let's try to break this into different lego blocks to understand what this overall process means.

The Markov property

In short, as per the **Markov property**, in order to know the information of near future (say, at time *t+1*) the present information at time *t* matters.

Given a sequence, $[x_1, x_2, \ldots, x_t]$, the first order of Markov says, $P(x_t|x_{t-1}, x_{t-2}, \ldots, x_1) = P(x_t|x_{t-1})$, that is, x_t depends only on x_{t-1}. Therefore, x_{t+1} will depend only on x_t. The second order of Markov says, $P(x_t|x_{t-1}, x_{t-2}, \ldots, x_1) = P(x_t|x_{t-1}, x_{t-2})$, that is, x_t depends only on x_{t-1} and x_{t-2}.

In our context, we will follow the first order of the Markov property from now on. Therefore, we can convert any process to a Markov property if the probability of the new state, say x_{t+1}, depends only on the current state, x_t, such that the current state captures and remembers the property and knowledge from the past. Thus, as per the Markov property, the world (that is, the environment) is considered to be stationary, that is, the rules in the world are fixed.

The S state set

The **S state set** is a set of different states, represented as **s**, which constitute the environment. States are the feature representation of the data obtained from the environment. Thus, any input from the agent's sensors can play an important role in state formation. State spaces can be either discrete or continuous. The starts from start state and has to reach the goal state in the most optimized path without ending up in bad states (like the red colored state shown in the diagram below).

Consider the following gridworld as having 12 discrete states, where the green-colored grid is the goal state, red is the state to avoid, and black is a wall that you'll bounce back from if you hit it head on:

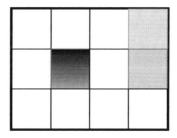

The states can be represented as 1, 2,....., 12 or by coordinates, (1,1),(1,2),.....(3,4).

Actions

The **actions** are the things an agent can perform or execute in a particular state. In other words, actions are sets of things an agent is allowed to do in the given environment. Like states, actions can also be either discrete or continuous.

Consider the following gridworld example having 12 discrete states and 4 discrete actions (**UP, DOWN, RIGHT**, and **LEFT**):

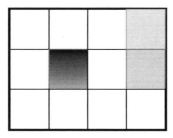

The preceding example shows the action space to be a discrete set space, that is, $a \in A$ where, $A = \{UP, DOWN, RIGHT, and LEFT\}$. It can also be treated as a function of state, that is, $a = A(s)$, where depending on the state function, it decides which action is possible.

Transition model

The transition model $T(s, a, s')$ is a function of three variables, which are the current state (s), action (a), and the new state (s'), and defines the rules to play the game in the environment. It gives probability $P(s'|s, a)$, that is, the probability of landing up in the new s' state given that the agent takes an action, a, in given state, s.

The transition model plays the crucial role in a stochastic world, unlike the case of a deterministic world where the probability for any landing state other than the determined one will have zero probability.

Let's consider the following environment (world) and consider different cases, determined and stochastic:

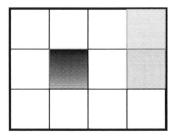

Since the actions $a \in A$ where, $A = \{UP, DOWN, RIGHT, and LEFT\}$.

The behavior of these two cases depends on certain factors:

- **Determined environment**: In a determined environment, if you take a certain action, say *UP*, you will certainly perform that action with probability 1.
- **Stochastic environment**: In a stochastic environment, if you take the same action, say *UP*, there will certain probability say 0.8 to actually perform the given action and there is 0.1 probability it can perform an action (either *LEFT* or *RIGHT*) perpendicular to the given action, *UP*. Here, for the s state and the *UP* action transition model, $T(s', UP, s) = P(s'| s, UP) = 0.8$.

Since $T(s,a,s') \sim P(s'|s,a)$, where the probability of new state depends on the current state and action only, and none of the past states. Thus, the transition model follows the first order Markov property.

We can also say that our universe is also a stochastic environment, since the universe is composed of atoms that are in different states defined by position and velocity. Actions performed by each atom change their states and cause changes in the universe.

Rewards

The **reward** of the state quantifies the usefulness of entering into a state. There are three different forms to represent the reward namely, $R(s)$, $R(s, a)$ and $R(s, a, s')$, but they are all equivalent.

For a particular environment, the domain knowledge plays an important role in the assignment of rewards for different states as minor changes in the reward do matter for finding the optimal solution to an MDP problem.

There are two approaches we reward our agent for when taking a certain action. They are:

- **Credit assignment problem**: We look at the past and check which actions led to the present reward, that is, which action gets the credit
- **Delayed rewards**: In contrast, in the present state, we check which action to take that will lead us to potential rewards

Delayed rewards form the idea of foresight planning. Therefore, this concept is being used to calculate the expected reward for different states. We will discuss this in the later sections.

Policy

Until now, we have covered the blocks that create an MDP problem, that is, states, actions, transition models, and rewards, now comes the solution. The policy is the solution to an MDP problem.

$$Policy : \pi(s) \to a$$

The policy is a function that takes the state as an input and outputs the action to be taken. Therefore, the policy is a command that the agent has to obey.

π^* is called the optimal policy, which maximizes the expected reward. Among all the policies taken, the optimal policy is the one that optimizes to maximize the amount of reward received or expected to receive over a lifetime. For an MDP, there's no end of the lifetime and you have to decide the end time.

Thus, the policy is nothing but a guide telling which action to take for a given state. It is not a plan but uncovers the underlying plan of the environment by returning the actions to take for each state.

The sequence of rewards - assumptions

The sequence of rewards play an important role in finding the optimal policy for an MDP problem, but there are certain assumptions that unveil how a sequence of rewards implements the concept of delayed rewards.

The infinite horizons

The first assumption is the infinite horizons, that is, the infinite amount of time steps to reach goal state from start state. Therefore,

$$\pi(s) \to a$$

The policy function doesn't take the remaining time steps into consideration. If it had been a finite horizon, then the policy would have been,

$$\pi(s, t) \to a$$

where t is the time steps left to get the task done.

Therefore, without the assumption of the infinite horizon, the notion of policy would not be stationary, that is, $\pi(s) \to a$, rather it would be $\pi(s, t) \to a$.

Utility of sequences

The utility of sequences refers to the overall reward received when the agent goes through the sequences of states. It is represented as $U(s_0, s_1, s_2, \ldots)$ where $s_0, s_1, s_2, \ldots$ represents the sequence of states.

The second assumption is that if there are two utilities, $U(s_0, s_1, s_2, \ldots)$ and $U(s_0, s_1', s_2', \ldots)$, such that the start state for both the sequences are the same and,

$$U(s_0, s_1, s_2, \ldots) > U(s_0, s_1', s_2', \ldots)$$

then,

$$U(s_1, s_2, \ldots) > U(s_1', s_2', \ldots)$$

This means, if the utility of sequence $U(s_0, s_1, s_2, \ldots)$ is greater than the other, $U(s_0, s_1', s_2', \ldots)$, provided the start state of both the sequences are the same then the sequences without that start state will hold the same inequality, that is, $U(s_1, s_2, \ldots)$ will be greater than $U(s_1', s_2', \ldots)$. This assumption is called the stationary of preferences.

Thus, the following equation satisfies the stationary of preferences,

$$U(s_0, s_1, s_2, \ldots) = \sum_{t=0}^{\infty} R(s_t)$$

The summation in the preceding formula is enough to satisfy our assumption, but it shares two disadvantages, which are as follows:

- Infinite time will make the summation infinite
- The summation doesn't differ in case or different order of sequences, that is, $U(a, b, c)$ and $U(a, c, b)$ both will have the same utility value, that is $R(a) + R(b) + R(c)$

Therefore, we implement the concept of delayed rewards by future rewards with a discount factor γ, such that,

$$U(s_0, s_1, s_2, \ldots\ldots) = \sum_{t=0}^{\infty} \gamma^t R(s_t)$$

, where $0 \leq \gamma < 1$

Let's consider that of all the $R(s_t)$, that is, rewards from different states in a given particular environment, R_{max} being the maximum value, then

$$\sum_{t=0}^{\infty} \gamma^t R(s_t) \leq \frac{R_{max}}{1 - \gamma}$$

How? Let's figure this upper limit out,

since, $R(s_t) \leq R_{max}$,

therefore, $\gamma^t R(s_t) \leq \gamma^t R_{max}$

therefore,

$$\sum_{t=0}^{\infty} \gamma^t R(s_t) \leq \sum_{t=0}^{\infty} \gamma^t R_{max}$$

$$\sum_{t=0}^{\infty} \gamma^t R_{max} = R_{max} [\sum_{t=0}^{\infty} \gamma^t]$$

$$\sum_{t=0}^{\infty} \gamma^t = [\gamma^0 + \gamma^1 + \gamma^2 + \ldots]$$

Let,

$$x = [\gamma^0 + \gamma^1 + \gamma^2 + \ldots\ldots\ldots\ldots]$$

then,

$$\gamma x = [\gamma^1 + \gamma^2 + \ldots\ldots\ldots\ldots]$$

thus,

$$x = \gamma^0 + \gamma x$$
$$x = 1 + \gamma x$$
$$(1 - \gamma)x = 1$$
$$x = \frac{1}{1 - \gamma}$$
$$R_{max}[\sum_{t=0}^{\infty} \gamma^t] = \frac{R_{max}}{1 - \gamma}$$

therefore,

$$\sum_{t=0}^{\infty} \gamma^t R(s_t) \leq \frac{R_{max}}{1 - \gamma}$$

The Bellman equations

Since the optimal π^* policy is the policy that maximizes the expected rewards, therefore,

$$\pi^* = argmax_{\pi} E[\sum_{\infty}^{t=0} \gamma^t R(s_t) \mid \pi]$$
,

where $E[\sum_{\infty}^{t=0} \gamma^t R(s_t) \mid \pi]$ means the expected value of the rewards obtained from the sequence of states agent observes if it follows the π policy. Thus, $argmax_{\pi}$ outputs the π policy that has the highest expected reward.

Similarly, we can also calculate the **utility of the policy of a state**, that is, if we are at the s state, given a π policy, then, the utility of the π policy for the s state, that is, $U^{\pi}(s)$ would be the expected rewards from that state onward:

$$U^{\pi}(s) = E[\sum_{t=0}^{\infty} \gamma^t R(s_t) \mid \pi, s_0 = s]$$

The immediate reward of the state, that is, $R(s)$ is different than the utility of the $U(s)$ state (that is, the utility of the optimal policy of the $U^{\pi^*}(s)$ state) because of the concept of delayed rewards. From now onward, the utility of the $U(s)$ state will refer to the utility of the optimal policy of the state, that is, the $U^{\pi^*}(s)$ state.

Moreover, the optimal policy can also be regarded as the policy that maximizes the expected utility. Therefore,

$$\pi^* = argmax_a \sum_{s'} T(s, a, s')U(s')$$

where, $T(s,a,s')$ is the transition probability, that is, $P(s'|s,a)$ and $U(s')$ is the utility of the new landing state after the a action is taken on the s state.

$$\sum_{s'} T(s, a, s')U(s')$$
refers to the summation of all possible new state outcomes for a particular action taken, then whichever action gives the maximum value of $\sum_{s'} T(s, a, s')U(s')$ that is considered to be the part of the optimal policy and thereby, the utility of the 's' state is given by the following **Bellman equation**,

$$U(s) = R(s) + \gamma \, max_a \sum_{s'} T(s, a, s')U(s')$$

where, $R(s)$ is the immediate reward and $max_a \sum_{s'} T(s, a, s')U(s')$ is the reward from future, that is, the discounted utilities of the 's' state where the agent can reach from the given s state if the action, a, is taken.

Solving the Bellman equation to find policies

Say we have some n states in the given environment and if we see the Bellman equation,

$$U(s) = R(s) + \gamma \, max_a \sum_{s'} T(s, a, s')U(s')$$

we find out that *n* states are given; therefore, we will have *n* equations and *n* unknown but the max_a function makes it non-linear. Thus, we cannot solve them as linear equations.

Therefore, in order to solve:

- Start with an arbitrary utility

- Update the utilities based on the neighborhood until convergence, that is, update the utility of the state using the Bellman equation based on the utilities of the landing states from the given state

Iterate this multiple times to lead to the true value of the states. This process of iterating to convergence towards the true value of the state is called **value iteration**.

For the terminal states where the game ends, the utility of those terminal state equals the immediate reward the agent receives while entering the terminal state.

Let's try to understand this by implementing an example.

An example of value iteration using the Bellman equation

Consider the following environment and the given information:

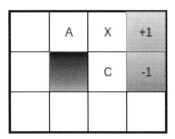

Given information:

- *A*, *C*, and *X* are the names of some states.

- The green-colored state is the goal state, *G*, with a reward of +1.

- The red-colored state is the bad state, *B*, with a reward of -1, try to prevent your agent from entering this state

- Thus, the green and red states are the terminal states, enter either and the game is over. If the agent encounters the green state, that is, the goal state, the agent wins, while if they enter the red state, then the agent loses the game.

- $\gamma = 1/2$, $R(s) = -0.04$ (that is, reward for all states except the G and B states is -0.04), $U_0(s) = 0$ (that is, the utility at the first time step is 0, except the G and B states).

- Transition probability $T(s,a,s')$ equals 0.8 if going in the desired direction; otherwise, 0.1 each if going perpendicular to the desired direction. For example, if the action is *UP* then with 0.8 probability, the agent goes *UP* but with 0.1 probability it goes *RIGHT* and 0.1 to the *LEFT*.

Questions:

1. Find $U_1(X)$, the utility of the X state at time step 1, that is, the agent will go through one iteration
2. Similarly, find $U_2(X)$

Solution:

$U_0(X) = 0$

$$U_1(X) = R(X) + \gamma\, max_a \sum_{s'} T(s, a, s')U_0(s')$$

$R(X) = -0.04$

Action a	s'	$T(s, a, s')$	$U_0(s')$	$T(s, a, s')U_0(s')$
RIGHT	G	0.8	+1	0.8 x 1 = 0.8
RIGHT	C	0.1	0	0.1 x 0 = 0
RIGHT	X	0.1	0	0.1 x 0 = 0

Thus, for action a = *RIGHT*,

$$[\sum_{s'} T(s, a, s')U_0(s') = 0.8 + 0 + 0 = 0.8]_{right}$$

Action a	s'	$T(s, a, s')$	$U_0(s')$	$T(s, a, s')U_0(s')$
DOWN	C	0.8	0	0.8 x 0 = 0
DOWN	G	0.1	+1	0.1 x 1 = 0.1
DOWN	A	0.1	0	0.1 x 0 = 0

Thus, for action a = DOWN,

$$[\sum_{s'} T(s, a, s')U_0(s') = 0 + 0.1 + 0 = 0.1]_{down}$$

Action a	s'	$T(s, a, s')$	$U_0(s')$	$T(s, a, s')U_0(s')$
UP	X	0.8	0	0.8 x 0 = 0
UP	G	0.1	+1	0.1 x 1 = 0.1
UP	A	0.1	0	0.1 x 0 = 0

Thus, for action a = UP,

$$[\sum_{s'} T(s, a, s')U_0(s') = 0 + 0.1 + 0 = 0.1]_{up}$$

Action a	s'	$T(s, a, s')$	$U_0(s')$	$T(s, a, s')U_0(s')$
LEFT	A	0.8	0	0.8 x 0 = 0
LEFT	X	0.1	0	0.1 x 0 = 0
LEFT	C	0.1	0	0.1 x 0 = 0

Thus, for action a = LEFT,

$$[\sum_{s'} T(s, a, s')U_0(s') = 0 + 0 + 0 = 0]_{left}$$

Therefore, among all actions,

$$max_a \sum_{s'} T(s,a,s')U_0(s') = [\sum_{s'} T(s,a,s')U_0(s') = 0.8 + 0 + 0 = 0.8]_{right} = 0.8$$

Therefore, $U_1(X) = -0.04 + 0.5 * 0.8 = 0.36$, where $R(X) = -0.04$ and $\gamma = 1/2 = 0.5$.

Similarly, calculate $U_1(A)$ and $U_1(C)$ and we get $U_1(A) = -0.04$ and $U_1(C) = -0.04$.

Since, $U_1(X) = 0.36, U_1(A) = -0.04, U_1(C) = -0.04, U_1(G) = 1, U_1(B) = -1$, and,

$$U_2(X) = R(X) + \gamma \, max_a \sum_{s'} T(s,a,s')U_1(s')$$
.

$R(X) = -0.04$

Action a	s'	$T(s,a,s')$	$U_0(s')$	$T(s,a,s')U_0(s')$
RIGHT	G	0.8	+1	0.8 x 1 = 0.8
RIGHT	C	0.1	-0.04	0.1 x -0.04 = -0.004
RIGHT	X	0.1	0.36	0.1 x 0.36 = 0.036

Thus, for action a = *RIGHT*,

$$[\sum_{s'} T(s,a,s')U_0(s') = 0.8 - 0.004 + 0.036 = 0.832]_{right}$$

Action a	s'	$T(s,a,s')$	$U_0(s')$	$T(s,a,s')U_0(s')$
DOWN	C	0.8	-0.04	0.8 x -0.04 = -0.032
DOWN	G	0.1	+1	0.1 x 1 = 0.1
DOWN	A	0.1	-0.04	0.1 x -0.04 = -0.004

Thus, for action $a = DOWN$,

$$[\sum_{s'} T(s, a, s')U_0(s') = -0.032 + 0.1 - 0.004 = 0.064]_{down}$$

Action a	s'	$T(s, a, s')$	$U_0(s')$	$T(s, a, s')U_0(s')$
UP	X	0.8	0.36	0.8 x 0.36 = 0.288
UP	G	0.1	+1	0.1 x 1 = 0.1
UP	A	0.1	-0.04	0.1 x -0.04 = -0.004

Thus, for action $a = UP$,

$$[\sum_{s'} T(s, a, s')U_0(s') = 0.288 + 0.1 - 0.004 = 0.384]_{up}$$

Action a	s'	$T(s, a, s')$	$U_0(s')$	$T(s, a, s')U_0(s')$
LEFT	A	0.8	-0.04	0.8 x -0.04 = -0.032
LEFT	X	0.1	0.36	0.1 x 0.36 = 0.036
LEFT	C	0.1	-0.04	0.1 x -0.04 = -0.004

Thus, for action $a = LEFT$,

$$[\sum_{s'} T(s, a, s')U_0(s') = -0.032 + 0.036 - 0.004 = 0]_{left}$$

Therefore, among all actions,

$$max_a \sum_{s'} T(s, a, s')U_0(s') = [\sum_{s'} T(s, a, s')U_0(s') = 0.8 - 0.004 + 0.036 = 0.832]_{right} = 0.832$$

Therefore, $U_2(X) = -0.04 + 0.5 * 0.832 = 0.376$, where $R(X) = -0.04$ and $\gamma = 1/2 = 0.5$.

Therefore, the answers to the preceding questions are:

1. $U_1(X) = 0.36$
2. $U_2(X) = 0.376$

Policy iteration

The process of obtaining optimal utility by iterating over the policy and updating the policy itself instead of value until the policy converges to the optimum is called **policy iteration**. The process of policy iteration is as follows:

- Start with a random policy, π_0

- For the given π_t policy at iteration step t, calculate $U_t = U_t^\pi$ by using the following formula:

$$U_t(s) = R(s) + \gamma \sum_{s'} T(s, \pi_t(s), s')U_{t-1}(s')$$

- Improve the π_{t+1} policy by

$$\pi_{t+1} = argmax_a \sum_{s'} T(s, a, s')U_t(s')$$

Partially observable Markov decision processes

In an MDP, the observable quantities are action, set A, the state, set S, transition model, T, and rewards, set R. This is not in case of **Partially observable MDP**, also known as **POMDP**. In a POMDP, there's an MDP inside that is not directly observable to the agent and takes the decision from whatever observations made.

In POMDP, there's an observation set, Z, containing different observable states and a observation function, O, which takes the s state and the z observation as inputs and outputs the probability of seeing that z observation in the s state.

POMDPs are basically a generalization of MDPs:

- **MDP**: {S,A,T,R}

- **POMDP**: {S,A,Z,T,R,O}

- where, S, A, T ,and R are the same. Therefore, for a POMDP to be a true MDP, following condition:

$Z = S$, that is, fully observe all states

$$O(s, z) = \begin{cases} 1 & ,if \ s = z \\ 0 & ,otherwise \end{cases}$$

POMDP are hugely intractable to solve optimally.

State estimation

If we expand the state spaces, this helps us to convert the POMDP into an MDP where Z contains fully observable state space. This gives the notion of **belief state b(s)**, which is the state that the decision maker is going to use in the context of a POMDP . The belief state, that is, $b(s)$ gives the probability of the agent being in the s state. Therefore, belief state, b, is a vector representing the probability distribution over all states. Thus, the belief state gets updated as soon as an action is taken.

Say, there's a belief state, b, the agent takes an action, a, and received some observations, z. This forms a new belief state. Therefore, we are converting a POMDP to belief MDP where it will consist of belief states as MDP states.

As per the preceding condition, the information given is the belief state, b, action, a, and observation, z. Therefore,

$b'(s')$ = probability of being in s state given after b, a, z, that is, $p(s'|b,a,z)$

$$p(s'|s, a, z) = \frac{p(z|b, a, s')}{p(z|b, a)} \sum_s b(s) . p(s'|s, b, a)$$

where, $p(z|b,a,s') = O(s',z)$ and $p(s'|s,b,a) = T(s,a,s')$. Thus,

$$p(s'|s,a,z) = \frac{O(s',z)}{p(z|b,a)} \sum_s b(s).T(s,a,s')$$

Value iteration in POMDPs

Value iteration in POMDPs is basically the value iteration on an infinite state space obtained from a belief MDP.

At *t=0*, $V_0(b) = 0$

At *t>0*, $V_t(b) = max_a[R(b,a) + \gamma \sum_z P(z|b,a).V_{t-1}(b')]$, where b' is $b'(s') = p(s'|b,a,z)$, that is, the state estimation for *(b,a,z)*, and *R(b,a)* is the expected reward over a belief state as shown here:

$$R(b,a) = \sum_s p(s).R(s,a) = \sum_s b(s).R(s,a)$$

where,

p(s) = probability of the *s* state

R(s,a) = reward in that state

$\sum_s b(s)R(s,a)$ = expected reward over a belief state

Training the FrozenLake-v0 environment using MDP

This is about a gridworld environment in OpenAI gym called **FrozenLake-v0**, discussed in Chapter 2, *Training Reinforcement Learning Agents Using OpenAI Gym*. We implemented Q-learning and Q-network (which we will discuss in future chapters) to get the understanding of an OpenAI gym environment.

Now, let's try to implement value iteration to obtain the utility value of each state in the FrozenLake-v0 environment, using the following code:

```
# importing dependency libraries
from __future__ import print_function
import gym
import numpy as np
import time

#Load the environment
env = gym.make('FrozenLake-v0')

s = env.reset()
print(s)
print()

env.render()
print()

print(env.action_space) #number of actions
print(env.observation_space) #number of states
print()

print("Number of actions : ",env.action_space.n)
print("Number of states : ",env.observation_space.n)
print()

# Value Iteration Implementation

#Initializing Utilities of all states with zeros
U = np.zeros([env.observation_space.n])

#since terminal states have utility values equal to their reward
U[15] = 1 #goal state
U[[5,7,11,12]] = -1 #hole states
termS = [5,7,11,12,15] #terminal states
#set hyperparameters
y = 0.8 #discount factor lambda

eps = 1e-3 #threshold if the learning difference i.e. prev_u - U goes below
this value break the learning

i=0
while(True):
    i+=1
    prev_u = np.copy(U)
    for s in range(env.observation_space.n):
```

```
        q_sa = [sum([p*(r + y*prev_u[s_]) for p, s_, r, _ in
env.env.P[s][a]]) for a in range(env.action_space.n)]
        if s not in termS:
            U[s] = max(q_sa)
    if (np.sum(np.fabs(prev_u - U)) <= eps):
        print ('Value-iteration converged at iteration# %d.' %(i+1))
        break

print("After learning completion printing the utilities for each states
below from state ids 0-15")
print()
print(U[:4])
print(U[4:8])
print(U[8:12])
print(U[12:16])
```


```
<<OUTPUT>>
[2018-04-16 20:59:03,661] Making new env: FrozenLake-v0
0


SFFF
FHFH
FFFH
HFFG

Discrete(4)
Discrete(16)

Number of actions : 4
Number of states : 16

Value-iteration converged at iteration# 25.
After learning completion printing the utilities for each states below from
state ids 0-15

[ 0.023482 0.00999637 0.00437564 0.0023448 ]
[ 0.0415207 -1. -0.19524141 -1. ]
[ 0.09109598 0.20932556 0.26362693 -1. ]
[-1. 0.43048408 0.97468581 1. ]
```

Analysing the output,

Let the state representation be as follows:

0 1 2 3

4 5 6 7

8 9 10 11

12 13 14 15

The start state of our agent is 0. Let's start from s=0,

$U[s=0] = 0.023482$, now the action can be either *UP*, *DOWN*, *LEFT*, or *RIGHT*.

At, $s=0$, if:

- action *UP* is taken, the s_new = 0, therefore, $u[s\_new]$ =0.023482
- action *DOWN* is taken, the s_new = 4, therefore, $u[s\_new]$ = 0.0415207
- action *LEFT* is taken, the s_new = 0, therefore, $u[s\_new]$ =0.023482
- action *RIGHT* is taken, the s_new = 1, therefore, $u[s\_new]$ = 0.00999637

The max is $u[s\_new = 4]$ =0.0415207, therefore, the action taken is *DOWN* and s_new = 4.

Now at $s=4$, if:

- action *UP* is taken, the s_new = 0, therefore, $u[s\_new]$ =0.023482
- action *DOWN* is taken, the s_new = 8, therefore, $u[s\_new]$ = 0.09109598
- action *LEFT* is taken, the s_new = 4, therefore, $u[s\_new]$ =0.0415207
- action *RIGHT* is taken, the s_new = 5, therefore, $u[s\_new]$ = -1.0

The max is $u[s\_new = 8]$ =0.09109598, then, the action taken would be *DOWN* and s_new = 8.

Now at $s=8$, if:

- action *UP* is taken, the s_new = 4, therefore, $u[s\_new]$ =0.0415207
- action *DOWN* is taken, the s_new = 12, therefore, $u[s\_new]$ = -1.0
- action *LEFT* is taken, the s_new = 8, therefore, $u[s\_new]$ =0.09109598
- action *RIGHT* is taken, the s_new = 9, therefore, $u[s\_new]$ = 0.20932556

The max is $u[s\_new = 9] = 0.20932556$, therefore, the action taken is *RIGHT* and $s\_new = 9$.

Now at $s=9$, if:

- action *UP* is taken, the $s\_new = 5$, therefore, $u[s\_new] = -1.0$
- action *DOWN* is taken, the $s\_new = 13$, therefore, $u[s\_new] = 0.43048408$
- action *LEFT* is taken, the $s\_new = 8$, therefore, $u[s\_new] = 0.09109598$
- action *RIGHT* is taken, the $s\_new = 10$, therefore, $u[s\_new] = 0.26362693$

The max is $u[s\_new = 13] = 0.43048408$, therefore, the action taken is *DOWN* and $s\_new = 13$.

Now at $s=13$, if:

- action *UP* is taken, the $s\_new = 9$, therefore, $u[s\_new] = 0.20932556$
- action *DOWN* is taken, the $s\_new = 13$, therefore, $u[s\_new] = 0.43048408$
- action *LEFT* is taken, the $s\_new = 12$, therefore, $u[s\_new] = -1.0$
- action *RIGHT* is taken, the $s\_new = 14$, therefore, $u[s\_new] = 0.97468581$

The max is $u[s\_new = 14] = 0.97468581$, therefore, the action taken is *RIGHT* and $s\_new = 14$.

Now at $s=14$, if:

- action *UP* is taken, the $s\_new = 10$, therefore, $u[s\_new] = 0.26362693$
- action *DOWN* is taken, the $s\_new = 14$, therefore, $u[s\_new] = 0.97468581$
- action *LEFT* is taken, the $s\_new = 13$, therefore, $u[s\_new] = 0.43048408$
- action *RIGHT* is taken, the $s\_new = 15(goal\ state)$, therefore, $u[s\_new] = 1.0$

The max is $u[s\_new = 15] = 1.0$, therefore, the action taken is *RIGHT* and $s\_new = 15$.

Therefore, our policy contains *DOWN, DOWN, RIGHT, DOWN, RIGHT,* and *RIGHT* to reach from $s=0(start\ state)$ to $s=15(goal\ state)$ by avoiding hole states (5, 7, 11, 12).

Summary

In this chapter, we covered the details of a gridworld type of environment and understood the basics of the Markov decision process, that is, states, actions, rewards, transition model, and policy. Moreover, we utilized this information to calculate the utility and optimal policy through value iteration and policy iteration approaches.

Apart from this, we got a basic understanding of what partially observable Markov decision processes look like and the challenges in solving them. Finally, we took our favorite gridworld environment from OpenAI gym, that is, FrozenLake-v0 and implemented a value iteration approach to make our agent learn to navigate that environment.

In the next chapter, we will start with policy gradients and move beyond **FrozenLake** to some other fascinating and complex environments.

4
Policy Gradients

So far, we have seen how to derive implicit policies from a value function with the value-based approach. Here, an agent will try to learn the policy directly. The approach is similar, any experienced agent will change the policy after witnessing it.

Value iteration, policy iteration, and Q-learning come under the value-based approach solved by dynamic programming, while the policy optimization approach involves policy gradients and union of this knowledge along with policy iteration, giving rise to actor-critic algorithms.

As per the dynamic programming method, there are a set of self-consistent equations to satisfy the Q and V values. Policy optimization is different, where policy learning happens directly, unlike deriving from the value function:

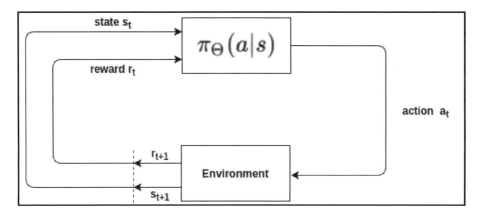

Thus, value-based methods learn the value function and we derive an implicit policy, but with policy-based methods, no value function is learned and the policy is learnt directly. The actor-critic method is more advanced because we learn both the value function and policy, and the network learning value function acts as a critic to the policy network, which is the actor. In this chapter, we will delve into the details of policy-based methods.

We will cover the following topics in this chapter:

- The policy optimization method
- Why policy optimization method?
- Policy objective functions
- Temporal difference rule
- Policy gradients
- Agent learning pong using policy gradient

The policy optimization method

The goal of the policy optimization method is to find the stochastic policy π_θ that is a distribution of actions for a given state that maximizes the expected sum of rewards. It aims to find the policy directly. The basic overview is to create a neural network (that is, policy network) that processes some state information and outputs the distribution of possible actions that an agent might take.

The two major components of policy optimization are:

- The weight parameter of the neural network is defined by θ vector, which is also the parameter of our control policy. Thus, our aim is to train the weight parameters to obtain the best policy. Since we value the policy as the expected sum of rewards for the given policy. Here, for different parameter values of θ, policy will differ and hence, the optimal policy would be the one having the maximum overall reward. Therefore, the θ parameter which has the maximum expected reward will be the optimal policy. Following is the formula for the expected sum of rewards:

$$max_\theta \ E[\sum_{t=0}^{H} \gamma^t R(s) \mid \pi_\theta]$$

That is maximize the expected sum of rewards.

Here, H = *time step at horizon*, so if the start time step $t = 0$, then the total time steps are $H+1$.

- The stochastic policy class smooths out the policy optimization problems, giving us a set of policies where the best can be chosen. In case of a deterministic policy in a grid-world environment, where changes owing to change in action is not smooth but if there would have been any distribution of actions for every state we can slightly shift the distribution which only slightly shifts the expected sum of rewards. This is the advantage of using a stochastic policy, where $\pi_\theta(a|s)$ gives the probability of action a for a given state s. Thus, π_θ gives the probabilistic distribution of actions for a given state.

Hence, because of the stochastic policy, we have a smooth optimization problem where gradient descent can be applied to obtain a good local optimum, thereby leading to an optimal policy.

Why policy optimization methods?

In this section, we will cover the pros and cons of policy optimization methods over value-based methods. The advantages are as follows:

- They provides better convergence.
- They are highly effective in case of high-dimensional/continuous state-action spaces. If action spaces are very big then a max function in a value-based method will be computationally expensive. So, the policy-based method directly changes the policy by changing the parameters instead of solving the max function at each step.
- Ability to learn stochastic policies.

The disadvantages associated with policy-based methods are as follows:

- Converges to local instead of global optimum
- Policy evaluation is inefficient and has high variance

We will discuss the approaches to tackle these disadvantages later in this chapter. For now, let's focus on the need for stochastic policies.

Why stochastic policy?

Let's go through two examples that will explain the importance of incorporating a stochastic policy compared to near to deterministic policy by value based methods.

Example 1 - rock, paper, scissors

Rock, paper, scissors is a two-player game comprising the following rules:

- Rock beats scissors
- Scissors beat paper
- Paper beat rock

Thus, there can't be a deterministic policy to win. Say, if there would have been a deterministic policy, that is rock will always win but that would be the case if an opponent has scissors. However, when an opponent has paper, then rock gets defeated. Thus, a determined solution is not possible in this environment. The only solution to this issue is using a uniform random policy that is stochastic in nature.

Example 2 - state aliased grid-world

Consider the following state aliased grid-world:

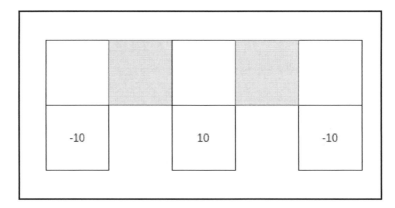

In the previous diagram, we see there are eight states, where two states with reward -10 are bad states to avoid and there's one state with reward 10 is a good state and also the goal state. However, our major concerns are the gray-shaded states, where the agent can't differentiate between these two states as they share the same features.

Say, the feature for any state s be $\phi(s, a)$ and actions are North, East, West, and South.

Considering these features, let's compare both value-based and policy-based methods:

- Value-based reinforcement learning will use the approximate value function
$Q(s, a) = f(\phi(s, a), w)$.
- Policy-based reinforcement learning will use parameterized policy
$\pi_\theta(s, a) = g(\phi(s, a), \theta)$.

Here, w is the parameter for the value function and θ is the parameter of the policy. As we know, the gray squares will have identical features, that is, have walls both in the North and South. Thus, this causes state aliasing owing to the same features. As a result, a value-based reinforcement learning method learns a near-deterministic policy as follows:

- Either move West in both the gray shaded states
- Or move East in both the gray shaded states

Either way, there is a high chance of getting stuck or taking a very long time to reach the goal state.

On the other hand, in case of a policy-based approach, an optimal stochastic policy will randomly choose East or West actions in the gray states because both actions will have the same probability as follows:

- π_θ(wall to North and South, action = East) = 0.5
- π_θ(wall to North and South, action = West) = 0.5

As a result, it will reach the goal state in fewer steps because both West and East will have an equal probability of occurring. Therefore, randomly different actions might occur for different gray shaded states leading to goal state faster compared to the value-based reinforcement learning approach. Thus, policy-based reinforcement learning can learn optimal stochastic policy.

Thus, from the previous examples, we have come to know that whenever state aliasing occurs, stochastic policy can perform better. So, whenever there is a case of state aliasing, that is, representation of the environment, state is partially observed (for example, you are in a partially observable Markov decision process) or the function approximator uses the features of the state, which limits the full view of the environment, then policy based methods using stochastic policy do better than value-based methods.

Policy objective functions

Let's discuss now how to optimize a policy. In policy methods, our main objective is that a given policy $\pi_\theta(s,a)$ with parameter vector θ finds the best values of the parameter vector. In order to measure which is the best, we measure $J(\theta)$ the quality of the policy $\pi_\theta(s,a)$ for different values of the parameter vector θ.

Before discussing the optimization methods, let's first figure out the different ways to measure the quality of a policy $\pi_\theta(s,a)$:

- If it's an episodic environment, $J(\theta)$ can be the value function of the start state $V^{\pi_\theta}(s_1)$ that is if it starts from any state s_1, then the value function of it would be the expected sum of reward from that state onwards. Therefore,

$$J(\theta) = V^{\pi_\theta}(s_1)$$

- If it's a continuing environment, $J(\theta)$ can be the average value function of the states. So, if the environment goes on and on forever, then the measure of the quality of the policy can be the summation of the probability of being in any state s that is $d^{\pi_\theta}(s)$ times the value of that state that is, the expected reward from that state onward. Therefore,

$$J(\theta) = \sum_s d^{\pi_\theta}(s) V^{\pi_\theta}(s)$$

- For the continuing environment, $J(\theta)$ can be the average reward per time step that is the summation of the probability of being in any state s that is $d^{\pi_\theta}(s)$ times the expected reward over different actions for that state that is $E[R_s^a] = \sum_a \pi_\theta(s,a) R_s^a$. Therefore:

$$J(\theta) = \sum_s d^{\pi_\theta}(s) \sum_a \pi_\theta(s,a) R_s^a$$

Here, R_s^a is the reward at state s for taking action a.

So far, we know that policy-based reinforcement learning is an optimization problem where the goal is to find that θ which maximizes the $J(\theta)$. Here also, we will use gradient-based method for optimization. The reason behind using gradient-based optimization is to get greater efficiency since a gradient points in the direction of greater efficiency comparative to a gradient free method.

Let $J(\theta)$ which measures the quality of a policy be our policy objective function. Thus, policy gradient algorithms look for the local maximum in $J(\theta)$ by ascending the gradient of the policy, with respect to the parameter θ. This is because our goal is to maximize $J(\theta)$ with respect to θ therefore, we go for gradient ascent where increment in the parameter that is $\triangle\theta$ is given by the following:

$$\triangle\theta = \alpha\nabla_\theta J(\theta)$$

Here, $\nabla_\theta J(\theta)$ is the policy gradient and α is the learning rate also called **the step size parameter**, which decides to what extent of the gradient the parameter should be shifted at each step. Policy gradient can also be elaborated in the following form:

$$\nabla_\theta J(\theta) = \begin{bmatrix} \frac{\nabla J(\theta)}{\nabla\theta_1} \\ \frac{\nabla J(\theta)}{\nabla\theta_2} \\ \ldots \\ \frac{\nabla J(\theta)}{\nabla\theta_n} \end{bmatrix}$$

Policy Gradient Theorem

Assuming our given policy $\pi_\theta(s, a)$ is differentiable whenever it's non zero, then the gradient of the given policy with respect to θ would be $\nabla_\theta\pi_\theta(s, a)$. Therefore, we can further exploit this gradient quantity in the form of the likelihood ratio as follows:

$$\nabla_\theta\pi_\theta(s, a) = \pi_\theta(s, a)\frac{\nabla_\theta\pi_\theta(s, a)}{\pi_\theta(s, a)}$$
$$= \pi_\theta(s, a)\,\nabla_\theta\, log\,\pi_\theta(s, a)$$

Here, $\nabla_\theta\, log\,\pi_\theta(s, a)$ is the score function for future reference.

Now, let's consider a simple one-step MDP, that is a Markov decision process, where:

- Starting state is s whose probability of occurring is $d^{\pi_\theta}(s)$
- Termination happens after one-time step only with reward $r = R_s^a$

Considering it a continuing environment, therefore:

$$J(\theta) = \sum_s d^{\pi_\theta}(s) \sum_a \pi_\theta(s,a) R_s^a$$

Therefore, policy gradient $\nabla_\theta J(\theta)$ would be as follows:

$$\nabla_\theta J(\theta) = \sum_s d^{\pi_\theta}(s) \sum_a \nabla_\theta \pi_\theta(s,a) R_s^a$$

Here, we have proved the following:

$$\nabla_\theta \pi_\theta(s,a) = \pi_\theta(s,a)\, \nabla_\theta\, log\, \pi_\theta(s,a)$$

As a result:

$$\begin{aligned}
\nabla_\theta J(\theta) &= \sum_s d^{\pi_\theta}(s) \sum_a \nabla_\theta \pi_\theta(s,a) R_s^a \\
&= \sum_s d^{\pi_\theta}(s) \sum_a \pi_\theta(s,a)\, \nabla_\theta\, log\, \pi_\theta(s,a) R_s^a \\
&= E_{\pi_\theta}[\nabla_\theta\, log\, \pi_\theta(s,a) r]
\end{aligned}$$

Thus, generalizing this approach to a multi-step Markov decision process will result in the replacement of the instantaneous reward r by the state-action Q value function $Q^\pi(s,a)$. This is called the **policy gradient theorem**. The theorem is valid for other types of policy objective functions discussed previously. Therefore, for any such policy objective function and any differentiable $\pi_\theta(s,a)$ the policy gradient is given by the following:

$$\nabla_\theta J(\theta) = E_{\pi_\theta}[\nabla_\theta\, log\, \pi_\theta(s,a) Q^{\pi_\theta}(s,a)]$$

Temporal difference rule

Firstly, **temporal difference (TD)** is the difference of the value estimates between two time steps. It is different from the outcome-based Monte Carlo approach where a full look ahead till the end of the episode is done in order to update the learning parameters. In case of temporal difference learning, only one step look ahead is done and a value estimate of the state at the next step is used to update the current state's value estimate. Thus, learning parameters update along the way. Different rules to approach temporal difference learning are the TD(1), TD(0), and TD(λ) rules. The basic notion in all the approaches is that the value estimate of the next step is used to update the current state's value estimate.

TD(1) rule

TD(1) incorporates the concept of eligibility trace. Let's go through the pseudo code of the approach and then we will discuss it in detail:

```
Episode T
    For all s, At the start of the episode : e(s) = 0 and $V_T(s) = V_{T-1}(s)$
        After $s_{t-1} \xrightarrow{r_t} s_t$ : (at step t)
            $e(s_{t-1}) = e(s_{t-1}) + 1$

        For all s,
                $V_T(s) = V_T(s) + \alpha_T[r_t + \gamma V_{T-1}(s_t) - V_{T-1}(s_{t-1})]e(s)$
                $e(s) = \gamma e(s)$
        $s_{t-1} \leftarrow s_t$
```

Each `Episode` T starts with the following initialization:

- For all the states s, eligibility score $e(s) = 0$

- For all the states s, the value of the state in the given `Episode` T that is $V_T(s)$ equals $V_{T-1}(s)$

At each time step of an episode that is at the current step t, we update the eligibility of the state s_{t-1} which we are leaving and then we update the following for all the states:

- The state value function using temporal difference error for the current leaving state s_{t-1} that is $r_t + \gamma V_{T-1}(s_t) - V_{T-1}(s_{t-1})$ and the eligibility score $e(s)$ of the state whose value we are going to change
- The eligibility score by discounting with the given discounting factor

Since these updates happen for all the states independently, these operations can be performed in parallel for all the states.

While expanding the calculated value estimates of each state after completing the final step of the episode we find that the value-based update is the same as the outcome-based update such as in the Monte Carlo approach where we do a full look ahead till the end of the episode. Thus, we need a better approach to update our value function estimate without doing more than one step look ahead. This brings us to the solution of this problem by incorporating the TD(0) rule.

TD(0) rule

The TD(0) rule finds the value estimate if the finite data is repeated infinitely, often that is if we take this finite data and keep running the following estimate update rule over and over again. Then in reality we are averaging out each of the transitions.

$$V_T(s_{t-1}) = V_T(s_{t-1}) + \alpha_T[r_t + \gamma V_{T-1}(s_t) - V_{T-1}(s_{t-1})]$$

Thus, value function is given by the following:

$$V_T(s_{t-1}) = E_{s_t}[r_t + \gamma V_{T-1}(s_t)]$$

This is not true in case of the outcome-based model where we don't use an estimate of the state, that is $V_T(s_t)$, rather we use use the whole sequence of rewards till the end of the episode. Thus, in case of the outcome-based model of the Monte Carlo approach the value function is given by the following:

$$V_T(s_{t-1}) = E[r_t + \gamma r_{t+1} + \gamma^2 r_{t+2} + \dots \dots \dots \dots]$$

Moreover, in the outcome-based approach we see a sequence once and repeating the process will not change the value of the value function. But, in the case of TD(0), at every step the value function estimate is being computed and refined as per the intermediate state.

The difference between TD(0) and TD(1) is the use of eligibility trace to update the state-value function in case of TD(1) but not in case of TD(0).

The pseudo code of the TD(0) rule is as follows:

```
Episode T
    For all s, At the start of the episode :  VT(s) = VT−1(s)
                              rt
        After  st−1 →  st  : (at step t)
        For s =  st−1 ,
                VT(s) = VT(s) + αT[rt + γVT−1(st) − VT−1(st−1)]e(s)
                e(s) = γe(s)
        st−1 ← st
```

Thus, here we only update the value function of the current leaving state s_{t-1} using the temporal difference error, $r_t + \gamma V_{T-1}(s_t) - V_{T-1}(s_{t-1})$.

TD(λ) rule

The TD(1) and TD(0) rules give rise to a generalized rule TD(λ) that is TD (lambda), such that for $\lambda \epsilon [0, 1]$ and should satisfy the following conditions:

- If λ=0, TD(λ) tends to TD(0)
- If λ=1, TD(λ) tends to TD(1)

Both TD(0) and TD(1) have updates based on differences between temporally successive predictions.

Therefore, the pseudo code of TD(λ) is as follows:

```
Episode T
    For all s, At the start of the episode : e(s) = 0 and  VT(s) = VT−1(s)
                              rt
        After  st−1 →  st  : (at step t)
                e(st−1) = e(st−1) + 1
```

For all s,
$$V_T(s) = V_T(s) + \alpha_T[r_t + \gamma V_{T-1}(s_t) - V_{T-1}(s_{t-1})]e(s)$$
$$e(s) = \lambda\gamma e(s)$$
$$s_{t-1} \leftarrow s_t$$

This satisfies the preceding two conditions and can incorporate any value for $\lambda\epsilon[0,1]$.

Policy gradients

As per the policy gradient theorem, for the previous specified policy objective functions and any differentiable policy $\pi_\theta(s,a)$ the policy gradient is as follows:

$$\nabla_\theta J(\theta) = E_{\pi_\theta}[\nabla_\theta \log \pi_\theta(s,a)Q^{\pi_\theta}(s,a)]$$

Steps to update parameters using the Monte Carlo policy gradient based approach is shown in the following section.

The Monte Carlo policy gradient

In the **Monte Carlo policy gradient** approach, we update the parameters by the stochastic gradient ascent method, using the update as per policy gradient theorem and v_t as an unbiased sample of $Q^{\pi_\theta}(s_t, a_t)$. Here, v_t is the cumulative reward from that time-step onward.

The Monte Carlo policy gradient approach is as follows:

```
Initialize θ arbitrarily
for each episode as per the current policy πθ do
    for step t=1 to T-1 do
        θ ← θ + α∇θlogπθ(st, at)vt
    end for
end for

Output: final θ
```

Actor-critic algorithms

The preceding policy optimization using the Monte Carlo policy gradient approach leads to high variance. In order to tackle this issue, we use a critic to estimate the state-action value function, that is as follows:

$$Q_w(s,a) \approx Q^{\pi_\theta}(s,a)$$

This gives rise to the famous **actor-critic algorithms**. The actor-critic algorithm, as the name suggests, maintains two networks for the following purposes:

- One network acts as a critic, which updates the weight w parameter vector of the function approximator of the state-action
- Other network acts as an **Actor**, which updates the policy parameter vector θ as per the direction given by the critic

The following image represents the actor-critic algorithm:

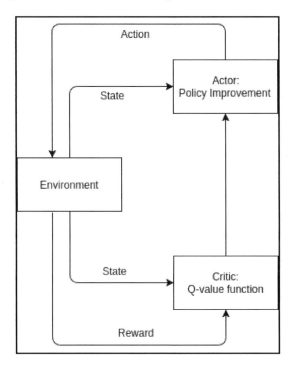

Thus, in case of actor-critic algorithms, the true state-action value function $Q^{\pi_\theta}(s,a)$ from the actual policy gradient formula is replaced with an approximate state-action value function, that is $Q_w(s,a)$. Therefore:

$$\nabla_\theta J(\theta) \approx E_{\pi_\theta}[\nabla_\theta \, log \, \pi_\theta(s,a)Q_w(s,a)] \text{ , and}$$

$$\triangle\theta = \alpha\nabla_\theta \, log \, \pi_\theta(s,a)Q_w(s,a)$$

Therefore, in order to estimate the state-action value function, the critic network uses TD(0) (discussed previously) to update the weight parameters w and in order to update the policy parameter vector θ actor network uses policy gradients. A simple approach to the actor-critic algorithm is shown as follows:

```
Initialize s, θ
for each episode
    Sample a ~ πθ(s) as per the current policy πθ
    for each step do
        Take action a and observe reward r and next state s'
        Sample action a' ~ πθ(s') as per the current policy πθ
        δ = r + γQw(s',a') − Qw(s,a)
        θ = θ + α∇θlogπθ(s,a)Qw(s,a)
        w = w + βδ∇wQw(s,a)
        a ← a', s ← s'
    end for
end for

Output : final θ
```

Thus, we can see that the actor-critic has both value-based optimization as well as policy-based optimization. So in case of the Monte Carlo policy gradient approach, policy improvement happens greedily. But in actor-critic, actor updates the policy parameter by taking a step in the direction as per the critic in order to get to a better policy.

Using a baseline to reduce variance

In addition to our initial effort to use an actor-critic method to reduce variance, we can also reduce variance by subtracting a **baseline function** $b(s)$ from the policy gradient. This will reduce the variance without affecting the expectation value as shown in the following:

$$E_{\pi_\theta}[\nabla_\theta log\pi_\theta(s,a)[Q^{\pi_\theta}(s,a)-b(s)]] = E_{\pi_\theta}[\nabla_\theta log\pi_\theta(s,a)Q^{\pi_\theta}(s,a)] - E_{\pi_\theta}[\nabla_\theta log\pi_\theta(s,a)b(s)]$$

$$= E_{\pi_\theta}[\nabla_\theta log\pi_\theta(s,a)Q^{\pi_\theta}(s,a)] - \sum_s d^{\pi_\theta}(s)\sum_a \nabla_\theta \pi_\theta(s,a)b(s)$$

$$= E_{\pi_\theta}[\nabla_\theta log\pi_\theta(s,a)Q^{\pi_\theta}(s,a)] - \sum_s d^{\pi_\theta}(s)b(s)\nabla_\theta \sum_a \pi_\theta(s,a)$$

$$= E_{\pi_\theta}[\nabla_\theta log\pi_\theta(s,a)Q^{\pi_\theta}(s,a)] - \sum_s d^{\pi_\theta}(s)b(s)\nabla_\theta 1$$

$$= E_{\pi_\theta}[\nabla_\theta log\pi_\theta(s,a)Q^{\pi_\theta}(s,a)] - \sum_s d^{\pi_\theta}(s)b(s)*0$$

$$= E_{\pi_\theta}[\nabla_\theta log\pi_\theta(s,a)Q^{\pi_\theta}(s,a)]$$

There are many options to choose a baseline function but state value function is regarded to be a good baseline function. Therefore:

$$b(s) = V^{\pi_\theta}(s)$$

Thus, we can rewrite the policy gradient formula by subtracting the baseline function as follows:

$$\nabla_\theta J(\theta) = E_{\pi_\theta}[\nabla_\theta \, log \, \pi_\theta(s,a)[Q^{\pi_\theta}(s,a) - V^{\pi_\theta}(s)]]$$

Here, $Q^{\pi_\theta}(s,a) - V^{\pi_\theta}(s)$ is termed the **advantage function** $A^{\pi_\theta}(s,a)$. Therefore, the policy gradient formula becomes the following:

$$\nabla_\theta J(\theta) = E_{\pi_\theta}[\nabla_\theta \, log \, \pi_\theta(s,a)A^{\pi_\theta}(s,a)]$$

Thus, by using a baseline function the expected value is under control by lowered variance without any change in the direction.

Vanilla policy gradient

In the vanilla policy gradient approach, the aim would be to update the policy using the policy gradient estimate with better baseline estimation.

Following is the pseudo code to implement the vanilla policy gradient to find the optimal policy:

```
Initialize: Policy parameter θ, and baseline b
for iteration = 1,2,......N   do
        Collect a set of trajectories using the current policy
        At each time step t in each trajectory, compute the following:
```

$$R_t = \sum_{t'=t}^{T-1} \gamma^{t'-t} r_{t'}$$

`returns`   `, and`

`advantage estimate` $\hat{A}_t = R_t - b(s_t)$

`Refit the baseline function` $b(s_t)$

$$\delta = \sum_{t=1}^{T-1} \nabla_\theta log \ \pi(a_t|s_t, \theta)\hat{A}_t$$

$$\theta = \theta + \alpha\delta$$

`end for`

Agent learning pong using policy gradients

In this section, we will create a policy network that will take raw pixels from our pong environment that is **pong-v0** from OpenAI gym as the input. The policy network is a single hidden layer neural network fully connected to the raw pixels of pong at the input layer and also to the output layer containing a single node returning the probability of the paddle going up. I would like to thank Andrej Karpathy for coming up with a solution to make the agent learn using policy gradients. We will try to implement a similar kind of approach.

A pixel image of size 80*80 in grayscale (we will not use RGB, which would be 80*80*3). Thus, we have a 80*80 grid that is binary and tells us the position of paddles and the ball, which we will feed as an input to the neural network. Thus a neural network would consist of the following:

- **Input layer (X)**: 80*80 squashed to 6400*1 that is 6400 nodes
- **Hidden layer**: 200 nodes
- **Output layer**: 1 node

Therefore, the total parameters would be as follows:

- **Weights and bias connecting input and hidden layer**: 6400*200 (weights) + 200 (bias) parameters
- **Weights and bias connecting hidden and output layer**: 200*1 (weights) + 1 (bias) parameters

Thus, the total parameters would be approximately 1.3 million.

This is huge, and as a result the training needs a couple of days to witness your agent playing pong fluently.

Pong can't be played from a static frame, therefore, some sort of motion information needs to be captured, which can be done by concatenating two such frames or the difference between the new and the previous frame. Since, we aren't using convolutional neural networks, no spatial information is available apart from the 6400 pixel values flipping between 0 and 1. That's the only thing the network can see; not the paddles and ball position.

A computationally efficient way to train 1.3 million parameters is by using policy gradients. You can relate this to supervised learning, where for each state an action label is mentioned. Therefore data and training would be as follows:

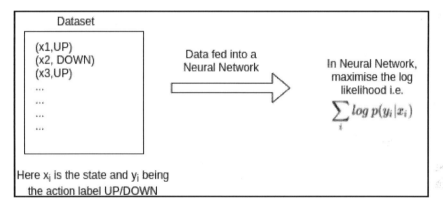

But, in reality we don't have the labels. Therefore, we will implement reinforcement learning where we will try lots of tasks and note down the observations. Then, perform the tasks that performed better, more often.

Let's put down the steps before we type in our Python code. They are as follows:

1. Initialize a random policy.
2. For the given current policy, we will collect different sample trajectories (rollouts) in the following way:
    1. Run a single episode of the game and capture the trajectories in that episode.

2. Similarly, collect a batch of trajectories which will look as follows:

Trajectories	Game Outcome	Trajectory Good/Bad
UP, DOWN, UP, UP, DOWN, DOWN, DOWN, UP	LOSE	BAD
DOWN, UP, UP, DOWN, UP, UP	WIN	GOOD
UP, UP, DOWN, DOWN, DOWN, DOWN, UP	LOSE	BAD
DOWN, UP, UP, DOWN, UP, UP	WIN	GOOD

Thus, we are able to create sample data, where the cases we won we consider to be the correct label for the action. Therefore, we will increase the log probability of those actions, that is $logp(y_i|x_i)$ and the cases where we lose each action are considered to be wrong label. Therefore, in those cases we will decrease the log probability of those actions.

Thus, after collecting the batch of trajectories we will maximize the product of advantage and log probability of actions, that is

$$\sum_i A_i \times log\, p(y_i|x_i)$$

Here, A_i is the advantage associated with a state action pair. Advantage is a scalar quantity, which quantifies how good the action eventually turned out. A_i would be high if we want to encourage the given action in future and low if we want to discourage the action. A positive advantage makes the action more likely to occur in future for that state, while a negative advantage makes the action less likely to occur in future for that state.

First, we will import the important dependencies required as follows:

```
#import dependencies
import numpy as np #for matrix math
import cPickle as pickle #to save/load model
import gym
```

- **Hyperparameter initialization**: Hyperparameters such as the number of hidden layer nodes, batch size, learning rate, discount factor gamma, decay rate since we are using RMSProp optimizer for gradient descent. We will use the following code for initialization:

```
#hyperparameters
H = 200 #number of nodes in the hidden layer
batch_size = 10
learning_rate = 1e-4
gamma = 0.99 #discount factor
decay_rate = 0.99 #for RMSProp Optimizer for Gradient Descent
resume = False #to resume from previous checkpoint or not
```

- **Policy neural network model Initialization**: Initialization of the weight parameters of the policy neural network. Here we are using one hidden layer neural network. We will use the following code for initialization:

```
#initialize : init model
D = 80*80 #input dimension
if resume:
    model = pickle.load(open('model.v','rb'))
else:
    model = {}
    #xavier initialisation of weights
    model['W1'] = np.random.randn(H,D)*np.sqrt(2.0/D)
    model['W2'] = np.random.randn(H)*np.sqrt(2.0/H)
    grad_buffer = {k: np.zeros_like(v) for k,v in model.iteritems()} #to
store our gradients which can be summed up over a batch
    rmsprop_cache = {k: np.zeros_like(v) for k,v in model.iteritems()} #to
store the value of rms prop formula
```

- **Activation functions**: The `sigmoid(x)` and `relu(x)` refer to the functions performing sigmoid and ReLU activation calculations respectively. We will use the following code for defining the function:

```
#activation function
def sigmoid(x):
    return 1.0/(1.0+np.exp(-x)) #adding non linearing + squashing

def relu(x):
    x[x<0] = 0
    return x
```

- **Preprocessing function**: The `preprocess(image)` function takes in the image pixels as the parameter and preprocesses them by cropping, downsampling, making it grayscale, erasing the background, and flattening the image to a one-dimensional vector. We will use the following code for defining the function:

```
#preprocessing function
def preprocess(image): #where image is the single frame of the game as the
input
    """ take 210x160x3 frame and returns 6400 (80x80) 1D float vector """
    #the following values have been precomputed through trail and error by
OpenAI team members
    image = image[35:195] #cropping the image frame to an extent where it
contains on the paddles and ball and area between them
    immage = image[::2,::2,0] #downsample by the factor of 2 and take only
the R of the RGB channel.Therefore, now 2D frame
    image[image==144] = 0 #erase background type 1
```

```
    image[image==109] = 0 #erase background type 2
    image[image!=0] = 1 #everything else(other than paddles and ball) set
to 1
    return image.astype('float').ravel() #flattening to 1D
```

- **Discount rewards**: The discount_rewards(r) function takes in the list of rewards r corresponding to different time-steps as the parameters and returns a list of discounted rewards corresponding to different time-steps, as shown in the following code:

```
def discount_rewards(r):
    """ take 1D float array of rewards and compute discounted reward """
    discount_r = np.zeros_like(r)
    running_add = 0 #addition of rewards
    for t in reversed(xrange(0,r.size)):
        if r[t] != 0: #episode ends
            running_add = 0
        running_add = gamma*running_add+r[t]
        discount_r[t] = running_add
    return discount_r
```

- **Forward propagation**: The policy_forward(x) function takes in the preprocessed image vector x, returns the probability of action being UP, and a vector containing the value of the hidden state nodes, as shown in the following code:

```
def policy_forward(x):
    h = np.dot(model['W1'],x)
    h = relu(h)
    logit = np.dot(model['W2'],h)
    p = sigmoid(logit)
    return p,h #probability of action 2(that is UP) and hidden layer state
that is hidden state
```

- **Backward propagation**: The policy_backward(arr_hidden_state, gradient_logp, observation_values) function takes in the hidden state values, the error, gradient_logp, and observations to compute the derivatives with respect to different weight parameters, as shown in the following code:

```
def policy_backward(arr_hidden_state,gradient_logp,observation_values):
    """ backward pass """
    #arr_hidden_state is array of intermediate hidden states shape [200x1]
    #gradient_logp is the loss value [1x1]
    dW2 = np.dot(arr_hidden_state.T,gradient_logp).ravel()
    # [200x1].[1x1] => [200x1] =>flatten=>[1x200]
    dh = np.outer(gradient_logp,model['W2']) # [1x1]outer[1x200] => [1x200]
```

```
dh = relu(dh) #[1x200]
dW1 = np.dot(dh.T,observation_values) #[200x1].[1x6400] => [200x6400]
return {'W1':dW1,'W2':dW2}
```

The final task, which creates the environment and incorporates the previous functions to make the agent learn step by step over multiple episodes, is as follows:

```
#implementation details
env = gym.make('Pong-v0')
observation = env.reset()
prev_x = None
#prev frame value in order to compute the difference between current and
previous frame
#as discussed frames are static and the difference is used to capture the
motion
#Intially None because there's no previous frame if the current frame is
the 1st frame of the game
episode_hidden_layer_values, episode_observations, episode_gradient_log_ps,
episode_rewards = [], [], [], []
running_reward = None
reward_sum = 0
episode_number = 0


#begin training
while True:
    env.render()
    #get the input and preprocess it
    cur_x = preprocess(observation)
    #get the frame difference which would be the input to the network
    if prev_x is None:
        prev_x = np.zeros(D)
    x = cur_x - prev_x
    prev_x = cur_x
    #forward propagation of the policy network
    #sample an action from the returned probability
    aprob, h = policy_forward(x)
    #stochastic part
    if np.random.uniform() < aprob:
        action = 2
    else:
        action = 3
    episode_observations.append(x) #record observation
    episode_hidden_layer_values.append(h) #record hidden state
    if action == 2:
        y = 1
    else:
        y = 0
```

```
        episode_gradient_log_ps.append(y-aprob) #record the gradient
        #new step in the environment
        observation,reward,done,info = env.step(action)
        reward_sum+=reward #for advantage purpose
        episode_rewards.append(reward) #record the reward
        if done: #if the episode is over
            episode_number+=1
            #stack inputs,hidden_states,actions,gradients_logp,rewards for the
episode
            arr_hidden_state = np.vstack(episode_hidden_layer_values)
            gradient_logp = np.vstack(episode_gradient_log_ps)
            observation_values = np.vstack(episode_observations)
            reward_values = np.vstack(episode_rewards)
            #reset the memory arrays
            episode_hidden_layer_values, episode_observations,
episode_gradient_log_ps, episode_rewards = [], [], [], []
            #discounted reward computation
            discounted_episoderewards = discount_rewards(reward_values)
            #normalize discounted_episoderewards
            discounted_episoderewards = (discounted_episoderewards -
np.mean(discounted_episoderewards))/np.std(discounted_episoderewards)
#advantage
            #modulate the gradient with the advantage
            gradient_logp *= discounted_episoderewards
            grad =
policy_backward(arr_hidden_state,gradient_logp,observation_values)
            #summing the gradients over the batch size
            for layer in model:
                grad_buffer[layer]+=grad[layer]
            #perform RMSProp to update weights after every 10 episodes
            if episode_number % batch_size == 0:
                epsilon = 1e-5
                for weight in model.keys():
                    g = grad_buffer[weight] #gradient
                    rmsprop_cache[weight] =
decay_rate*rmsprop_cache[weight]+(1-decay_rate)*g**2
model[weight]+=learning_rate*g/(np.sqrt(rmsprop_cache[weight]) + epsilon)
                    grad_buffer[weight] = np.zeros_like(model[weight])
            if running_reward is None:
                running_reward = reward_sum
            else:
                running_reward = running_reward*learning_rate+reward_sum*(1-
learning_rate)
            print('Episode Reward : {}, Running Mean Award :
{}'.format(reward_sum,running_reward))
            if episode_number % 100 == 0:
                pickle.dump(model,open('model.v','wb'))
            reward_sum = 0
```

```
        prev_x = None
        observation = env.reset() #resetting the environment since episode
has ended
    if reward != 0: #if reward is either +1 or -1 that is an episode has
ended
        print("Episode {} ended with reward
{}".format(episode_number,reward))
```

The screenshot of the game played by the agent:

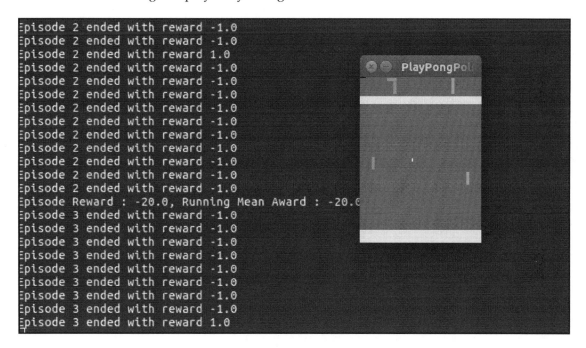

Convergence might take a couple of days if you are running the previous code on your laptop. Try using a GPU-powered cloud instance to get better results in approximately 5-6 hours.

Summary

In this chapter, we covered the most famous algorithms in reinforcement learning, the policy gradients and actor-critic algorithms. There is a lot of research going on in developing policy gradients to benchmark better results in reinforcement learning. Further study of policy gradients include **Trust Region Policy Optimization (TRPO)**, **Natural Policy Gradients**, and **Deep Dependency Policy Gradients (DDPG)**, which are beyond the scope of this book.

In the next chapter, we will take a look at the building blocks of Q-Learning, applying deep neural networks, and many more techniques.

Q-Learning and Deep Q-Networks

5

In Chapter 3, *Markov Decision Process*, we discussed the transition model of the environment, which follows the Markov property, and the concept of delayed rewards and value (or utility) functions. Well, in this chapter we take a look at the Markov decision process, learn about Q-learning, and a modified approach called the deep Q-network for generalizing in different environments.

We will cover the following topics in this chapter:

- Supervised and unsupervised learning for artificial intelligence
- Model based learning and model free learning
- Q-learning
- Deep Q-networks
- Monte Carlo tree search algorithm
- SARSA algorithm

Why reinforcement learning?

In 2014, Google acquired a London-based startup named DeepMind for a whopping $500 million. In the news, we read that they had created an AI agent to beat any Atari game, but the main reason why Google paid so much to acquire it was because this breakthrough was a step closer toward **general artificial intelligence**. General artificial intelligence is referred to as an AI agent. It is capable of doing a variety of tasks and generalizing just like a human. When it surpasses that, that point of singularity is termed, artificial super intelligence. At present, the work done by the AI community is what we term, artificial narrow intelligence, where an AI agent is capable of acing a couple of tasks but not able to generalize over a variety of tasks.

DeepMind published their paper, *Human Level Control through Deep Reinforcement Learning* in the research journal **Nature** (http://www.davidqiu.com:8888/research/nature14236. pdf) showing that their deep reinforcement learning algorithm could be successfully applied to 50 different Atari games and achieve above human-level performance in 30 of them. Their AI agent was called **deep-Q learner**. Let's recall the basics of reinforcement learning before diving into deep reinforcement learning in detail.

Supervised and unsupervised learning are well known to the applied AI community. **Supervised learning** deals with a labelled dataset containing input features and target labels (either continuous or discrete), and creates a model that maps these input features to the target labels. On the other hand, **unsupervised learning** deals with unlabeled datasets containing only input features and no target labels, where the objective is to discover the underlying pattern to segregate data among different clusters and define their utility separately, as per the specific types of data in different clusters.

Thus, using supervised and unsupervised learning we can either create data classifiers/regressors or data generators, where the learning happens via a batch of data in one go. In order to enhance learning over time, the batch needs to incorporate more and more data, causing the supervised and unsupervised learning to become slow and difficult to generalize. Let's consider a situation where you want an AI agent to play a particular video/virtual game for you but the catch is that the algorithm should become intelligent over the time.

So, how to tackle this problem?

Let's say, we take videos of all the best players of a particular video game and input the data in the form of image frames and target labels as the sets of different possible actions. Since we have input features and target labels, these forms a supervised learning classification problem. Assuming the data is huge, and we have access to very high end machines having state-of-the-art GPUs, then it totally makes sense to create a deep neural network for this task.

But what's the catch here?

In order to create a deep neural network that can solve this classification problem such that the resultant AI agent can beat any opponent at any level in that game, our input data would require thousands of hours of video data distributed over different levels of the game by different players, catering to different approaches to win that game so that our neural network can generalize the mapping in the best possible way. The reason behind obtaining more data is to avoid under fitting. Moreover, a high volume of data over fitting can also be an issue, but regularization is a possible solution to generalize the model to the best possible as per the given data. Thus, we see that even after obtaining thousands of hours of video data (that is, very high data volume) of expert players, still this supervised learning approach doesn't seem to be an elegant solution. This is because, unlike other applied AI problems, here the dataset is dynamic and not static.

The training data is continuous here and new frames emerge continuously in a gaming world. Now, ask yourself how we humans learn this task and the answer is simple, that is, we learn best by interacting with the environment and not by watching others interacting with it. Thus, an AI agent can try to learn better by interacting with the environment and evolve its learning through a series of trial and error over the course of time.

Environments are generally *stochastic* in the real world and also in the gaming world, where any number of events can occur. Since all the events are associated with some probability of occurrence, therefore, they can be statistically analyzed but cannot be precisely determined. Say, in a given environment e, we have only three actions to perform a, b, and c but each action has some sort of uncertainty associated with it, that is, their chances of occurrence are random and any one of them can occur but the outcome for each is not determined. For the supervised classification problem, we regard the environment to be deterministic, where the outcome associated with a particular action is determined and the result is a precise prediction, that is, a particular class (target label). Before proceeding further with the topic, let's have a look at the differences between the two environments:

- **Deterministic environment**: Environment where the agent's actions can uniquely determine the outcome since there's no uncertainty. For example, in chess you move a piece from one square to another square. Therefore, the outcome is determined, that is, the resultant square. There is no randomness.
- **Stochastic environment**: Environments where each action is associated with some amount of randomness, owing to which, the outcome is not determined, whatever action we take. For example, throwing a dart at a rotating disc-board or rolling a dice. In both these cases, the outcome is not determined.

Thus, for a problem based in a stochastic environment it seems the best way to learn is by trying out different possibilities. Therefore, instead of solving it as a pattern recognition problem through supervised classification, it would be better by trial and error, where the outcome labels would be replaced by rewards that quantify the usefulness of a particular action to accomplish the ulterior objective of the given problem statement.

This gives rise to the environment-agent interaction approach, which we discussed in Chapter 1, *Deep Reinforcement – Architectures and Frameworks,* where we devise the system such that an agent interacts with the environment first by perceiving the state through the sensors, performing some action through effectors on the environment, and receiving feedback, that is, a reward for the action taken, as shown in the following diagram:

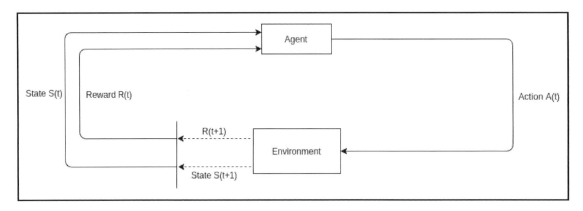

The state here is basically the agent's view of the environment as per the signals received by the sensors while sensing the environment at a particular time step.

Model based learning and model free learning

In Chapter 3, *Markov Decision Process,* we used states, actions, rewards, transition models, and discount factors to solve our Markov decision process, that is, the MDP problem. Thus, if all these elements of an MDP problem are available, we can easily use a planning algorithm to come up with a solution to the objective. This type of learning is called **model based learning,** where an AI agent will interact with the environment and based on its interactions, will try to approximate the environment's model, that is, the state transition model. Given the model, now the agent can try to find the optimum policy through value iteration or policy iteration.

But its not necessary for our AI agent to learn an explicit model of the environment. It can derive optimal policy directly from its interactions with the environment without building a model. This type of learning is called **model free learning**. Model free learning involves predicting the value function of a certain policy without having a concrete model of the environment.

Model free learning can be done using two approaches, namely:

- Monte Carlo learning
- Temporal difference learning

We will discuss both of them in the following topics.

Monte Carlo learning

Monte Carlo is the simplest approach for model free learning, where the agent observes rewards for all steps ahead in an episode, that is, a full look ahead. Thus, total estimate reward at time t would be R_t given by:

$$R_t = r_{t+1} + \gamma\, r_{t+2} + \gamma^2\, r_{t+3} + \ldots\ldots\ldots + \gamma^{T-t+1}\, r_T$$

Here, γ is the discount factor and T being the time step when the episode ends. We can initialize the Monte Carlo learning technique using the following code:

```
Initialize:

    π i.e. the policy to be evaluated
    V i.e. an arbitrary state-value function
    Returns(s) = empty list ∀ s ∈ S
    #here Returns(s) refer to returns for a particular state i.e. the
series of rewards the agent receives from that state onward

Repeat forever:

    Generate an episode using the current π
    For each state 's' appearing in the episode perform the following:
        R = returns following the first occurrence of 's'
        Append R to Returns(s)
        V(s) = Average(Returns(s))
    Update policy as per V
```

Temporal difference learning

Unlike in Monte Carlo learning where we do a full look ahead, here, in temporal difference learning, there is only one look ahead, that is, we observe only the next step in the episode:

$$R_t = r_{t+1} + \gamma V(s_{t+1})$$

Temporal difference learning is the one used for learning the value function in value and policy iteration methods and the Q-function in Q-learning.

If we want our AI agent to always choose an action that maximizes the discounted future rewards, then we need some sort of temporal difference learning. For that, we need to define a function Q that represents the maximum discounted future rewards when we take an action *a* at state *s*. Thus, the Q-function represents the quality of the action at a given state. Using it, we can estimate the end score by just knowing the current state and action and there's no need for the actions after that. Thus, the goal would be to take that action for a state that has the highest Q-value. Therefore, we have to learn this Q-function by a process called Q-learning.

On-policy and off-policy learning

Off-policy learning as the name suggests, is the learning of optimal policy independent of the agent's actions. Therefore, you don't need a specific policy to start with and the agent will learn the optimal policy even by starting with a random action, finally converging to the optimal one. Q-learning is an example of off-policy learning.

On the other hand, **on-policy** learning learns the optimal policy by carrying out the current policy and updating it through exploration methods. Thus, on-policy learning is dependent on the policy you start with. The SARSA algorithm is an example of on-policy learning.

Q-learning

In reinforcement learning, we want the Q-function $Q(s,a)$ to predict the best action for a state *s* in order to maximize the future reward. The Q-function is estimated using Q-learning, which involves the process of updating the Q-function using Bellman equations through a series of iterations as follows:

$$Q(s,a) \leftarrow (1 - \alpha)Q(s,a) + \alpha[R + \gamma \, max_{a'} Q(s',a')]$$

Here:

$Q(s,a)$ = Q value for the current state s and action a pair

α = learning rate of convergence

γ = discounting factor of future rewards

$Q(s',a')$ = Q value for the state action pair at the resultant state s' after action a was taken at state s

R = refers to immediate reward

$\gamma\,max_{a'}\,Q(s',a')$ = future reward

In simpler cases, where state space and action space are discrete, Q-learning is implemented using a Q-table, where rows represent the states and columns represent the actions.

Steps involved in Q-learning are as follows:

1. Initialize Q-table randomly
2. For each episode, perform the following steps:
    1. For the given state s, choose action a from the Q-table
    2. Perform action a
    3. Reward R and state s' is observed
    4. Update Q-value for the current state-action pair, that is, $Q(s,a)$ by:

$$Q(s, a) \leftarrow (1 - \alpha)Q(s, a) + \alpha[R + \gamma\,max_{a'}\,Q(s', a')]$$

But here exploration of a new path is not happening, and most of the time the agent is exploiting the known paths. Therefore, some amount of randomness is implemented so that the AI agent explores a new path randomly by taking random actions sometimes, instead of the current optimal action. The reason behind exploration is that it increases the possibility of getting a better path (that is, new optimal policy) than the current:

```
Create Q-table where rows represent different states and columns represent
different actions
Initialize Q(s,a) arbitrarily
For each episode:
    Start with the starting state i.e. Initialize s to start
    Repeat for each step in the episode:
        Choose action a for s using the policy derived from Q
        [e.g. €-greedy, either for the given 's' which 'a' has the max Q-
```

```
value or choose a random action]
        Take the chosen action a, observe reward R and new state s'
        Update  Q(s,a) ← (1 − α)Q(s,a) + α[R + γ max_{a'} Q(s',a')]
        s ← s'
    until s is the terminal state
end
```

The exploration exploitation dilemma

The following table summarizes the dilemma between exploration and exploitation:

Exploration	Exploitation
To choose other actions randomly apart from the current optimal action and hope to obtain a better reward.	To choose the current optimal action without trying other actions.

Thus, the dilemma is whether the AI should only trust the learned Q-values based on the actions as per the current optimal policy or it should try other actions randomly in a hope for a better reward resulting in improvement in Q-values and thereby, deriving better optimal policy.

Q-learning for the mountain car problem in OpenAI gym

The **mountain car** is a standard testing problem in the domain of reinforcement learning. It consists of an under-powered car, which has to drive up a steep hill to the flag point as shown in the following diagram:

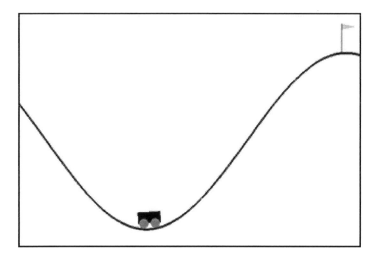

The catch here is that gravity is stronger than the car's engine, so even at full throttle the car cannot accelerate up that steep slope. Therefore, the car has to make use of the potential energy by driving in reverse, in the opposite direction and then utilize that to reach the flag point at the top right.

Here, state space is continuous and is defined by two points: position and velocity. For a given state (that is, position and velocity) the agent can take three discrete actions, which are move forward (towards top-right in the diagram), move opposite (towards top-left in the diagram) or not use the engine, that is, the car is in neutral. The agent receives a negative reward until it reaches the goal state.

Q-learning can be easily applied to the environment having discrete state space and actions, but this problem became the test bed for reinforcement learning algorithms as it has continuous state space and requires either discretization of continuous state space or function approximation to map it to a discrete class.

The technical details of the mountain car problem are listed as follows for your reference:

The state space is two dimensional and continuous. It consists of position and velocity, with the following values:

- **Position**: (-1.2,0.6)
- **Velocity**: (-0.07,0.07)

Action space is discrete and one-dimensional and has three options:

- (left, neutral, right)

Reward -1 for every timestep.

Start state:

- **Position**: -0.5
- **Velocity**: 0.0

Terminal state condition:

- **An episode ends at**: Position $\geq$ 0.6

As we have now seen the parameters of Q-learning, we will now look at the implementation of Q-learning to solve the mountain car problem.

First, we will import the dependencies and examine the mountain car environment, using the following code:

```
#importing the dependencies

import gym
import numpy as np

#exploring Mountain Car environment

env_name = 'MountainCar-v0'
env = gym.make(env_name)

print("Action Set size :",env.action_space)
print("Observation set shape :",env.observation_space)
print("Highest state feature value :",env.observation_space.high)
print("Lowest state feature value:",env.observation_space.low)
print(env.observation_space.shape)
```

The previous print statements output the following:

```
Making new env: MountainCar-v0
('Action Set size :', Discrete(3))
('Observation set shape :', Box(2,))
('Highest state feature value :', array([ 0.6 , 0.07]))
('Lowest state feature value:', array([-1.2 , -0.07]))
(2,)
```

Thus, we see the action space is a discrete set showing three possible actions, and the state space is a two-dimensional continuous space, where one dimension caters to the position while the other, the velocity of the car. Next, we will assign the hyperparameters such as number of states, number of episodes, learning rate (both initial and minimum), discount factor gamma, maximum steps in an episode, and epsilon for epsilon-greedy, using the following code:

```
n_states = 40   # number of states
episodes = 10 # number of episodes

initial_lr = 1.0 # initial learning rate
min_lr = 0.005 # minimum learning rate
gamma = 0.99 # discount factor
max_steps = 300
epsilon = 0.05

env = env.unwrapped
env.seed(0)          #setting environment seed to reproduce same result
np.random.seed(0)    #setting numpy random number generation seed to
reproduce same random numbers
```

Our next task would be to create a function to perform discretization of the continuous state space. Discretization is the conversion of continuous states space observation to a discrete set of state space:

```
def discretization(env, obs):
    env_low = env.observation_space.low
    env_high = env.observation_space.high
    env_den = (env_high - env_low) / n_states
    pos_den = env_den[0]
    vel_den = env_den[1]
    pos_high = env_high[0]
    pos_low = env_low[0]
    vel_high = env_high[1]
    vel_low = env_low[1]
    pos_scaled = int((obs[0] - pos_low)/pos_den)   #converts to an integer
value
    vel_scaled = int((obs[1] - vel_low)/vel_den)   #converts to an integer
value
    return pos_scaled,vel_scaled
```

Now, we will start implementing our Q-learning algorithm by initializing a Q-table and updating the Q-values accordingly. Here, we have updated the reward value as absolute differences between current position and position at the lowest point, that is, start point so that it maximizes the reward by going away from the central, that is, lowest point. This has been done for better convergence:

```
#Q table
#rows are states but here state is 2-D pos,vel
#columns are actions
#therefore, Q- table would be 3-D

q_table = np.zeros((n_states,n_states,env.action_space.n))
total_steps = 0
for episode in range(episodes):
        obs = env.reset()
        total_reward = 0
        # decreasing learning rate alpha over time
        alpha = max(min_lr,initial_lr*(gamma**(episode//100)))
        steps = 0
        while True:
            env.render()
            pos,vel = discretization(env,obs)
            #action for the current state using epsilon greedy
            if np.random.uniform(low=0,high=1) < epsilon:
                a = np.random.choice(env.action_space.n)
            else:
                a = np.argmax(q_table[pos][vel])
            obs,reward,terminate,_ = env.step(a)
            total_reward += abs(obs[0]+0.5)
            #q-table update
            pos_,vel_ = discretization(env,obs)
            q_table[pos][vel][a] = (1-alpha)*q_table[pos][vel][a] +
alpha*(reward+gamma*np.max(q_table[pos_][vel_]))
            steps+=1
            if terminate:
                break
        print("Episode {} completed with total reward {} in {}
steps".format(episode+1,total_reward,steps))

while True: #to hold the render at the last step when Car passes the flag
        env.render()
```

The preceding program for Q-learning will print output in the following manner as per the learning:

```
Episode 1 completed with total reward 8433.30289388 in 26839 steps
Episode 2 completed with total reward 3072.93369963 in 8811 steps
Episode 3 completed with total reward 1230.81734028 in 4395 steps
Episode 4 completed with total reward 2182.31111239 in 6629 steps
Episode 5 completed with total reward 2459.88770998 in 6834 steps
Episode 6 completed with total reward 720.943914405 in 2828 steps
Episode 7 completed with total reward 389.433014729 in 1591 steps
Episode 8 completed with total reward 424.846699654 in 2362 steps
Episode 9 completed with total reward 449.500988781 in 1413 steps
Episode 10 completed with total reward 222.356805259 in 843 steps
```

This will also render the environment showing the car moving and taking the optimal path and reaching the goal state as shown in the following screenshot:

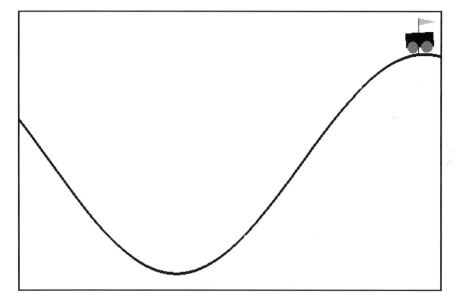

Final state view of the mountain car game

Thus, we see model free learning can derive an optimal policy from its interactions with the environment without any need to create a model of the environment. Thus, we have learnt that Q-learning is a type of model free temporal difference learning that finds the optimal state action selection policy by estimating the Q-function.

Deep Q-networks

If we recall `Chapter 2`, *Training Reinforcement Learning Agents Using OpenAI Gym*, where we tried to implement a basic Q-network, we studied that for a real-world problem, Q-learning using a Q-table is not a feasible solution owing to continuous state and action spaces. Moreover, a Q-table is environment-specific and not generalized. Therefore, we need a model which can map the state information provided as input to Q-values of the possible set of actions. This is where a neural network comes to play the role of a function approximator, which can take state information input in the form of a vector, and learn to map them to Q-values for all possible actions.

Let's discuss the issues with Q-learning in a gaming environment and evolution of deep Q-networks. Consider applying Q-learning to a gaming environment, the state would be defined by the location of the player, obstacles, opponents, and so on, but this would be game-specific and cannot be generalized over other gaming environments, even if we create a Q-table for all possible states for this game somehow.

Well, the gaming environments have one thing in common and, that is, all are made of pixels. If the pixels can be fed into a model that can be mapped to actions then it can be generalized across all games. DeepMind's implementation of convolutional neural networks had game image frames, where the inputs and the outputs were the Q-values for each possible action in that environment. The convolutional neural networks consisted of three convolution layers and two fully connected layers. One element of a **convolution neural network (CNN)** is the pooling layer, which has been avoided here. The main reason for using a pooling layer is in case of object detection in images where the location of the object in the images is not important, but not here, where the location of the objects in a game frame is highly important.

Therefore, for a gaming environment, a **deep Q-network (DQN)** consists of consecutive game frames as the input to capture the motion and outputs Q-values for all possible actions in the game. Since a deep neural network is being used as a function approximator of the Q-function, this process is called deep-Q learning.

Deep Q-networks are much more capable of generalization compared to Q-networks. In order to convert a Q-network into a deep Q-network we need the following improvements:

- Use a convolution neural network instead of a single layer neural network
- Use of experience replay
- Separate target network to compute target Q-values

We will discuss each of these parameters in detail, in the following topics:

Using a convolution neural network instead of a single layer neural network

Our gaming environment is videos and convolution neural networks have shown state-of-the-art results when it comes to computer vision. Moreover, the level of object detection in game frames should be close to human level ability and convolution neural networks learn representation from images similar to the way the primal visual cortex of humans does.

DeepMind used three convolution layers and two fully connected layers in their DQN network that achieves superhuman level performance in Atari games as shown in the following flowchart:

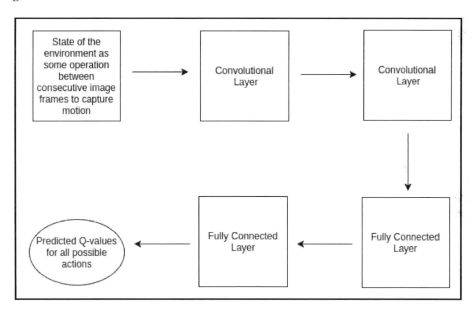

Use of experience replay

Another important feature added to deep Q-networks is **experience replay**. The idea behind this feature is that the agent can store its past experiences and use them in batches to train the deep neural network. Storing the experiences allows the agent to randomly draw the batches and help the network to learn from a variety of data instead of just formalizing decisions on immediate experiences. Each of these experiences are stored in a form of four dimensional vector comprising of **state, action, reward,** and **next state**.

In order to avoid storage issues, the buffer of experience replay is fixed, and as the new experiences get stored the old experiences get removed. For training neural networks, uniform batches of random experiences are drawn from the buffer.

Separate target network to compute the target Q-values

A separate network to generate target Q-values is an important feature and makes deep Q-networks unique. The Q-values generated by this separate target network is used to compute loss after every action taken by the agent during training. The reason behind the use of two networks instead of one is that the primary Q-network values shift constantly at every step owing to the change in weights at every step, and this makes the Q-values generated from this network unstable.

In order to get stable Q-values, another neural network is used whose weights are changed slowly compared to the primary Q-network. In this way, the training process is more stable. This was also published in a post (http://www.davidqiu.com:8888/research/ nature14236.pdf) by DeepMind. They found this approach was able to stabilize the training process.

Adapted from Minh et. al (2015) (http://www.davidqiu.com:8888/research/nature14236. pdf), here's the pseudo code for DQN:

```
Input: the image(game frame) pixels

Initialize replay memory D for experience replay
Initialize action-value function Q i.e. primary neural network with random
weight θ
Initialize target action-value function Qᵀ i.e. target neural network with
weights θ_T = θ

for each episode do
    Initialize sequence s₁ = x₁ and preprocessed sequence φ₁ = φ(s₁)
    for t = 0 to max_step in an episode do
        Choose aₜ using ε-greedy such that
```

$$a_t = \begin{cases} a\ random\ action & ,with\ probability\ \epsilon \\ argmax_{a'}\,Q(\phi(s_1),a';\theta) & ,otherwise \end{cases}$$

```
        Perform action aₜ
        Observe reward rₜ and image xₜ₊₁
        Set sₜ₊₁ = sₜ, aₜ, xₜ₊₁ and preprocess φₜ₊₁ = φ(sₜ₊₁)
```

```
Store transition (φ(s_t), a_t, r_t, φ(s_{t+1})) in D
// experience replay
Sample random batch of transitions (φ_j, a_j, r_j, φ_{j+1}) from D
```

$$y_j = \begin{cases} r_j & , \; if \; episode \; terminates \; at \; j+1 \\ r_j + \gamma \, max_{a'} Q(\phi(s_{j+1}), a'; \theta_T) & , \; otherwise \end{cases}$$

Set

$$\sum_j (y_j - Q(\phi(s_j), a_j; \theta))^2$$

```
Compute the cost function =
Perform gradient descent on the cost function w.r.t. the primary
```
network parameter θ

```
// periodic update of target network
After every C steps reset Q^T = Q, i.e., set θ_T = θ
    until end of episode
end
```

Advancements in deep Q-networks and beyond

With more research and time, deep Q-networks have undergone many improvements, thereby deriving better architectures providing greater performance and stability. In this section, we will discuss only two famous architectures, which are **Double DQN** and **Dueling DQN**.

Double DQN

The reason behind the use of **Double DQN (DDQN)** is that the regular DQN overestimates the Q-values of potential actions to take in a given state. Overestimation is not equal across all the actions in a regular DQN. Therefore the issue persisted: otherwise, equal estimation across all actions would not have been an issue. As a result, certain suboptimal actions were getting higher values so the time to learn optimal policy increased. This led to small modifications in our regular DQN architecture and it resulted in what we call DDQN , that is, double deep Q-network.

In DDQN, instead of taking the max over Q-values while computing the target Q-value during training, we use a primary network to choose the action and target network to generate a target Q-value for that action. This decouples the action; choosing from a target Q-network, which generates target Q-values, results in reducing the overestimation, and helps to train faster. The target Q-value in DDQN is updated by the following equation:

$$Q_{target} = r + \gamma \, Q(s', argmax_a(Q(s', a; \theta)); \theta_T)$$

Here:

θ represents the weights of the primary network, and

θ_T represents the weights of the target network.

Dueling DQN

In case of **Dueling DQN**, the Q value has been modified as the summation of the value function of the state and advantage function of the action. The value function $V(s)$ quantifies the usefulness or goodness of being in state s and the advantage function $A(a)$ quantifies the advantage of action a over other possible actions. Therefore,

$$Q(s, a) = V(s) + A(a)$$

Dueling DQN has separate networks to compute the value and advantage functions and then combine them back to fetch the value for the Q-function. The reason behind decoupling the computation of value and advantage is that the agent doesn't have to take care of the unnecessary value function computations for each action in a given state. Therefore, decoupling these computations can lead to robust state action Q-values.

Deep Q-network for mountain car problem in OpenAI gym

We have already discussed the environment while implementing Q-learning for the mountain car problem. Let's dive directly into implementing a deep Q-network to solve the mountain car problem. First, we will import the required libraries, using the following code:

```
#importing the dependencies

import numpy as np
import tensorflow as tf
import gym
```

Let's discuss our class DQN, which holds the architecture of the deep Q-network:

- `__init__(self, learning_rate, gamma, n_features, n_actions, epsilon, parameter_changing_pointer, memory_size)`: Default constructor to assign the hyperparameters such as:
  - `learning_rate`
  - gamma, that is, the discount factor
  - `n_feature`: Number of features in state, that is, number of dimensions in state
  - `epsilon`: Threshold value for epsilon greedy condition to exploit or explore actions
- `build_networks()`: To create primary and target networks using Tensorflow
- `target_params_replaced(self)`: To replace the target network parameters with primary network parameters
- `store_experience(self, obs, a, r, obs_)`: To store experiences, that is, tuple of (state, action, reward, new state)
- `fit(self)`: To train our deep Q-network
- `epsilon_greedy(self, obs)`: For a given observation state, which action to take, that is, either exploit action as per existing policy or explore new actions randomly

The architecture of the DQN class with the main function can be defined using the following code:

```
class DQN:
    def __init__(self, learning_rate, gamma, n_features,
                    n_actions, epsilon, parameter_changing_pointer, memory_size):
    . . . .
    def build_networks(self):
    . . . .
    def target_params_replaced(self):
    . . . .
    def store_experience(self, obs, a, r, obs_):
    . . . .
    def fit(self):
    . . . .
    def epsilon_greedy(self, obs):
    . . . .

if __name__ == "__main__":
    . . . .
```

The __init__: The default constructor is explained along with the comments in the following code snippet:

```
def
__init__(self,learning_rate,gamma,n_features,n_actions,epsilon,parameter_ch
anging_pointer,memory_size):
        self.learning_rate = learning_rate
        self.gamma = gamma
        self.n_features = n_features
        self.n_actions = n_actions
        self.epsilon = epsilon
        self.batch_size = 100
        self.experience_counter = 0
        self.experience_limit = memory_size
        self.replace_target_pointer = parameter_changing_pointer
        self.learning_counter = 0
        self.memory = np.zeros([self.experience_limit,self.n_features*2+2])
#for experience replay

        self.build_networks()
        #to fetch parameters under the collection :
'primary_network_parameters'
        p_params = tf.get_collection('primary_network_parameters')
        #to fetch parameters under the collection :
'target_network_parameters'
        t_params = tf.get_collection('target_network_parameters')
        #replacing tensor replace the target network parameters with
primary network parameters
        self.replacing_target_parameters = [tf.assign(t,p) for t,p in
zip(t_params,p_params)]
        self.sess = tf.Session()
        self.sess.run(tf.global_variables_initializer())
```

Now let's initialize `build_networks(self)`. It is a function to build primary and target networks:

- Primary network parameters are created under `variable_scope`:
  `primary_network` and collection `primary_network_parameters`
- Target network parameters are created under
  `variable_scope`: `target_network` and
  collection `target_network_parameters`
- Both parameters have the same structure, namely:
  - w1: Weight matrix associated with input layer
  - b1: Bias vector associated with input layer

- ReLU: Activation function for the signals moving from input to the hidden layer
- w2: Weight matrix associated with hidden layer
- b2: Bias vector associated with input layer
- Calculating loss between the Q-value output by the primary network and the Q-value output by the target network
- Minimize this loss using **adam** optimizer

We will use the following code to define the build_networks(self) function:

```
def build_networks(self):
        #primary network
        hidden_units = 10
        self.s = tf.placeholder(tf.float32,[None,self.n_features])
        self.qtarget = tf.placeholder(tf.float32,[None,self.n_actions])
        with tf.variable_scope('primary_network'):
                c = ['primary_network_parameters',
tf.GraphKeys.GLOBAL_VARIABLES]
                # first layer
                with tf.variable_scope('layer1'):
                        w1 =
tf.get_variable('w1',[self.n_features,hidden_units],initializer=tf.contrib.
layers.xavier_initializer(),dtype=tf.float32,collections=c)
                        b1 =
tf.get_variable('b1',[1,hidden_units],initializer=tf.contrib.layers.xavier_
initializer(),dtype=tf.float32,collections=c)
                        l1 = tf.nn.relu(tf.matmul(self.s, w1) + b1)

                # second layer
                with tf.variable_scope('layer2'):
                        w2 =
tf.get_variable('w2',[hidden_units,self.n_actions],initializer=tf.contrib.l
ayers.xavier_initializer(),dtype=tf.float32,collections=c)
                        b2 =
tf.get_variable('b2',[1,self.n_actions],initializer=tf.contrib.layers.xavie
r_initializer(),dtype=tf.float32,collections=c)
                        self.qeval = tf.matmul(l1, w2) + b2


        with tf.variable_scope('loss'):
                self.loss =
tf.reduce_mean(tf.squared_difference(self.qtarget,self.qeval))

        with tf.variable_scope('optimizer'):
                self.train =
```

```
tf.train.AdamOptimizer(self.learning_rate).minimize(self.loss)
        #target network
        self.st = tf.placeholder(tf.float32,[None,self.n_features])

        with tf.variable_scope('target_network'):
                c = ['target_network_parameters',
tf.GraphKeys.GLOBAL_VARIABLES]
                # first layer
                with tf.variable_scope('layer1'):
                        w1 = tf.get_variable('w1',
[self.n_features,hidden_units],initializer=tf.contrib.layers.xavier_initial
izer(),dtype=tf.float32,collections=c)
                        b1 = tf.get_variable('b1',
[1,hidden_units],initializer=tf.contrib.layers.xavier_initializer(),dtype=t
f.float32,collections=c)
                        l1 = tf.nn.relu(tf.matmul(self.st, w1) + b1)

                # second layer
                with tf.variable_scope('layer2'):
                        w2 =
tf.get_variable('w2',[hidden_units,self.n_actions],initializer=tf.contrib.l
ayers.xavier_initializer(),dtype=tf.float32,collections=c)
                        b2 =
tf.get_variable('b2',[1,self.n_actions],initializer=tf.contrib.layers.xavie
r_initializer(),dtype=tf.float32,collections=c)
                        self.qt = tf.matmul(l1, w2) + b2
```

Now we will define the `target_params_replaced(self)`, using the following code. It is function to run the tensor operation of assigning primary network parameters to target network parameters:

```
def target_params_replaced(self):
        self.sess.run(self.replacing_target_parameters)
```

Now we will define the `store_experience(self,obs,a,r,obs_)`, which is a function to store each experience, that is, tuple of (state, action, reward, new state) in its experience buffer through which the primary target will get trained, as shown in the following code:

```
def store_experience(self,obs,a,r,obs_):
        index = self.experience_counter % self.experience_limit
        self.memory[index,:] = np.hstack((obs,[a,r],obs_))
        self.experience_counter+=1
```

Here we will define `fit(self)`, which is a function to train the network by selecting a batch from an experience buffer, calculate the tensor value for `q_target`, and then minimize the loss between the `qeval` (that is, the output from the primary network) and `q_target`(that is, the Q-value calculated using the target network). We will use the following code to define the function:

```
def fit(self):
        # sample batch memory from all memory
        if self.experience_counter < self.experience_limit:
                indices = np.random.choice(self.experience_counter,
size=self.batch_size)
        else:
                indices = np.random.choice(self.experience_limit,
size=self.batch_size)
        batch = self.memory[indices,:]
        qt,qeval =
self.sess.run([self.qt,self.qeval],feed_dict={self.st:batch[:,-
self.n_features:],self.s:batch[:,:self.n_features]})
        qtarget = qeval.copy()
        batch_indices = np.arange(self.batch_size, dtype=np.int32)
        actions = self.memory[indices,self.n_features].astype(int)
        rewards = self.memory[indices,self.n_features+1]
        qtarget[batch_indices,actions] = rewards + self.gamma *
np.max(qt,axis=1)
        self.sess.run(self.train,feed_dict =
{self.s:batch[:,:self.n_features],self.qtarget:qtarget})

        #increasing epsilon
        if self.epsilon < 0.9:
                self.epsilon += 0.0002
        #replacing target network parameters with primary network
parameters
        if self.learning_counter % self.replace_target_pointer == 0:
                self.target_params_replaced()
                print("target parameters changed")
        self.learning_counter += 1
```

We have already discussed the exploration and exploitation dilemma. The **epsilon-greedy approach** is one of the approaches for selecting a threshold value epsilon and generating a random number. If it's less than epsilon we follow the same policy, and if it's greater we randomly explore actions or vice-versa. Here, in `epsilon_greedy(self,obs)`, we have implemented the epsilon-greedy approach in a dynamic way, where in the fit(self) function we increment the value of epsilon every learning step:

```
def epsilon_greedy(self,obs):
        #epsilon greedy implementation to choose action
```

```
        if np.random.uniform(low=0,high=1) < self.epsilon:
            return
np.argmax(self.sess.run(self.qeval,feed_dict={self.s:obs[np.newaxis,:]}))
        else:
            return np.random.choice(self.n_actions)
```

Following is the main function, which creates an object of the preceding class of DQN, uses gym to fetch the `MountainCar-v0` environment, and trains the agent to solve the problem. Like in Q-learning, here also we have updated the reward value as absolute difference between current position and position at lowest point, that is, start point so that it maximizes reward by going away from central:

```
if __name__ == "__main__":
    env = gym.make('MountainCar-v0')
    env = env.unwrapped
    dqn =
DQN(learning_rate=0.001,gamma=0.9,n_features=env.observation_space.shape[0]
,n_actions=env.action_space.n,epsilon=0.0,parameter_changing_pointer=500,me
mory_size=5000)
    episodes = 10
    total_steps = 0
    for episode in range(episodes):
        steps = 0
        obs = env.reset()
        episode_reward = 0
        while True:
            env.render()
            action = dqn.epsilon_greedy(obs)
            obs_,reward,terminate,_ = env.step(action)
            reward = abs(obs_[0]+0.5)
            dqn.store_experience(obs,action,reward,obs_)
            if total_steps > 1000:
                dqn.fit()
            episode_reward+=reward
            if terminate:
                break
            obs = obs_
            total_steps+=1
            steps+=1
        print("Episode {} with Reward : {} at epsilon {} in steps
{}".format(episode+1,episode_reward,dqn.epsilon,steps))
    while True: #to hold the render at the last step when Car passes the
flag
        env.render()
```

The preceding program will print the following:

```
target parameters changed
target parameters changed
target parameters changed
target parameters changed
target parameters changed
target parameters changed
Episode 1 with Reward : 1399.25710453 at epsilon 0.5948 in steps 3974
target parameters changed
Episode 2 with Reward : 168.166352703 at epsilon 0.6762 in steps 406
target parameters changed
Episode 3 with Reward : 67.6246277944 at epsilon 0.7568 in steps 402
Episode 4 with Reward : 53.1292577484 at epsilon 0.7942 in steps 186
target parameters changed
Episode 5 with Reward : 38.90009005 at epsilon 0.818 in steps 118
Episode 6 with Reward : 60.9286778233 at epsilon 0.8738 in steps 278
target parameters changed
Episode 7 with Reward : 72.433268035 at epsilon 0.9002 in steps 257
Episode 8 with Reward : 80.7812592557 at epsilon 0.9002 in steps 251
target parameters changed
Episode 9 with Reward : 92.123978864 at epsilon 0.9002 in steps 234
Episode 10 with Reward : 38.7923903502 at epsilon 0.9002 in steps 126
```

Here, it converges quickly but it also depends on the exploration and exploitation of the actions as well as the initialization of the parameters and hyperparameters. This will also render the environment showing the car moving and taking the optimal path and reaching the goal state as shown in the following screenshot:

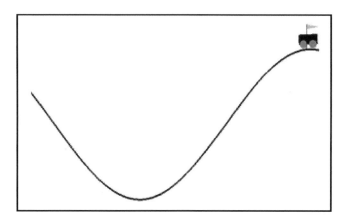

Next, let's try to implement a deep Q-network to solve the Cartpole problem from OpenAI gym in the following topic.

Deep Q-network for Cartpole problem in OpenAI gym

The **Cartpole** is one the simplest problems in an MDP environment, as shown in the following screenshot. It consist of a cart that moves in a horizontal axis with a pole anchored at the center of the cart, which rotates. The goal is to take actions in such a way that the pole remains near to vertical and not rotate down.

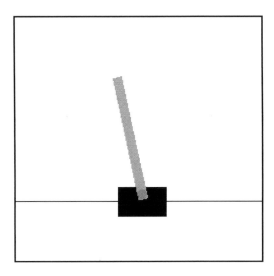

A state in a cart pole environment is a 4-dimensional continuous space where each dimension is as follows:

- x: It denotes the cart position (minimum = -2.4, maximum = 2.4)
- x_dot: Denotes the cart velocity (minimum = -∞, maximum = ∞)
- theta: Shows the angle in radians (minimum = -0.73, maximum = 0.73)
- theta_dot: Shows the angular velocity (minimum = -∞, maximum = ∞)

At every step in a given state, there are two possible actions, that is, the cart can either move left or right, and the reward received for each step is 1. Here, the reward is received as long as the pole is near to vertical and the cart is within the boundaries. An episode is considered to be over if:

- The pole falls beyond a certain angle, that is, beyond ± 0.20944 radians
- The cart goes too far either to the left or to the right out of the frame, that is, beyond ± 2.4

Hence, the goal of the problem is to hold the pole to near to vertical without the cart going beyond the boundary for as long as possible.

In order to implement a deep Q-network for the Cartpole problem, we will import the DQN class previously created. Please follow the following code to implement a deep Q-network in the Cartpole environment. The problem is considered to be solved if the average reward over 100 consecutive trials is greater than or equal to 195:

```
#Importing dependencies
import gym
import numpy as np

#Importing the DQN class created preceding
from Deep_Q_Network_Mountain_Car import DQN
```

Now we will explore the Cartpole environment, using the following code:

```
env = gym.make('CartPole-v0')
env = env.unwrapped

print(env.action_space)
print(env.observation_space)
print(env.observation_space.high)
print(env.observation_space.low)
print("Position extreme threshold value:",env.x_threshold)
print("Angle extreme threshold value:",env.theta_threshold_radians)
```

The previous print statements output the following:

```
Making new env: CartPole-v0
Discrete(2)
Box(4,)
[ 4.80000000e+00 3.40282347e+38 4.18879020e-01 3.40282347e+38]
[ -4.80000000e+00 -3.40282347e+38 -4.18879020e-01 -3.40282347e+38]
Position extreme threshold value: 2.4
Angle extreme threshold value: 0.20943951023931953
```

Here, the observation space high/low values follow the following order (position, velocity, angle, angular velocity)

The following code is the main part where we create an object of the preceding class of DQN, use gym to fetch the Cartpole-v0 environment, and train the agent to solve the problem. Here, we have updated the reward value as the sum of the difference of position from the extreme, and difference of the angle from the extreme pole angle, because away it would be from the extreme position and smaller will be the angle and will be closer to the center of the cart, therefore higher should be the reward. This has been done for better primary network convergence. We will use this reward for learning, but for the calculation of the overall success measure we will use the original reward:

```
dqn =
DQN(learning_rate=0.01,gamma=0.9,n_features=env.observation_space.shape[0],
n_actions=env.action_space.n,epsilon=0.0,parameter_changing_pointer=100,mem
ory_size=2000)

episodes = 150
total_steps = 0
rew_ep = []

for episode in range(episodes):
    steps = 0
    obs = env.reset()
    episode_reward = 0
    while True:
        env.render()
        action = dqn.epsilon_greedy(obs)
        obs_,reward,terminate,_ = env.step(action)
        #smaller the theta angle and closer to center then better should be
the reward
        x, vel, angle, ang_vel = obs_
        r1 = (env.x_threshold - abs(x))/env.x_threshold - 0.8
        r2 = (env.theta_threshold_radians -
abs(angle))/env.theta_threshold_radians - 0.5
        reward = r1 + r2
        dqn.store_experience(obs,action,reward,obs_)
        if total_steps > 1000:
            dqn.fit()
        episode_reward+=reward
        if terminate:
            break
        obs = obs_
        total_steps+=1
        steps+=1
    print("Episode {} with Reward : {} at epsilon {} in steps
{}".format(episode+1,episode_reward,dqn.epsilon,steps))
    rew_ep.append(episode_reward)
```

```
print("Mean over last 100 episodes are: ",np.mean(rew_ep[50:]))
while True: #to hold the render at the last step when Car passes the flag
    env.render()
```

The preceding program will print output as follows:

```
. . . . . . . . . . . . . . . .
. . . . . . . . . . . . . . . .
. . . . . . . . . . . . . . .
Episode 145 with Reward : 512.0 at epsilon 0.9002 in steps 511
target parameters changed
target parameters changed
target parameters changed
target parameters changed
target parameters changed
target parameters changed
Episode 146 with Reward : 567.0 at epsilon 0.9002 in steps 566
target parameters changed
target parameters changed
target parameters changed
target parameters changed
target parameters changed
target parameters changed
target parameters changed
target parameters changed
target parameters changed
target parameters changed
target parameters changed
target parameters changed
target parameters changed
Episode 147 with Reward : 1310.0 at epsilon 0.9002 in steps 1309
Episode 148 with Reward : 22.0 at epsilon 0.9002 in steps 21
target parameters changed
target parameters changed
target parameters changed
target parameters changed
target parameters changed
target parameters changed
target parameters changed
target parameters changed
target parameters changed
target parameters changed
target parameters changed
target parameters changed
Episode 149 with Reward : 1171.0 at epsilon 0.9002 in steps 1170
target parameters changed
target parameters changed
target parameters changed
```

```
target parameters changed
target parameters changed
target parameters changed
target parameters changed
target parameters changed
target parameters changed
target parameters changed
Episode 150 with Reward : 1053.0 at epsilon 0.9002 in steps 1052
Mean over last 100 episodes are: 248.72999999999999
```

Because the output log is too long, here we have the output catering to the last six episodes along with the average reward per episode for the last 100 episodes.

Deep Q-network for Atari Breakout in OpenAI gym

The **Breakout** environment was developed by the team of Nolan Bushnell, Steve Bristow, and Steve Wozniak at Atari, Inc. The Atari Breakout environment has a lot bigger state size compared to what we have seen in mountain car, Cartpole, or Frozen Lake. The state space is in a similar range to what we saw in Atari Pong. Therefore, it takes a long time for the learning to converge. The following screenshot illustrates the initial image frame of the Atari Breakout environment:

Screenshot of the Breakout-v0 environment

The observation space is continuous, contains pixel values of the image frame, and the action space is discrete comprising of four distinct actions. Each image frame is of size *210*160*3* (210 pixels height, 160 pixels width, 3 color channels, that is, RGB). Therefore, we can take the grayscale image frame as there will be no loss of information and the size will become *210*160*. Only taking an image frame for a state will not work as it doesn't capture any motion information. Therefore, we will stack four consecutive image frames per state. Thus, the state size will be *4*210*160 = 134,440*. For Atari Breakout, downsampling to a certain extent will not cause any loss of information. Moreover, we can also crop the image frame to avoid unnecessary sections of the image and retain important ones that would contain sufficient information to play the game.

Let's examine the environment first, using the following code:

```
import gym

env = gym.make('Breakout-v0')
s = env.reset()
print("State space shape : ",env.observation_space)
print("Action space shape : ",env.action_space)
print("Type of actions : ",env.unwrapped.get_action_meanings())
```

This will output the following statements:

```
State space shape : Box(210, 160, 3)
Action space shape : Discrete(4)
Type of actions : ['NOOP', 'FIRE', 'RIGHT', 'LEFT']
```

Thus we get the shape of state space and action space, and also the four different types of action the paddle can take, that is, noop (short for no operation), fire (the ball at the target bricks above), going right, or going left to stop the ball going down.

Let's also check a sample cropping and see the difference, as shown in the following image:

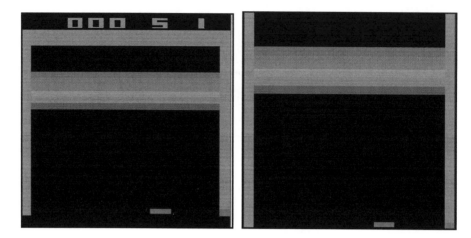

Before cropping (left) and after cropping (right)

The game proceeds in the following way:

- The paddle at the bottom fires the ball up and it hits the bricks to destroy them at the top layers of the screen
- After hitting the bricks the ball bounces back
- The paddle should move left or right to hit the ball and to stop it falling
- If the ball falls below, that is, goes off the screen below the paddle, the game is over and the player loses
- If the ball bounces of the paddle it will again go up, bouncing off the walls and hitting more bricks

Thus, the objective is to win the game by destroying all the bricks without allowing the ball to go below the paddle.

Let's start implementing a deep Q-network to make our agent learn the game of Atari Breakout. First, we will import the necessary libraries, using the following code:

```
#Importing the dependencies

import numpy as np
import tensorflow as tf
import gym
from scipy.misc import imresize
```

The architecture of the `class DQN` with main functions can be defined using the following code:

```
class DQN:

    def
__init__(self,learning_rate,gamma,n_features,n_actions,epsilon,parameter_ch
anging_pointer,memory_size,epsilon_incrementer):
        ....
    def
add_layer(self,inputs,w_shape=None,b_shape=None,layer=None,ctivation_fn=Non
e,c=None,isconv=False:
        ....
    def weight_variable(self,w_shape,layer,c):
        ....
    def bias_variable(self,b_shape,layer,c):
        ....
    def conv(self,inputs,w):
        ....
    def build_networks(self):
        ....
    def target_params_replaced(self):
        ....
    def store_experience(self,obs,a,r,obs_):
        ....
    def fit(self):
        ....
    def epsilon_greedy(self,obs):
        ....

if __name__ == "__main__":
    ....
```

Let's discuss our class DQN and its parameters, which holds the architecture of a deep Q-network:

- `__init__(self,learning_rate,gamma,n_features,n_actions,epsilon ,parameter_changing_pointer,memory_size)`: Default constructor to assign the hyperparameters such as:
    - `learning_rate`
    - `gamma`: That is, the discount factor
    - `n_feature`: It is the number of features in state, that is, number of dimensions in state
    - `epsilon`: The threshold value for epsilon greedy condition to exploit or explore actions

- `parameter_changing_pointer`: An integer value(say *n*) specifying that after every *n* iterations, the parameters of primary network is copied to the target network
- `memory_size`: Maximum length of the experience reply

- `add_layer(self,inputs,w_shape=None,b_shape=None,layer=None,acti vation_fn=None,c=None,isconv=False)`: Function to create the layer in the neural network
- `weight_variable(self,w_shape,layer,c)`: Function to create weight parameters
- `bias_variable(self,b_shape,layer,c)`: Function to create bias parameters
- `conv(self,inputs,w)`: Function to perform the convolution operation on an image frame
- `build_networks()`: This function is used to create the primary and target networks using TensorFlow
- `target_params_replaced(self)`: Used to replace the target network parameters with primary network parameters
- `store_experience(self,obs,a,r,obs_)`: Helps to store experiences, that is, tuple of (state, action, reward, new state)
- `fit(self)`: Used to train our deep Q-network
- `epsilon_greedy(self,obs)`: It helps us in choosing the right action for a given observation state, that is, either exploit the action as per existing policy or explore new actions randomly

Now let's define the `__init__` `default` constructor, using the following code:

```
def
__init__(self,learning_rate,gamma,n_features,n_actions,epsilon,parameter_ch
anging_pointer,
          memory_size,epsilon_incrementer):

    tf.reset_default_graph()
    self.learning_rate = learning_rate
    self.gamma = gamma
    self.n_features = n_features
    self.n_actions = n_actions
    self.epsilon = epsilon
    self.batch_size = 32
    self.experience_counter = 0
    self.epsilon_incrementer = epsilon_incrementer
    self.experience_limit = memory_size
    self.replace_target_pointer = parameter_changing_pointer
```

```
        self.learning_counter = 0
        self.memory = [] #np.zeros([self.experience_limit,4]) #for
experience replay

        self.build_networks()
        p_params = tf.get_collection('primary_network_parameters')
        t_params = tf.get_collection('target_network_parameters')
        self.replacing_target_parameters = [tf.assign(t,p) for t,p in
zip(t_params,p_params)]
        self.sess = tf.Session()
        self.sess.run(tf.global_variables_initializer())
```

The following code defines the `add_layer` function, which helps in creating different layers as per the requirement of convolution, or fully connected layers by providing the boolean parameter of `isconv`, where if `isconv` is true, it means it's the convolution layer:

```
def
add_layer(self,inputs,w_shape=None,b_shape=None,layer=None,activation_fn=No
ne,c=None,isconv=False):
        w = self.weight_variable(w_shape,layer,c)
        b = self.bias_variable(b_shape,layer,c)
        eps = tf.constant(value=0.000001, shape=b.shape)
        if isconv:
            if activation_fn is None:
                return self.conv(inputs,w)+b+eps
            else:
                h_conv = activation_fn(self.conv(inputs,w)+b+eps)
                return h_conv
        if activation_fn is None:
            return tf.matmul(inputs,w)+b+eps
        outputs = activation_fn(tf.matmul(inputs,w)+b+eps)
        return outputs
```

Next, we have the `weight_variable` and `bias_variable` functions. The following code is used to define the weight parameters:

```
def weight_variable(self,w_shape,layer,c):
        return
tf.get_variable('w'+layer,w_shape,initializer=tf.contrib.layers.xavier_init
ializer(),
                                        dtype=tf.float32,collections=c)
```

Code to define the bias parameters:

```
def bias_variable(self,b_shape,layer,c):
        return
tf.get_variable('b'+layer,b_shape,initializer=tf.contrib.layers.xavier_init
```

```
ializer(),
                                       dtype=tf.float32,collections=c)
```

Now let's define `conv(self,inputs,w)`, a function that calls the `tf.nn.conv2d` function of TensorFlow and takes:

- Inputs as a 2-D vector
- **Weights**: Weight of shape
  [`patch_size,patch_size,input_vector_depth,output_vector_depth`]
- **Strides**: A list in form of [1, `x_movement,y_movement`, 1], where:
  - `x_movement`: Defines the number of steps for the patch moved in a horizontal direction
  - `y_movement`: Defines the number of steps for the patch moved in a vertical direction
- **Padding**: SAME or VALID (we have discussed this and valid padding in `Chapter 1`, *Deep Learning – Architectures and Frameworks*)

We will use the following code to define the function:

```
def conv(self,inputs,w):
        #strides [1,x_movement,y_movement,1]
        #stride[0] = stride[3] = 1
        return tf.nn.conv2d(inputs,w,strides=[1,1,1,1],padding='SAME')
```

Now, let us define `build_networks(self)`. It is a function to build the primary and target networks where:

- The primary network parameters are created under `variable_scope` namely: `primary_network` and collection `primary_network_parameters`
- The target network parameters are created under `variable_scope` namely: `target_network` and collection `target_network_parameters`
- Both have the same structure namely:
  - Convolution Layer 1
  - Convolution Layer 2
  - Fully connected Layer 1
  - Fully connected Layer 2
  - Activation function used: ReLU

The function also helps in:

- Calculating loss between the Q-value output by the primary network and the Q-value output by the target network

We can minimize this loss using the adam optimizer.

Now as we have learned about the function, let's define it:

```
def build_networks(self):
        #primary network
        shape = [None] + self.n_features
        self.s = tf.placeholder(tf.float32,shape)
        self.qtarget = tf.placeholder(tf.float32,[None,self.n_actions])
        with tf.variable_scope('primary_network'):
                c = ['primary_network_parameters',
tf.GraphKeys.GLOBAL_VARIABLES]
                #first convolutional layer
                with tf.variable_scope('convlayer1'):
                        l1 =
self.add_layer(self.s,w_shape=[5,5,4,32],b_shape=[32],layer='convL1',activa
tion_fn=tf.nn.relu,c=c,isconv=True)

                #first convolutional layer
                with tf.variable_scope('convlayer2'):
                        l2 =
self.add_layer(l1,w_shape=[5,5,32,64],b_shape=[64],layer='convL2',activatio
n_fn=tf.nn.relu,c=c,isconv=True)
                #first fully-connected layer
                l2 = tf.reshape(l2,[-1,80*80*64])
                with tf.variable_scope('FClayer1'):
                        l3 =
self.add_layer(l2,w_shape=[80*80*64,128],b_shape=[128],layer='fclayer1',act
ivation_fn=tf.nn.relu,c=c)

                #second fully-connected layer
                with tf.variable_scope('FClayer2'):
                        self.qeval =
self.add_layer(l3,w_shape=[128,self.n_actions],b_shape=[self.n_actions],lay
er='fclayer2',c=c)

        with tf.variable_scope('loss'):
                self.loss =
tf.reduce_mean(tf.squared_difference(self.qtarget,self.qeval))

        with tf.variable_scope('optimizer'):
                self.train =
```

```
tf.train.AdamOptimizer(self.learning_rate).minimize(self.loss)

        #target network
        self.st = tf.placeholder(tf.float32,shape)

    with tf.variable_scope('target_network'):
        c = ['target_network_parameters',
tf.GraphKeys.GLOBAL_VARIABLES]
        #first convolutional layer
        with tf.variable_scope('convlayer1'):
            l1 =
self.add_layer(self.st,w_shape=[5,5,4,32],b_shape=[32],layer='convL1',activ
ation_fn=tf.nn.relu,c=c,isconv=True)

        #first convolutional layer
        with tf.variable_scope('convlayer2'):
            l2 =
self.add_layer(l1,w_shape=[5,5,32,64],b_shape=[64],layer='convL2',activatio
n_fn=tf.nn.relu,c=c,isconv=True)
        #first fully-connected layer
        l2 = tf.reshape(l2,[-1,80*80*64])
        with tf.variable_scope('FClayer1'):
            l3 =
self.add_layer(l2,w_shape=[80*80*64,128],b_shape=[128],layer='fclayer1',act
ivation_fn=tf.nn.relu,c=c)

        #second fully-connected layer
        with tf.variable_scope('FClayer2'):
            self.qt =
self.add_layer(l3,w_shape=[128,self.n_actions],b_shape=[self.n_actions],lay
er='fclayer2',c=c)
```

Now, let's define `target_params_replaced(self)`, which is a function to run the tensor operation of assigning primary network parameters to target network parameters:

```
def target_params_replaced(self):
    self.sess.run(self.replacing_target_parameters)
```

Now, we will define the `store_experience(self,obs,a,r,obs_)` function, to store each experience, that is, tuple of (state, action, reward, new state) in its experience buffer over which the primary target will get trained:

```
def store_experience(self,obs,a,r,obs_):
    if len(obs.shape)<3 or len(obs_.shape)<3:
        print("Wrong shape entered :
",obs.shape,obs_.shape,len(self.memory))
    else:
```

```
        index = self.experience_counter % self.experience_limit
        if self.experience_counter < self.experience_limit:
                self.memory.append([obs,a,r,obs_])
        else:
                self.memory[index] = [obs,a,r,obs_]
    self.experience_counter+=1
```

Now we will define the `fit(self)` function to train the network by selecting a batch from the experience buffer, calculate the tensor value for `q_target`, and then minimize the loss between the `qeval` (that is, the output from the primary network) and `q_target`(that is, the Q-value calculated using the target network):

```
def fit(self):
        # sample batch memory from all memory
        indices = np.random.choice(len(self.memory), size=self.batch_size)
        batch = [self.memory[i] for i in indices]
        obs_nlist = np.array([i[3] for i in batch])
        obs_list = np.array([i[0] for i in batch])
        qt,qeval =
self.sess.run([self.qt,self.qeval],feed_dict={self.st:obs_nlist,self.s:obs_
list})
        qtarget = qeval.copy()
        batch_indices = np.arange(self.batch_size, dtype=np.int32)
        actions = np.array([int(i[1]) for i in batch])
        rewards = np.array([int(i[2]) for i in batch])
        qtarget[batch_indices,actions] = rewards + self.gamma *
np.max(qt,axis=1)
        _ = self.sess.run(self.train,feed_dict =
{self.s:obs_list,self.qtarget:qtarget})
     print(self.learning_counter+1," learning done")
        #increasing epsilon
        if self.epsilon < 0.9:
                self.epsilon += self.epsilon_incrementer

        #replacing target network parameters with primary network
parameters
        if self.learning_counter % self.replace_target_pointer == 0:
            self.target_params_replaced()
            print("target parameters changed")

        self.learning_counter += 1
```

Now we will define `epsilon_greedy(self,obs)`, which is a function similar to what we implemented in DQN for the mountain car and Cartpole:

```
def epsilon_greedy(self,obs):
    new_shape = [1]+list(obs.shape)
```

```
    obs = obs.reshape(new_shape)
        #epsilon greedy implementation to choose action
        if np.random.uniform(low=0,high=1) < self.epsilon:
            return
np.argmax(self.sess.run(self.qeval,feed_dict={self.s:obs})) #[np.newaxis,:]
        else:
            return np.random.choice(self.n_actions)
```

Outside the class, we have a function `preprocessing_image`, which is used to preprocess the following parameters:

- Cropping the image
- Converting it to grayscale
- Downsampling the image
- Normalizing the image

We will use the following code to define the function:

```
def preprocessing_image(s):
    s = s[31:195]  #cropping
    s = s.mean(axis=2)  #converting to greyscale
    s = imresize(s,size=(80,80),interp='nearest')  #downsampling
    s = s/255.0  #normalizing
    return s
```

The following code defines the `main` function, which creates an object of the previous class of DQN, uses `gym` to fetch the `Breakout-v0` environment, and trains the agent to solve the problem:

```
if __name__ == "__main__":
    env = gym.make('Breakout-v0')
    env = env.unwrapped
    epsilon_rate_change = 0.9/500000.0
    dqn = DQN(learning_rate=0.0001,
            gamma=0.9,
            n_features=[80,80,4],
            n_actions=env.action_space.n,
            epsilon=0.0,
            parameter_changing_pointer=100,
            memory_size=50000,
            epsilon_incrementer=epsilon_rate_change)

    episodes = 100000
    total_steps = 0

    for episode in range(episodes):
```

```
steps = 0
obs = preprocessing_image(env.reset())
s_rec = np.stack([obs]*4,axis=0)
s = np.stack([obs]*4,axis=0)
s = s.transpose([1,2,0])
episode_reward = 0
while True:
    env.render()
    action = dqn.epsilon_greedy(s)
    obs_,reward,terminate,_ = env.step(action)
    obs_ = preprocessing_image(obs_)
    a = s_rec[1:]
    a = a.tolist()
    a.append(obs_)
    s_rec = np.array(a)
    s_ = s_rec.transpose([1,2,0])
    dqn.store_experience(s,action,reward,s_)
    if total_steps > 1999 and total_steps%500==0:
        dqn.fit()
    episode_reward+=reward
    if terminate:
        break
    s = s_
    total_steps+=1
    steps+=1
print("Episode {} with Reward : {} at epsilon {} in steps
{}".format(episode+1,episode_reward,dqn.epsilon,steps))

while True: #to hold the render at the last step when Car passes the
flag
    env.render()
```

Owing to the many weight parameters, the convergence takes a lot of time on a normal machine, and a GPU-powered machine is expensive to run. However, to witness the possibility of converging on your normal machine, run your code for 5-6 hours to see the agent getting better. I would suggest, if affordable, running it on a machine with a GPU. Anyways, the sample output of the preceding main function will look as follows:

```
. . . .
. . . .

. . . .
Episode 992 with Reward : 0.0 at epsilon 0.0008766 in steps 174
Episode 993 with Reward : 2.0 at epsilon 0.0008766 in steps 319
(488, ' learning done')
Episode 994 with Reward : 0.0 at epsilon 0.0008784 in steps 169
Episode 995 with Reward : 1.0 at epsilon 0.0008784 in steps 228
Episode 996 with Reward : 1.0 at epsilon 0.0008784 in steps 239
```

```
(489, ' learning done')
Episode 997 with Reward : 4.0 at epsilon 0.0008802 in steps 401
(490, ' learning done')
Episode 998 with Reward : 0.0 at epsilon 0.000882 in steps 171
Episode 999 with Reward : 4.0 at epsilon 0.000882 in steps 360
(491, ' learning done')
Episode 1000 with Reward : 0.0 at epsilon 0.0008838 in steps 171
Episode 1001 with Reward : 1.0 at epsilon 0.0008838 in steps 238
(492, ' learning done')
Episode 1002 with Reward : 1.0 at epsilon 0.0008856 in steps 249
Episode 1003 with Reward : 1.0 at epsilon 0.0008856 in steps 232
. . . .
. . . .
. . . .
```

Try using different parameters to witness better convergence.

The Monte Carlo tree search algorithm

The **Monte Carlo Tree Search** (**MCTS**) is a planning algorithm and a way of making optimal decisions in case of artificial narrow intelligence problems. MCTS works on a planning ahead kind of approach to solve the problem.

The MCTS algorithm gained importance after earlier algorithms such as **minimax** and **game trees** failed to show results with complex problems. So what makes the MCTS different and better than past decision making algorithms such as minimax?

Let's first discuss what minimax is.

Minimax and game trees

Minimax was the algorithm used by IBM Deep Blue to beat the world champion Gary Kasparov on February 10, 1996 in a chess game. This win was a very big milestone back then. Both minimax and game trees are directed graphs, where each node represents the game states, that is, position in the game as shown in the following diagram of a game of tic-tac-toe:

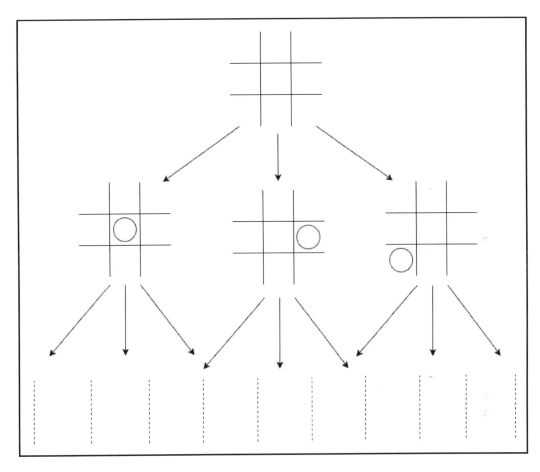

Game tree for tic-tac-toe. The top node represents the start position of the game. Following down the tree leads to outcome positions of the game

Therefore, by searching the game tree an AI agent can pick the best possible move because of the combination of nodes and their path present in the tree. This is good for problems where the game complexity is at an acceptable mark, because with an increase in complexity the size of the game tree increases. For example, the game tree of chess has more nodes than there are atoms in the universe. Therefore, only potential searches are possible in such cases. Thus, as the complexity increases the usability of minimax and game trees decreases.

Another good example is the open ended Chinese game of Go, that has a complexity of 10^{360} compared to 10^{123} for chess. With such high complexity, minimax fails to draw an evaluation function, and even create such big game trees. Therefore, approximately 20 years after Deep Blue's achievement, no algorithm was able to master the game of Go. The reason was simple, the current, state-of-the-art algorithms of that time such as minimax could not solve problems that had very high complexity such as the game of Go. Moreover, solving Go would require a more human way of learning, that is, interaction based.

Therefore, Google DeepMind's **AlphaGo** is regarded as the state-of-the-art AI agent that was able to successfully defeat Lee Sedol in 2016 using deep reinforcement learning, which is used in neural networks, reinforcement learning, and Monte Carlo Tree Search. This was the first time an AI task was achieved in a way a human would achieve it, that is, through a continuous number of interactions, and gaining knowledge through this process of continuous trial and error.

The Monte Carlo Tree Search

So, how is Monte Carlo Tree Search different to minimax's approach, and how is it able to plan ahead in a highly complex game of Go, which has an immense number of potential counter moves? The MCTS builds a statistical tree that looks exactly like a game tree but whereas game trees or minimax have game positions, that is, game states in the node of the directed graph, in MCTS the node of the directed graph is the quantity for that game state that tells us the number of successful simulations (that is, moves that lead to a win at the end of the game) with respect to the total number of simulations that game state has been through. Therefore, the higher the number of simulations, the more nodes get the chance to become a part of the simulations, thereby leading to convergence. Thus, the value of each node is dependent on the number of simulations.

Post convergence, this statistics tree guides the AI agent to look at the best possible node at each level and proceed till the goal. At the start, the statistics tree goes for expansion, to add more nodes for possible game states through multiple simulations. Post gathering a sufficient number of nodes, the selection of better nodes starts simultaneously, and if the nodes result in successful achievement of the problem objective then their value increases with every simulation, making their utility higher.

In the selection strategy, MCTS also incorporates an exploration-exploitation trade off by maintaining a balance between the existing, promising nodes and the unexplored nodes that could be more promising. Therefore, the higher the number of simulations, the bigger the statistics tree, the more accurately converged the node values, and the better the optimal decisions.

MCTS is domain independent and doesn't need complex handwritten heuristics. Thus, it is a powerful algorithm for a variety of open-ended AI problems.

The SARSA algorithm

The **State–Action–Reward–State–Action (SARSA)** algorithm is an on-policy learning problem. Just like Q-learning, SARSA is also a temporal difference learning problem, that is, it looks ahead at the next step in the episode to estimate future rewards. The major difference between SARSA and Q-learning is that the action having the maximum Q-value is not used to update the Q-value of the current state-action pair. Instead, the Q-value of the action as the result of the current policy, or owing to the exploration step like ϵ-greedy is chosen to update the Q-value of the current state-action pair. The name SARSA comes from the fact that the Q-value update is done by using a quintuple $Q(s,a,r,s',a')$ where:

- **s,a:** current state and action
- **r:** reward observed post taking action a
- **s':** next state reached after taking action a
- **a':** action to be performed at state s'

Steps involved in the SARSA algorithm are as follows:

1. Initialize Q-table randomly

2. For each episode:

    1. For the given state s, choose action a from Q-table

    2. Perform the action a

    3. Reward R and new state s' observed

    4. For the new state s' choose action a' from Q-table

    5. Update Q-value for the current state-action, that is, Q(s,a) pair by:

$$Q(s, a) \leftarrow (1 - \alpha)Q(s, a) + \alpha[R + \gamma Q(s', a')]$$

The pseudo code of the SARSA algorithm is as follows:

```
Create Q-table where rows represent different states and columns represent
different actions

Initialize Q(s,a) arbitrarily, e.g. 0 for all states
set action value for terminal states as 0

For each episode:
    Start with the starting state that is Initialize s to start
    Choose action a for s using the policy derived from Q [e.g. -greedy,
either for the given 's' which 'a' has the max Q-value or choose a random
action]
    Repeat for each step in the episode:
        Take the chosen action a, observe reward R and new state s'
        Choose action a' for s' using the policy derived from Q
        [e.g. Є-greedy]
```

$$\text{Update} \quad Q(s,a) \leftarrow (1-\alpha)Q(s,a) + \alpha[R + \gamma Q(s',a')]$$

$$s \leftarrow s'$$

$$a \leftarrow a'$$

```
    until s is the terminal state
end
```

SARSA algorithm for mountain car problem in OpenAI gym

Let's try to implement the SARSA algorithm explained previously in the mountain car problem. The initial part of the program shares similarities with the previous Q-learning program.

First, we will import the dependencies and examine the mountain car environment, using the following code:

```
#importing the dependencies

import gym
import numpy as np

#exploring Mountain Car environment

env_name = 'MountainCar-v0'
env = gym.make(env_name)

print("Action Set size :",env.action_space)
```

```
print("Observation set shape :",env.observation_space)
print("Highest state feature value :",env.observation_space.high)
print("Lowest state feature value:",env.observation_space.low)
print(env.observation_space.shape)
```

The previous print statements outputs the following:

```
Making new env: MountainCar-v0
('Action Set size :', Discrete(3))
('Observation set shape :', Box(2,))
('Highest state feature value :', array([ 0.6 , 0.07]))
('Lowest state feature value:', array([-1.2 , -0.07]))
(2,)
```

Next, we will assign the hyperparameters, such as number of states, number of episodes, learning rate (both initial and minimum), discount factor gamma, maximum steps in an episode, and the epsilon for epsilon-greedy, using the following code:

```
n_states = 40   # number of states
episodes = 10 # number of episodes

initial_lr = 1.0 # initial learning rate
min_lr = 0.005 # minimum learning rate
gamma = 0.99 # discount factor
max_steps = 300
epsilon = 0.05

env = env.unwrapped
env.seed(0)          #setting environment seed to reproduce same result
np.random.seed(0)    #setting numpy random number generation seed to
reproduce same random numbers
```

Our next task would be create a function to perform discretization of the continuous state space. Discretization is the conversion of continuous states space observation to a discrete set of state space. We will use the following code to perform discretization:

```
def discretization(env, obs):
    env_low = env.observation_space.low
    env_high = env.observation_space.high
    env_den = (env_high - env_low) / n_states
    pos_den = env_den[0]
    vel_den = env_den[1]
    pos_high = env_high[0]
    pos_low = env_low[0]
    vel_high = env_high[1]
    vel_low = env_low[1]
    pos_scaled = int((obs[0] - pos_low)/pos_den)   #converts to an integer
```

```
value
    vel_scaled = int((obs[1] - vel_low)/vel_den)   #converts to an integer
value
    return pos_scaled,vel_scaled
```

Till now, every task has been similar to what we did in the Q-learning algorithm. Now the SARSA implementation starts with initializing the Q-table and updating the Q-values accordingly, as shown in the following code. Here also, we have updated the reward value as an absolute difference between the current position and position at the lowest point, that is, start point so that it maximizes the reward by going away from the central, that is, lowest point:

```
#Q table
#rows are states but here state is 2-D pos,vel
#columns are actions
#therefore, Q- table would be 3-D

q_table = np.zeros((n_states,n_states,env.action_space.n))
total_steps = 0
for episode in range(episodes):
    obs = env.reset()
    total_reward = 0
    # decreasing learning rate alpha over time
    alpha = max(min_lr,initial_lr*(gamma**(episode//100)))
    steps = 0

    #action for the initial state using epsilon greedy
    if np.random.uniform(low=0,high=1) < epsilon:
        a = np.random.choice(env.action_space.n)
    else:
        pos,vel = discretization(env,obs)
        a = np.argmax(q_table[pos][vel])
    while True:
        env.render()
        pos,vel = discretization(env,obs)
        obs,reward,terminate,_ = env.step(a)
        total_reward += abs(obs[0]+0.5)
        pos_,vel_ = discretization(env,obs)

        #action for the next state using epsilon greedy
        if np.random.uniform(low=0,high=1) < epsilon:
            a_ = np.random.choice(env.action_space.n)
        else:
            a_ = np.argmax(q_table[pos_][vel_])

        #q-table update
        q_table[pos][vel][a] = (1-alpha)*q_table[pos][vel][a] +
```

```
alpha*(reward+gamma*q_table[pos_][vel_][a_])
        steps+=1
        if terminate:
            break
        a = a_
    print("Episode {} completed with total reward {} in {}
steps".format(episode+1,total_reward,steps))
while True: #to hold the render at the last step when Car passes the flag
    env.render()
```

The preceding program will print in the following manner:

```
Episode 1 completed with total reward 11167.6296185 in 36605 steps
Episode 2 completed with total reward 830.204697241 in 2213 steps
Episode 3 completed with total reward 448.46977318 in 1899 steps
Episode 4 completed with total reward 930.154976751 in 3540 steps
Episode 5 completed with total reward 6864.96292351 in 20871 steps
Episode 6 completed with total reward 677.449030827 in 3995 steps
Episode 7 completed with total reward 2994.99152751 in 7401 steps
Episode 8 completed with total reward 724.212076546 in 3267 steps
Episode 9 completed with total reward 192.502071909 in 928 steps
Episode 10 completed with total reward 213.212231118 in 786 steps
```

Thus, we have been able to successfully implement the SARSA algorithm for the mountain car problem.

Summary

We knew that reinforcement learning optimizes the reward for an agent in the environment, and the **Markov decision process** (**MDP**) is a type of environment representation and mathematical framework for modeling the decisions using states, actions, and rewards. In this chapter, we understood that Q-learning is an approach that finds the optimal action selection policy for any MDP without any transition models. On the other hand, value iteration finds the optimal action selection policy for any MDP if a transition model is given.

We also learned another important topic called the deep-Q network, which is a modified Q-learning approach that takes a deep neural network as a function approximator to generalize across different environments, unlike a Q-table, which is environment specific. Moreover, we also learnt to implement Q-learning, deep Q-networks, and SARSA algorithms in OpenAI gym environments. Most of the implementation shown previously might work better with better hyperparameter values and more episodes for training.

In the following chapter, we will cover the famous, asynchronous advantage actor-critic algorithms in detail.

6
Asynchronous Methods

So far, we have covered most of the important topics, such as the Markov Decision Processes, Value Iteration, Q-learning, Policy Gradients, deep-Q networks, and Actor Critic Algorithms. These form the core of the reinforcement learning algorithms. In this chapter, we will continue our search from where we left off in Actor Critic Algorithms, and delve into the advanced **asynchronous methods used in deep reinforcement learning**, and its most famous variant, the **asynchronous advantage actor-critic algorithm**, better known as the **A3C Algorithm**.

But, before we start with the A3C algorithm, let's revise the basics of the Actor Critic Algorithm covered in Chapter 4, *Policy Gradients*. If you remember, the Actor Critic Algorithm has two components:

- Actor
- Critic

The **Actor** takes the current environment state and determines best action to take, while the **Critic** plays a policy-evaluation role by taking in the environment state and action, and returns a score depicting how good an action is for the state. This is illustrated in the following diagram:

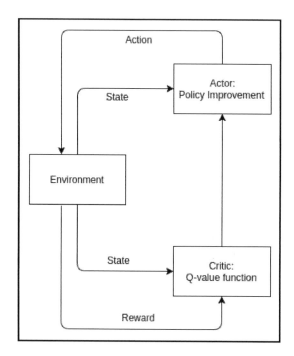

In other words, the **Actor** acts like a child while the **Critic** acts like a parent, where the child explores multiple actions and the parent criticizes bad actions and complements good actions. Thus, the actor-critic algorithm learns both the policy and state-action value function. Like policy gradients, the actor-critic algorithm also updates its parameters by gradient ascent. Actor-critic methods work very well in case of high-dimensional continuous state and action spaces.

So, let's start with the asynchronous method in deep reinforcement learning published by Google DeepMind, which surpassed DQN in terms of performance and computational efficiency.

We will cover the following topics in this chapter:

- Why asynchronous methods?
- Asynchronous one-step Q-learning

- Asynchronous one-step SARSA
- Asynchronous n-step Q-learning
- Asynchronous advantage actor critic
- A3C for pendulum-v0 in OpenAI gym

Why asynchronous methods?

Asynchronous methods for deep reinforcement learning was published in June 2016 by the combined team of Google DeepMind and MILA (`https://arxiv.org/pdf/1602.01783.pdf`). It was faster and was able to show good results on a multi-core CPU instead of using a GPU. Asynchronous methods also work on continuous as well as discrete action spaces.

If we recall the approach of deep Q-network, we use experience replay as a storage to store all the experiences, and then use a random sample from that to train our deep neural network, which in turn predicts maximum Q-value for the most favorable action. But, it has the drawbacks of high memory usage and heavy computation over time. The basic idea behind this was to overcome this issue. Therefore, instead of using experience replay, multiple instances of the environment are created and multiple agents asynchronously execute actions in parallel (shown in the following diagram):

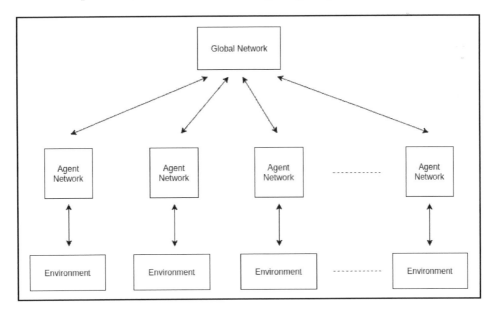

High-level diagram of the asynchronous method in deep reinforcement learning

In the asynchronous approach, each thread is assigned the process that contains a learner representing an agent network that interacts with its own copy of the environment. Therefore, these multiple learners run in parallel exploring their own version of the environment. This approach of parallelism allows the agent to experience varied different states simultaneously at any given time-step, and covers the fundamentals of both off-policy and on-policy learning algorithms.

As we have mentioned above, asynchronous methods were able to show good results in multi-core CPUs instead of using a GPU. Therefore, asynchronous methods are very fast and thus became the new state of the art-reinforcement learning algorithm, because till now implementation of deep-reinforcement learning algorithms relied on GPU-powered machines and distributed architectures to witness faster convergence of the algorithms implemented.

These multiple learners running in parallel use different exploration policies, which maximizes the diversity. Different exploration policies by different learners changes the parameters, and these updates have the least chance to be correlated in time. Therefore, experience replay memory is not required, and we rely on this parallel learning using different exploration policies performing the role of experience replay used in DQN earlier.

The benefits of using parallel learners are as follows:

- Reduction in training time.
- No use of experience replay. Therefore, on-policy reinforcement learning methods can also be used to train neural networks.

Different variants of asynchronous methods in deep reinforcement learning are:

- Asynchronous one-step Q-learning
- Asynchronous one-step SARSA
- Asynchronous n-step Q-learning
- **Asynchronous advantage actor critic (A3C)**

Applying the variant A3C to variety Atari 2600 games benchmarked better results on multi-core CPU that too in far less time relative to the earlier deep reinforcement learning algorithms, which needed to be run on GPU-powered machines. Thus, it solved the issue owing to the dependency on expensive hardware resources like GPUs, and also different complex distributed architectures. As a result of all these advantages, an A3C learning agent is the most advanced reinforcement learning agent at present.

Asynchronous one-step Q-learning

The architecture of asynchronous one-step Q-learning is very similar to DQN. An agent in DQN was represented by a set of primary and target networks, where one-step loss is calculated as the square of the difference between the state-action value of the current state s predicted by the primary network, and the target state-action value of the current state calculated by the target network. The gradients of the loss is calculated with respect to the parameters of the policy network, and then the loss is minimized using a gradient descent optimizer leading to parameter updates of the primary network.

The difference here in asynchronous one-step Q-learning is that there are multiple such learning agents, for instance, learners running and calculating this loss in parallel. Thus, the gradient calculation also occurs in parallel in different threads where each learning agent interacts with its own copy of the environment. The accumulation of these gradients in different threads over multiple time steps are used to update the policy network parameters after a fixed time step, or when an episode is over. The accumulation of gradients is preferred over policy network parameter updates because this avoids overwriting the changes perform by each of the learner agents.

Moreover, adding a different exploration policy to different threads makes the learning diverse and robust. This improves the performance owing to better exploration, because each of the learning agents in different threads is subjected to a different exploration policy. Though there are many ways to do this, a simple approach is to use different sample of epsilon ϵ for different threads while using ϵ-greedy.

The pseudo-code for asynchronous one-step Q-learning is shown as follows. Here, the following are the global parameters:

- θ: the parameters (weights and biases) of the policy network
- θ^t: parameters (weights and biases) of the target network
- T: overall time step counter

```
// Globally shared parameters θ,θᵗ and T
// θ is initialized arbitrarily
// T is initialized 0

pseudo-code for each learner running parallel in each of the threads:

Initialize thread level time step counter t=0
Initialize θᵗ = θ
Initialize network gradients dθ = 0
Start with the initial state s
```

```
repeat until T > Tmax :
    Choose action a with ε-greedy policy such that:
```
$$a = \begin{cases} a \; random \; action & , with \; probability \; \epsilon \\ argmax_{a'} Q(s,a';\theta) & , otherwise \end{cases}$$

```
    Perform action a
    Receive new state s' and reward r
```
$$y = \begin{cases} r & , for \; terminal \; s' \\ r + \gamma_{max \; a'} \, Q(s',a';\theta^t) & , otherwise \end{cases}$$

```
    Compute target y :
    Compute the loss, L(θ) = (y − Q(s,a;θ))²
```

```
    Accumulate the gradient w.r.t. θ :
```
$$d\theta = d\theta + \frac{\nabla L(\theta)}{\nabla \theta}$$

```
    s = s'
    T = T + 1
    t = t + 1

    if T mod Itarget == 0 :
        Update the parameters of target network : θ* = θ
        # After every Itarget time steps the parameters of target network is
updated

    if t mod IAsyncUpdate == 0 or s = terminal state:
        Asynchronous update of θ using dθ
        Clear gradients : dθ = 0
        #at every IAsyncUpdate time step in the thread or if s is the
terminal state
        #update θ using accumulated gradients dθ
```

Asynchronous one-step SARSA

The architecture of asynchronous one-step SARSA is almost similar to the architecture of asynchronous one-step Q-learning, except the way target state-action value of the current state is calculated by the target network. Instead of using the maximum Q-value of the next state s' by the target network, SARSA uses ε-greedy to choose the action a' for the next state s' and the Q-value of the next state action pair, that is, $Q(s',a';\theta^t)$ is used to calculate the target state-action value of the current state.

The pseudo-code for asynchronous one-step SARSA is shown below. Here, the following are the global parameters:

- θ : the parameters (weights and biases) of the policy network
- θ^t : parameters (weights and biases) of the target network
- T : overall time step counter

```
// Globally shared parameters θ,θᵗ and T
// θ is initialized arbitrarily
// T is initialized 0

pseudo-code for each learner running parallel in each of the threads:

Initialize thread level time step counter t=0
Initialize θᵗ = θ
Initialize network gradients dθ = 0
Start with the initial state s
Choose action a with €-greedy policy such that:
```
$$a = \begin{cases} a \; random \; action & , with \; probability \; \epsilon \\ argmax_{a'} Q(s, a'; \theta) & , otherwise \end{cases}$$
```
repeat until T > Tₘₐₓ :
    Perform action a
    Receive new state s' and reward r
    Choose action a' with €-greedy policy such that:
```
$$a' = \begin{cases} a \; random \; action & , with \; probability \; \epsilon \\ argmax_{a''} Q(s, a''; \theta) & , otherwise \end{cases}$$
```
Compute target y :
```
$$y = \begin{cases} r & , for \; terminal \; s' \\ r + \gamma \, Q(s', a'; \theta^t) & , otherwise \end{cases}$$
```
Compute the loss,
```
$$L(\theta) = (y - Q(s, a; \theta))^2$$
```
Accumulate the gradient w.r.t. θ :
```
$$d\theta = d\theta + \frac{\nabla L(\theta)}{\nabla \theta}$$
```
    s = s'
    T = T + 1
    t = t + 1
    a = a'

if T mod Iₜₐᵣ𝓰ₑₜ == 0 :
        Update the parameters of target network : θᵗ = θ
        # After every Iₜₐᵣ𝓰ₑₜ time steps the parameters of target network is
updated

if t mod I_AsyncUpdate == 0 or s = terminal state:
```

```
        Asynchronous update of θ using dθ
        Clear gradients : dθ = 0
        #at every I_AsyncUpdate time step in the thread or if s is the
terminal state
        #update θ using accumulated gradients dθ
```

Asynchronous n-step Q-learning

The architecture of asynchronous n-step Q-learning is, to an extent, similar to that of asynchronous one-step Q-learning. The difference is that the learning agent actions are selected using the exploration policy for up to t_{max} steps or until a terminal state is reached, in order to compute a single update of policy network parameters. This process t_{max} lists rewards from the environment since its last update. Then, for each time step, the loss is calculated as the difference between the discounted future rewards at that time step and the estimated Q-value. The gradient of this loss with respect to thread-specific network parameters for each time step is calculated and accumulated. There are multiple such learning agents running and accumulating the gradients in parallel. These accumulated gradients are used to perform asynchronous updates of policy network parameters.

The pseudo-code for asynchronous n-step Q-learning is shown below. Here, the following are the global parameters:

- θ : the parameters(weights and biases) of the policy network
- θ^t : parameters(weights and biases) of the target network
- T : overall time step counter
- t : thread level time step counter
- T_{max} : maximum number of overall time steps
- t_{max} : maximum number of time steps in a thread

```
// Globally shared parameters θ,θᵗ and T
// θ is initialized arbitrarily
// T is initialized 0

pseudo-code for each learner running parallel in each of the threads:

Initialize thread level time step counter t = 1
Initialize θᵗ = θ
Initialize θ′ = θ
Initialize network gradients dθ = 0

repeat until T > Tₘₐₓ :
```

```
Clear gradient :
```
$d\theta = 0$

```
Synchronize thread-specific parameters:
```
$\theta' = \theta$

$t_{start} = t$

```
Get state
```
s_t

```
r = []  //list of rewards
a = []  //list of actions
s = []  //list of actions
repeat until
```
s_t
```
is a terminal state or
```
$t - t_{start} == t_{max}$:

```
        Choose action
```
a_t
```
with
```
ϵ
```
-greedy policy such that:
```

$$a_t = \begin{cases} a \ random \ action & , with \ probability \ \epsilon \\ argmax_{a'} Q(s_t, a'; \theta') & , otherwise \end{cases}$$

```
        Perform action
```
a_t

```
        Receive new state
```
s_{t+1}
```
and reward
```
r_t

```
        Accumulate rewards by appending
```
r_t
```
to r
        Accumulate actions by appending
```
a_t
```
to a
        Accumulate actions by appending
```
s_t
```
to s
        t = t + 1
        T = T + 1
```
$s_t = s_{t+1}$

$$R = \begin{cases} 0 & , for \ terminal \ s_t \\ max_a \ Q(s_t, a; \theta^t) & , otherwise \end{cases}$$

```
Compute returns, R :
for
```
$i \epsilon [t-1, \ldots \ldots, t_{start}] \ do$:

$R = r_i + \gamma R$

```
        Compute loss,
```
$L(\theta') = (R - Q(s_i, a_i; \theta'))^2$

```
        Accumulate gradients w.r.t.
```
θ' :

$$d\theta = d\theta + \frac{\nabla L(\theta)}{\nabla \theta'}$$

```
Asynchronous update of
```
θ
```
using
```
$d\theta$

```
if T mod
```
$I_{target} == 0$:

```
        Update the parameters of target network :
```
$\theta^t = \theta$

```
        # After every
```
I_{target}
```
time steps the parameters of target network is
```
```
updated
```

Asynchronous advantage actor critic

In the architecture of asynchronous advantage actor-critic, each learning agent contains an actor-critic learner that combines the benefits of both value- and policy-based methods. The actor network takes in the state as input and predicts the best action of that state, while the critic network takes in the state and action as the inputs and outputs the action score to quantify how good the action is for that state. The actor network updates its weight parameters using policy gradients, while the critic network updates its weight parameters using *TD(0)*, in other words, the difference of value estimates between two time steps, as discussed in `Chapter 4`, *Policy Gradients*.

In `Chapter 4`, *Policy Gradients*, we studied how updating the policy gradients by subtracting a baseline function from the expected future rewards in the policy gradients reduces the variance without affecting the expectation value of the gradient. The difference between the expected future rewards and the baseline function is called the **advantage function**; it not only tells us the good or bad status, but also how good or bad that action was expected to be.

The convolution neural network is used for both actor and critic networks. The policy and action value parameters are updated after every t_{max} steps or until a terminal state is reached. The network updates, entropy, and the objective function will be explained along with the following pseudo-code. Moreover, an entropy H of the policy π is added to the objective function in order to improve the exploration by avoiding early convergence to sub-optimal policies.

Thus, there are multiple such learning agents running each containing actor-critic network where the policy network parameters, that is, actor network parameters, are updated using policy gradients where the advantage function is used to calculate those policy gradients.

The pseudo-code for asynchronous one-step SARSA is shown as follows. Here, the following are the global parameters:

- θ : the parameters(weights and biases) of the policy network
- θ_v: parameters(weights and biases) of the value function approximator
- T : overall time step counter

The thread-specific parameters are as follows:

- θ' : Thread specific parameter of the policy network
- θ'_v: Thread specific parameter of the value function approximator

```
//Globally shared parameters θ,θv and T
// θ is initialized arbitrarily
// θv is initialized arbitrarily
// T is initialized 0

pseudo-code for each learner running parallel in each of the threads:

//Thread specific parameters θ' and θ'v
Initialize thread level time step counter t = 1
repeat until T > Tmax :
    reset gradients : dθ = 0 and dθv = 0
    synchronize thread specific parameters : θ' = θ and θ'v = θv
    tstart = t
    Get state st
    r = [] //list of rewards
    a = [] //list of actions
    s = [] //list of actions
    repeat until st is a terminal state or t - tstart == tmax :
        Perform at according to policy π(at|at;θ')
        Receive new state st+1 and reward rt
        Accumulate rewards by appending rt to r
        Accumulate actions by appending at to a
        Accumulate actions by appending st to s
        t = t + 1
        T = T + 1
        st = st+1
    Compute returns, that is expected future rewards R such that:
```

$$R = \begin{cases} 0 & , \text{for terminal } s_t \\ V(s_t; \theta_v) & , \text{otherwise} \end{cases}$$

```
    for i ∈ [t - 1,......,tstart] do :
```

$$R = r_i + \gamma R$$

```
        Accumulate gradients w.r.t. θ' :
```

$$d\theta = d\theta + \frac{\nabla log\, \pi(s_i, a_i; \theta')(R - V(s_i; \theta'_v))}{\nabla \theta'}$$

```
        Accumulate gradients w.r.t. θ'v :
```

$$d\theta_v = d\theta_v + \frac{\nabla(R - V(s_i; \theta'_v))^2}{\nabla \theta'_v}$$

```
    Asynchronous update of θ using dθ and θv using dθv
```

A3C for Pong-v0 in OpenAI gym

We have already discussed the pong environment before in Chapter 4, *Policy Gradients*. We will use the following code to create the A3C for Pong-v0 in OpenAI gym:

```
import multiprocessing
import threading
import tensorflow as tf
import numpy as np
import gym
import os
import shutil
import matplotlib.pyplot as plt

game_env = 'Pong-v0'
num_workers = multiprocessing.cpu_count()
max_global_episodes = 100000
global_network_scope = 'globalnet'
global_iteration_update = 20
gamma = 0.9
beta = 0.0001
lr_actor = 0.0001 # learning rate for actor
lr_critic = 0.0001 # learning rate for critic
global_running_rate = []
global_episode = 0

env = gym.make(game_env)

num_actions = env.action_space.n


tf.reset_default_graph()
```

The input state image preprocessing function:

```
def preprocessing_image(obs): #where I is the single frame of the game as
the input
    """ prepro 210x160x3 uint8 frame into 6400 (80x80) 1D float vector """
    #the values below have been precomputed through trail and error by
OpenAI team members
    obs = obs[35:195]
    #cropping the image frame to an extent where it contains on the paddles
and ball and area between them
    obs = obs[::2,::2,0]
    #downsample by the factor of 2 and take only the R of the RGB
channel.Therefore, now 2D frame
    obs[obs==144] = 0 #erase background type 1
```

```
obs[obs==109] = 0 #erase background type 2
obs[obs!=0] = 1 #everything else(other than paddles and ball) set to 1
return obs.astype('float').ravel() #flattening to 1D
```

The `actor-critic` class, containing the architecture of `actor` and `critic` network, is shown in the following code:

```
class ActorCriticNetwork(object):
    def __init__(self, scope, globalAC=None):

        if scope == global_network_scope: # get global network
            with tf.variable_scope(scope):
                self.s = tf.placeholder(tf.float32, [None,6400], 'state')
                self.a_params, self.c_params = self._build_net(scope)[-2:]
        else: # local net, calculate losses
            with tf.variable_scope(scope):
                self.s = tf.placeholder(tf.float32, [None,6400], 'state')
                self.a_his = tf.placeholder(tf.int32, [None,], 'action')
                self.v_target = tf.placeholder(tf.float32, [None, 1],
'target_vector')

                self.a_prob, self.v, self.a_params, self.c_params =
self._build_net(scope)

                td = tf.subtract(self.v_target, self.v,
name='temporal_difference_error')
                with tf.name_scope('critic_loss'):
                    self.c_loss = tf.reduce_mean(tf.square(td))

                with tf.name_scope('actor_loss'):
                    log_prob = tf.reduce_sum(tf.log(self.a_prob) *
tf.one_hot(self.a_his, num_actions, dtype=tf.float32), axis=1,
keep_dims=True)
                    exp_v = log_prob * td
                    entropy = -tf.reduce_sum(self.a_prob *
tf.log(self.a_prob + 1e-5),
                                             axis=1, keep_dims=True)
#exploration
                    self.exp_v = beta * entropy + exp_v
                    self.a_loss = tf.reduce_mean(-self.exp_v)

            with tf.name_scope('local_grad'):
                self.a_grads = tf.gradients(self.a_loss, self.a_params)
                self.c_grads = tf.gradients(self.c_loss, self.c_params)

        with tf.name_scope('sync'):
            with tf.name_scope('pull'):
```

```
                    self.pull_a_params_op = [l_p.assign(g_p) for l_p, g_p
    in zip(self.a_params, globalAC.a_params)]
                    self.pull_c_params_op = [l_p.assign(g_p) for l_p, g_p
    in zip(self.c_params, globalAC.c_params)]
              with tf.name_scope('push'):
                    self.update_a_op =
    actor_train.apply_gradients(zip(self.a_grads, globalAC.a_params))
                    self.update_c_op =
    critic_train.apply_gradients(zip(self.c_grads, globalAC.c_params))

       def _build_net(self, scope):
           w_init = tf.random_normal_initializer(0., .1)
           with tf.variable_scope('actor_network'):
               l_a = tf.layers.dense(self.s, 300, tf.nn.relu6,
    kernel_initializer=w_init, name='actor_layer')
               a_prob = tf.layers.dense(l_a, num_actions, tf.nn.softmax,
    kernel_initializer=w_init, name='ap')
           with tf.variable_scope('critic_network'):
               l_c = tf.layers.dense(self.s, 100, tf.nn.relu6,
    kernel_initializer=w_init, name='critic_layer')
               v = tf.layers.dense(l_c, 1, kernel_initializer=w_init,
    name='v') # state value
           a_params = tf.get_collection(tf.GraphKeys.TRAINABLE_VARIABLES,
    scope=scope + '/actor')
           c_params = tf.get_collection(tf.GraphKeys.TRAINABLE_VARIABLES,
    scope=scope + '/critic')
           return a_prob, v, a_params, c_params

    def update_global(self, feed_dict): # run local
        session.run([self.update_a_op, self.update_c_op], feed_dict) #
    local gradient applied to global net

    def pull_global(self): # run local
        session.run([self.pull_a_params_op, self.pull_c_params_op])

    def choose_action(self, s): # run local
        s = np.reshape(s, [-1])
        prob_weights = session.run(self.a_prob, feed_dict={self.s:
    s[np.newaxis, :]})
        action = np.random.choice(range(prob_weights.shape[1]),
                                  p=prob_weights.ravel()) # select action
    w.r.t the actions prob
        return action
```

The worker class, representing the process in each thread, is shown as follows:

```
class Worker(object):
    def __init__(self, name, globalAC):
```

```
        self.env = gym.make(game_env).unwrapped
        self.name = name
        self.AC = ActorCriticNetwork(name, globalAC)

    def work(self):
        global global_running_rate, global_episode
        total_step = 1
        buffer_s, buffer_a, buffer_r = [], [], []
        while not coordinator.should_stop() and global_episode <
max_global_episodes:
            obs = self.env.reset()
            s = preprocessing_image(obs)
            ep_r = 0
            while True:
                if self.name == 'W_0':
                    self.env.render()
                a = self.AC.choose_action(s)
                #print(a.shape)
                obs_, r, done, info = self.env.step(a)
                s_ = preprocessing_image(obs_)
                if done and r<=0:
                    r = -20
                ep_r += r
                buffer_s.append(np.reshape(s,[-1]))
                buffer_a.append(a)
                buffer_r.append(r)

                if total_step % global_iteration_update == 0 or done: #
update global and assign to local net
                    if done:
                        v_s_ = 0 # terminal
                    else:
                        s_ = np.reshape(s_,[-1])
                        v_s_ = session.run(self.AC.v, {self.AC.s:
s_[np.newaxis, :]})[0, 0]
                    buffer_v_target = []
                    for r in buffer_r[::-1]: # reverse buffer r
                        v_s_ = r + gamma * v_s_
                        buffer_v_target.append(v_s_)
                    buffer_v_target.reverse()

                    buffer_s, buffer_a, buffer_v_target =
np.vstack(buffer_s), np.array(buffer_a), np.vstack(buffer_v_target)
                    feed_dict = {
                        self.AC.s: buffer_s,
                        self.AC.a_his: buffer_a,
                        self.AC.v_target: buffer_v_target,
                    }
```

```
                            self.AC.update_global(feed_dict)

                            buffer_s, buffer_a, buffer_r = [], [], []
                            self.AC.pull_global()

                    s = s_
                    total_step += 1
                    if done:
                            if len(global_running_rate) == 0: # record running
    episode reward
                                global_running_rate.append(ep_r)
                            else:
                                global_running_rate.append(0.99 *
    global_running_rate[-1] + 0.01 * ep_r)
                            print(
                                self.name,
                                "Ep:", global_episode,
                                "| Ep_r: %i" % global_running_rate[-1],
                                )
                            global_episode += 1
                            break
```

The `main` function, which creates the thread pool and assigns workers to different threads, is shown in the following code:

```
if __name__ == "__main__":
    session = tf.Session()

    with tf.device("/cpu:0"):
        actor_train = tf.train.RMSPropOptimizer(lr_actor,
name='RMSPropOptimiserActor')
        critic_train = tf.train.RMSPropOptimizer(lr_critic,
name='RMSPropOptimiserCritic')
        acn_global = ActorCriticNetwork(global_network_scope) # we only
need its params
        workers = []
        # Create worker
        for i in range(num_workers):
            i_name = 'W_%i' % i # worker name
            workers.append(Worker(i_name, acn_global))

    coordinator = tf.train.Coordinator()
    session.run(tf.global_variables_initializer())

    worker_threads = []
    for worker in workers:
        job = lambda: worker.work()
```

```
    t = threading.Thread(target=job)
    t.start()
    worker_threads.append(t)
coordinator.join(worker_threads)

plt.plot(np.arange(len(global_running_rate)), global_running_rate)
plt.xlabel('step')
plt.ylabel('Total moving reward')
plt.show()
```

The screenshot of the output as per the learning(green paddle is our learning agent):

```
'W_1', 'Ep:', 152, '| Ep_r: -24')
'W_2', 'Ep:', 153, '| Ep_r: -24')
'W_3', 'Ep:', 154, '| Ep_r: -24')
'W_2', 'Ep:', 155, '| Ep_r: -24')
'W_1', 'Ep:', 156, '| Ep_r: -24')
'W_0', 'Ep:', 157, '| Ep_r: -24')
'W_3', 'Ep:', 158, '| Ep_r: -24')
'W_2', 'Ep:', 159, '| Ep_r: -24')
'W_1', 'Ep:', 160, '| Ep_r: -24')
'W_3', 'Ep:', 161, '| Ep_r: -24')
'W_2', 'Ep:', 162, '| Ep_r: -24')
'W_1', 'Ep:', 163, '| Ep_r: -24')
'W_3', 'Ep:', 164, '| Ep_r: -24')
'W_2', 'Ep:', 165, '| Ep_r: -24')
'W_0', 'Ep:', 166, '| Ep_r: -24')
'W_3', 'Ep:', 167, '| Ep_r: -24')
'W_1', 'Ep:', 168, '| Ep_r: -23')
'W_2', 'Ep:', 169, '| Ep_r: -23')
'W_3', 'Ep:', 170, '| Ep_r: -23')
'W_2', 'Ep:', 171, '| Ep_r: -23')
'W_1', 'Ep:', 172, '| Ep_r: -23')
```

Summary

We saw that using parallel learners to update a shared model produced a great improvement on the learning process. We learned about the reason behind the use of asynchronous methods in deep learning and their different variants, including asynchronous one-step Q-learning, asynchronous one-step SARSA, asynchronous n-step Q-learning, and asynchronous advantage actor-critic. We also learned to implement the A3C algorithm, where we made an agent learn to play the games Breakout and Doom.

In the coming chapters, we will focus on different domains and how deep reinforcement learning is being, and can be, applied.

7
Robo Everything – Real Strategy Gaming

In recent times, the video gaming industry has grown at a tremendous rate. As per the 2017 year in review report by SuperData, the global gaming industry generated revenue of $108.4 billion. Newzoo, a global gaming market researcher forecast that the revenue of the video gaming industry will exceed $140 billion by 2020.

Real-time strategy games form a sub-category of the strategy video game genre and is now gaining higher importance relative to turn-based strategy games. In this chapter, we will discuss why the AI community is behind solving real-time strategy games and how reinforcement learning is better at solve this problem statement compared to the other algorithms in terms of learning and performance.

We will cover the following topics in this chapter:

- Real-time strategy games
- Reinforcement learning and other approaches
- Reinforcement learning in RTS gaming

Real-time strategy games

The term **real-time strategy (RTS)** was first used by Brett Sperry as a tagline to market their game Dune II. Real-time strategy games involve the player using real-time tactics to increase assets, and save them, and utilizing them to destroy the assets of the opponent. It is associated with the many complex tactical decisions that need to be taken in a very short period of time.

This is different from turn-based strategy games, where each opponent has time to analyze and take action while other opponents couldn't perform any actions. In real-time strategy games, the action and reaction both take place in real time, since the other entities in the environment, that is, opponents, are also active and will be performing actions simultaneously. In a real strategy game environment, there are varied forms of entities, which include players, structures, and their varied high dimensional features. Thus, the goal would be to take the optimal actions to survive in the gaming environment until you are victorious, while an entity or entities in the environment are acting against you.

The properties of real-time strategy games that make traditional planning approaches inefficient are as follows:

- High dimensional and continuous action space
- High dimensional and continuous state space
- The environment is non-deterministic
- The environment is partially observable, where the player can only perceive only a part of the environment (that is, the game map/world)
- It is in real time, therefore, the system should be capable of deciding on, and executing, actions in real time, since the state of the gaming environment changes continuously

Real-time strategy games have evolved a lot and now have complex virtual environments containing many entities and can model diverse real-world problems. Thus, real-world strategy games have become a good testing ground for researchers in the AI community as they provide a simulation of complex, diverse, real-world environments to test their algorithms in order to create more robust and efficient algorithms. Thus, these simulated environments actually help in creating better learning agents that can survive and win in these environments without the need to test in the real world, which is very expensive to create and maintain.

The increase in computational power in recent decades has made it possible to implement advanced AI algorithms. Therefore, it has made them the most valid choice of candidate to ace the problem of state-action complexity and time in real strategy gaming. Most of the techniques, such as minimax and online case-based planning have been derived to approach this problem, but they operated efficiently under limited conditions.

Among the techniques available, reinforcement learning performed better in learning and planning. We already know that reinforcement learning has many successful cases when it comes to high dimensional and continuous state-action spaces.

Reinforcement learning and other approaches

There have been many approaches devised for solving the problem of real-time strategy gaming. One of the major approaches before reinforcement learning was **online case-based planning**. Online case-based planning involves real-time case-based reasoning. In a case-based reasoning, a set of methods are used to learn the plans. Online case-based planning implemented this property along with the implementation of plan acquisition and execution, and that too in real time.

Online case-based planning

Case-based reasoning consists of four steps:

- Retrieve

- Reuse

- Revise

- Retain

These steps are illustrated in the following image:

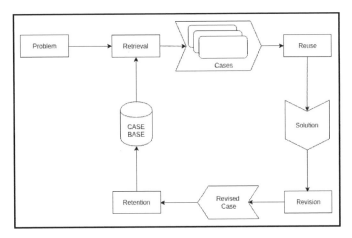

Case-based reasoning

In the retrieval step, a subset of cases that are relevant to the problem are selected from the case base. In the reuse step, the solution as per the cases selected is adapted. Then, in the revision step, the adapted solution is verified through testing it in a real-world environment and observes a feedback quantifying the accuracy of the predicted solution. The retention step decides whether or not to store this new solved case in the case base. Thus, case-based reasoning and planning involves reusing the previous plans and adapting them to match new situations.

Case-based reasoning has mainly been applied to static domains, that is, the agent has time to decide which action to take and in the meantime, the state of the environment doesn't change. But real-world problems are dynamic and have time constraints. Thus case-based reasoning is not suitable for real strategy gaming and this leads to **online case-based planning,** where planning and execution happens in real time, unlike case-based reasoning. The architecture of online case-based planning is given in the following image:

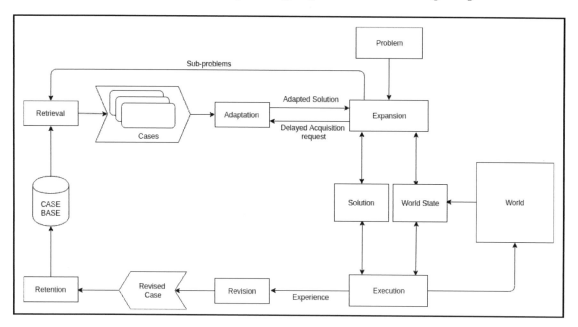

Online case-based planning

As shown, online case-based planning has two additional processes with small changes relative to the case-based reasoning to implement planning and execution in real time. These two processes are as follows:

- **Expansion**: This process takes the current adapted solution as the input and finds open sub-problems, that is, sub-goals if there are any open sub goals available to retrieve and can be solved. It also monitors the world state and sends a signal to the adaption module if there's a change in the world state that is significant enough for the current solution to change. This is called **delayed adaptation** and is performed during runtime. This process module makes online case-based planning work in dynamic environments.
- **Execution**: This executes the current solution and updates its status as per the result of the execution. If a sub-problem fails causing the current solution to fail when executed, then this process updates the current solution to mitigate this by sending this information to the expansion module to find an alternative solution.

Drawbacks to real-time strategy games

The reason behind the inefficiency of all the previous approaches is because the decision making happens in real time, where the state-action spaces are huge and continuous. The previous approaches were efficient under limited conditions as they were not able to fulfill all of the following conditions:

- High dimensional state-action spaces
- Adversarial environment
- Partially observable environment
- Stochastic environment
- Real time

In order to cover the large state-action spaces, a large number of rules would be required in the solution base. Moreover, no exploration strategy is there to find an optimal solution. Thus, these traditional AI approaches found it difficult because of all the previously mentioned issues and complications associated with real-time strategy games.

Why reinforcement learning?

The reason why reinforcement learning stands out relative to other AI approaches are as follows:

- Avoids hand coded rule-based approach.
- Reinforcement learning doesn't require any need to store the game's specific rules. A reinforcement learning agent learns over multiple interactions and reinforces its understanding to act in an environment each time it interacts with the environment.
- For high-dimensional state-action spaces, a neural network can be used as a function approximator to derive optimal actions.
- Always explores different policies to find the optimal one.
- Reinforcement learning has been applied to various domains that require state-action planning, such as robotics, self driving cars, and so on.
- Moreover, reinforcement learning is a highly active and large research domain, therefore it's certain that many better algorithms are yet to evolve.

Reinforcement learning in RTS gaming

Here we will discuss how reinforcement learning algorithms can be implemented to solve the real-time strategy gaming problem. Let's recall the basic components of reinforcement learning again, they are are follows:

- States S
- Actions A
- Rewards R
- Transition model (if on-policy, not required for off-policy learning)

If these components are perceived and processed by the sensors present on the learning agent while receiving signals from the given gaming environment, then a reinforcement learning algorithm can be successfully applied. The signals perceived by the sensors can be processed to form the current environment state, predict the action as per the state information, and receive feedback, that is, reward where the action taken was good or bad. This updates that state-action pair value that is, reinforces its learning as per the feedback received.

Moreover, the higher dimension state and action spaces can be encoded to compact lower dimensions by using deep autoencoders. This reduces the feature size of the state and action spaces to important features.

Deep autoencoder

A **deep autoencoder** is a type of deep neural network composed of two symmetrical neural networks, as shown in the following diagram, which is capable of converting input data to a more compact representation that is also lower in dimension. The encoder network first encodes the input into a compact compressed representation and the decoder network decodes that representation back to output the original input. As shown in the following diagram, there are two neural networks (encoder and decoder) connected by a middle layer, which contains the compact compressed representation of the input data:

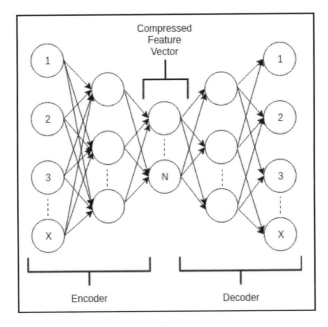

Architecture of an autoencoder

Here, X represents the number of nodes in the input and output layer, which is equal to the number of features (dimensions) of the input data, and N represents the number of nodes in the middle layer, which is equal to the number of required features (dimensions) of the compact compressed representation.

For example, say your input is a 28x28 pixel image of the game environment that is, 784 pixels. Therefore, a sample encoder network architecture can have nodes in the following order (it's not necessary to follow the order):

$$784 \rightarrow 1024 \rightarrow 512 \rightarrow 256 \rightarrow 128 \rightarrow 64 \rightarrow 32$$

In the previous example encoder network, we have taken an input of dimension 784, then expanded it to 1024 dimensions, then reduced to 512, 256, 128, 64, and finally 32 dimensions respectively through successive layers of the network. Here, X is 784 and N is 32. Here, our compact compressed representation is represented by 32 dimensions only relative to the input data of 784 dimensions.

Similarly, our decoder network architecture for this would be the reverse of this as follows:

$$32 \rightarrow 64 \rightarrow 128 \rightarrow 256 \rightarrow 512 \rightarrow 1024 \rightarrow 784$$

Post training a deep autoencoder, decoder network is not required. Thus, our goal here is to train the network in such a way that the loss between the output of the decoder network and the input to the encoder network is minimized. As a result, the middle layer learns to create better representation of the input. Thus, we can retrieve better, compact, and low dimensional representation of the feature vector for the input feature vector.

How is reinforcement learning better?

Earlier, with online case-based planning, human traces provided by experts were the most important component in the learning process. These were provided by the experts to create a list of solutions. This created the case base and consumed high space storage. Moreover, it also came with a demerit that they didn't capture all possible traces, that is, combinations of states and actions specifically in case of continuous state-action spaces.

However, with reinforcement learning, storage of these traces is not required and moreover, the high dimensional and continuous state-action spaces can deal with a deep neural network, which incorporates them as input and outputs the optimal actions. Moreover, if the state-action space is huge and there is a need to reduce the dimensions to further reduce computational time, then the use of deep autoencoders as shown previously converts the input data into a compact and low dimensional vector.

The reward function in reinforcement learning has to be associated with each state in such a way that the action taken from the start state leads to a goal state through a series of intermediate states, such that the expected sum of rewards is maximized, thereby resulting in an optimal path.

Basic reinforcement learning algorithms, such as Q-learning and SARSA algorithms (explained in Chapter 5, *Q-Learning and Deep Q Networks*) have performed better in terms of time to converge and ratio of winning compared to the earlier online case-based learning.

Moreover, much research is going on in the field of deep reinforcement learning, which is focused on using images for agent perception to work better in more complex domains. The previous autoencoder approach helped in transforming a very complex domain into a simpler one. Moreover, the learning reward function and other variations of autoencoders especially denoising stacked auto-encoders will further improve the results.

Furthermore, using asynchronous or distributed multi-agent reinforcement learning approaches (discussed in Chapter 6, *Asynchronous Methods*), where learning agents work in parallel with their own copy of the environment will further reduce the convergence time with better results.

Summary

In this chapter, we discussed real strategy games and why researchers from the AI community are trying to solve them. We also covered the complexity and properties of real strategy games and the different traditional AI approaches, such as case-based reasoning and online case-based planning to solve them and their drawbacks. We discussed the reason behind reinforcement learning being the perfect candidate for the problem and how it is successful in fulfilling the complexity and issues related to real-time strategy games where earlier traditional AI approaches failed. We also learnt about deep autoencoders and how they can be used to reduce the dimensionality of the input data and obtain a better representation of the input.

In the next chapter, we will cover the most famous topic that brought deep reinforcement learning into the limelight and made it the flag bearer of AI algorithms, that is, Alpha Go.

8

AlphaGo – Reinforcement Learning at Its Best

Games have the best testing environment for many **artificial intelligence (AI)** algorithms. These simulated environments are cost effective, and algorithms can be tested in a safe way. The major goal of AI is to solve the biggest problems in the world. The major global objectives for AI are:

- Eradicate poverty
- Eradicate hunger
- Primary personalized healthcare for all
- Quality education
- Clean energy
- Good infrastructure
- Innovation and creativity
- Reduced inequalities
- Protecting the planet
- Tackle climatic change
- Peace and justice
- Good jobs
- Economic growth
- Solve water crisis

There are many more global objectives that the research technology and industrial community are trying to achieve. Now with AI algorithms and better computational power, the strides towards these objectives have become longer with time. Though it's a very long path to walk, with recent advancements and discoveries we can at least say we are on the right path and in a better place than we were a decade ago.

As discussed previously, games are the best test bed for testing these AI algorithms. Apart from being cost effective, no two games are alike, so being able to use the knowledge learned from one game and apply it to another is a sign of general intelligence. The more games a single algorithm can be applied to, the more generalized it becomes.

The first time we witnessed a huge step towards **artificial general intelligence (AGI)** was when DeepMind demonstrated that their AI could beat a bunch of Atari games making it the most generalized AI system in existence. DeepMind published their paper, *Human-level control through deep reinforcement learning* in the research journal **Nature** (`http://www.davidqiu.com:8888/research/nature14236.pdf`) by Silver et. al. showing that their AI agent, called **deep Q-learner**, used deep reinforcement learning algorithm, was successfully applied to 50 different Atari games, and achieved above human-level performance in 30 of them shown in the following screenshot. This direction towards generalized AI was the reason that Google bought DeepMind:

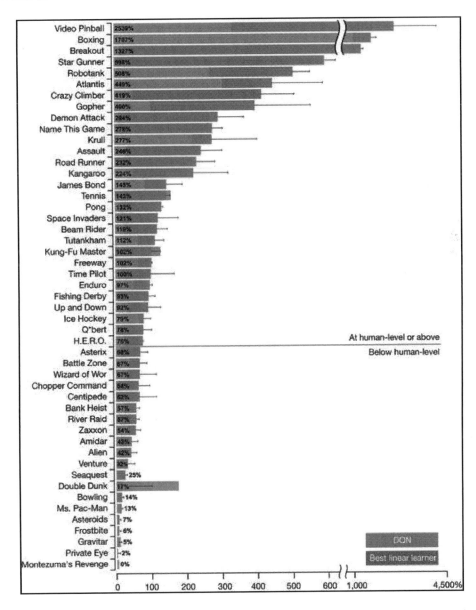

Comparing performance in 50 different Atari Games: The performance of DQN is normalized with respect to a professional human games tester in *Human-level control through deep reinforcement learning*(http://www.davidqiu.com:8888/research/nature14236.pdf) by Silver et. al.

On 9th March, 2016 we witnessed history when Google DeepMind's AlphaGo defeated the 18-times world champion Lee Sedol in the ancient Chinese game of Go. This was a great milestone for the whole AI community. This is because people have dedicated their lives to mastering the game of Go. The game of Go is highly challenging because of its complexity. As per a 1997 New York Times article (`http://www.nytimes.com/1997/07/29/science/to-test-a-powerful-computer-play-an-ancient-game.html`) scientists said that Go is the highest intellectual game and it would take at least a century for a computer to beat humans at Go. But thanks to Google DeepMind here we are, this feat was achieved in less than two decades. The following are the topics that we will be covering in this chapter:

- What is Go?
- AlphaGo - Mastering Go
- AlphaGo Zero

What is Go?

The game of Go originated in China around 3000 years ago. The rules of the game are simple as follows:

- Go is a two player game
- The default board size is 19x19 lines
- One player places a black stone, while the other player places a white stone
- The goal is to surround the opponent's stones and cover most of the empty spaces on the board

The following is a default board size, which is of 19x19 lines:

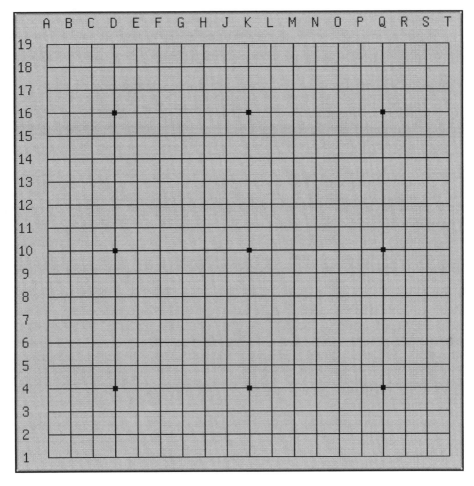

19x19 Go board

Even with those simple rules, the game of Go is highly complex. There are around 2.08 x 10^{170} possible moves in a 19x19 Go compared to 10^{80} atoms in universe and 10^{120} possible moves in chess. Thus, the intellectual depth required to play the game of Go has captured human imagination for ages.

Go versus chess

In 1997, IBM's DeepBlue defeated the then world champion Gary Kasparov in the game of chess. Almost two decades later, Google DeepMind's AI program AlphaGo defeated the 9-dan Go player and former world champion Lee Sedol. In order to understand the giant leap and achievement of Google DeepMind through AlphaGo, let's first understand the difference between these two games and then the architecture used behind the AI of DeepBlue and AlphaGo.

Both chess and Go need two players. In chess, each player has sixteen pieces that are of six different types possessing different strengths as per the game rules. The goal is to capture the opponent's King. On the other hand, Go starts with a blank board where each player places a stone one by one in turn and all the stones possess the same strength obeying the same rules. The goal here is to capture as much territory possible on the board.

Thus, we see that the game of Go is simpler than chess in terms of rules but what we don't see is the complexity, which is very high for Go relative to chess. At each game state, a Go player has to choose a move from 250 possible choices compared to 35 choices in chess. A game of Go lasts for approximately 150 moves while a game of chess lasts for roughly around 80 moves.

As we have studied previously, there are around 2.08×10^{170} possible moves in a 19x19 Go compared to 10^{80} atoms in the universe and 10^{120} possible moves in chess.

How did DeepBlue defeat Gary Kasparov?

In Chapter 5, *Q-Learning and Deep Q Networks*, we studied game trees and minimax algorithms. Let's recall those approaches to understand the architecture behind the AI program of IBM DeepBlue.

A game tree represents the full end-to-end representation of a game, where each node in the tree represents a particular game state (position) and the edges linking the nodes represent the moves (actions) taken at previous game states leading to a new game state. The root node represents the start of the game and nodes in the next level represent the possible states generated after all different possible actions have been taken at the start state of the game and similarly nodes in the further layers are generated.

For simple games such as tic-tac-toe, it is easy to create the game tree because of lower complexity. As soon as the complexity of the game increases, the creation of a game tree becomes impossible. For chess it would require 10^{120} different nodes to create the game tree. Such huge game trees are impossible to store.

As per the traditional approaches, knowing a game tree for a game was very important to create game playing AI as it helps to pick the best possible move at any given state. The best possible set of moves were picked using the minimax algorithm, where at each turn it tries to figure out which move would minimize the worst possible cases (which also includes losing the game).

In order to do that, it first finds out the node representing the current game state and then picks up the action in such a way that the loss suffered is minimized. For this, traversing the whole game tree down to the leaf nodes (end game states) is required to evaluate the losses. Therefore, minimax algorithm requires traversing down the game tree to evaluate the losses (worst case scenarios) for each move and then selecting the one with minimum loss.

DeepBlue searched the game tree of chess to the lowest possible depth (since creating the whole game tree of chess is impossible). Then it uses an evaluation function to calculate a value, which replaces the sub-tree below. This evaluation function is used to summarize the sub-tree below into a single value. Then it uses a minimax algorithm to lead toward the minimum worst case scenario till this maximum possible depth.

The evaluation function relies on some heuristics. In DeepBlue, the evaluation function was divided into 8000 parts to design specifically for certain particular positions. Thus, in order to go to deeper depths in the game tree computation power should be high, and even after that the game specific evaluation function is designed according to different game positions under supervision. Thus, it cannot be generalized over other domains (or games) since there is no learning.

In short, to tackle the complexity of chess, DeepBlue used a brute force approach to a game tree with a well designed evaluation function.

Why is the game tree approach no good for Go?

Go cannot be approached in a game tree way. The reason is that the bigger complexity and brute force approach used don't perform any sort of learning. The only task it performs is mapping the game state to a node in the game tree. Moreover, the brute force approach used in DeepBlue didn't have a generalized evaluation function rather it was hand-crafted for different game positions. Thus the preceding approach is too game specific and such approaches can't be scaled up to play Go.

AlphaGo – mastering Go

Traditional AI approaches based on search trees covering all possible position fail in the case of Go. The reason being the enormously huge search space because of 2.08×10^{170} possible moves and thereby, the difficulty in evaluating the strength of each possible board position. Thus, the traditional brute force approaches fail for the enormous search space of Go.

Therefore, advanced tree search such as Monte Carlo Tree Search with Deep Neural Networks was considered to be the novel approach to capture the intuition that humans use to play the game of Go. These neural networks are **convolutional neural networks** (**CNNs**) and take an image of the board, that is, the description of the board and activates it through the series of layers to find the best move as per the given state of the game.

There are two neural networks used in the architecture of AlphaGo, which are:

- **Policy network**: This neural network decides what next move/action to take
- **Value network**: This neural network predicts the winner of the game from the current position

The way AlphaGo uses the policy and value network is to reduce the enormous complexity of the search tree down to a small manageable search space. Therefore, instead of considering hundreds of different moves at each step, it considers some of the best possible moves suggested by the policy network.

Moreover, the value network reduces the depth of the search. At each position, the value network tries to predict which player is going to win instead of traversing the search tree down to evaluate that. Therefore, it is able to return a value that quantifies how good the moves are suggested by the possible network.

Humans have weaknesses in terms of longevity of the game, that is, they get tired during long matches leading to mistakes, which is not an issue with computing machines. Moreover, humans have limited time; they can play around thousand games of Go in a lifetime, while AlphaGo can play a million games in a day. Therefore, after given enough processing, enough training, enough search, and enough computation power AlphaGo was able to beat the best professional Go players across the world.

Thus, acing the given enormous complexity of Go can also pave the path for using this type of approach in medicine, to help patients with personalized treatments using deep reinforcement learning to understand the sequences of the treatments, which can lead to the best outcomes based on the patient medical and biological history.

Monte Carlo Tree Search

In `Chapter 5`, *Q-Learning and Deep Q Networks* we studied the Monte Carlo Tree Search. Here, let's revise it again and see how it was used by AlphaGo to achieve better results.

Monte Carlo Tree Search is an alternative approach to game tree search. In this approach, we run many simulations of the game, where each simulation starts with the current game state and ends with one of the two players being the winner. At the start, simulations are random where actions are chosen randomly for both players. At each simulation, for each game state of that simulation, corresponding values are stored. This value of a game state (node) represents the frequency of occurrence of this node and frequency of how many of these occurrences lead to a win. These values act as a guide in action selection for later simulations. The more simulations that are run, the more optimal these values will become in selecting winning moves.

Monte Carlo Tree Search focuses more on the actions leading to a win once it encounters one and tends to that direction, therefore, leading to exploitation of the existing actions explored. In order to explore new actions, it's important to add a randomness while taking the next action. This helps in adding exploration of new moves in a search.

One of the big advantages is that Monte Carlo Tree Search doesn't need any domain knowledge. The only thing it requires is to go through numerous simulations of the game and update the values of different games states when encountered accordingly. Moreover, it doesn't require the whole game tree to keep knowledge of each and every possible game state. It's impossible to store a game tree for games such as chess and Go. Instead Monte Carlo Tree Search just runs more and more simulations to optimize the node (game state) values leading to better results.

The AI programs of Go before AlphaGo totally relied on Monte Carlo Tree Search. These were Fuego, Pachi, Zen, and Crazy Stone. Out of which, Pachi was the strongest until AlphaGo defeated it using only policy network without using any search methods. The aforementioned AI programs of Go also relied on some domain knowledge to select better results during Monte Carlo simulations and achieve strong amateur levels. Pure Monte Carlo Tree Search doesn't learn through simulations experienced, it just optimizes the position (game state/node).

Architecture and properties of AlphaGo

All methods have relied on a tree search combined with some domain knowledge and human intervention. AlphaGo uses both a tree search and two kinds of CNNs (policy and value networks) to guide the tree search. These CNNs are kind of similar to the evaluation function used in DeepBlue, with one difference, that is, CNNs learn the evaluation function while the evaluation function used in DeepBlue was hand-crafted.

The tree search used earlier was a brute force approach, while CNN is a learning-based approach, which provides a sort of intuition-based game playing. Thus, the first task would be reducing the search space (which is in the order of 10^{170} for Go). This can be done by two approaches:

- Reducing *action candidates,* that is breadth reduction (avoid unnecessary moves that come up if we explore them in a game tree)
- Reducing evaluation function before time, that is depth reduction (avoid full game tree traversal to evaluate the move taken and predict the winning status as per current game state)

The policy network incorporates the current game state and outputs the probability of each possible action for that given state. Actions with higher probability have higher chances of winning. First, the policy network is trained using supervised learning using the dataset of the games played by expert players. Input data contains the image of the game board and output would be the action taken. A training dataset of approximately 30 million board positions from 160000 expert games was used to initially train the policy network of AlphaGo. Post training on an expert dataset, the model to predict possible actions learnt is improved through self-playing, where it was made to play against itself innumerable times to learn from past mistakes using policy gradients. Thus a policy network helps in reducing the action candidates by providing probabilities of possible moves.

The value network provides an estimate value of the current state that is the probability of the black player to win the game given the current state. The input to both policy and value networks are the same that is the current game state (image of the game of board with current stone positions). The output of the policy network is the probability of winning. Thus, a value network acts like an evaluation function that has been learnt through a supervised learning set of 30 million board positions.

Thus, a value network outputs intuition (chances of winning and losing) and policy network outputs reflection (training game knowledge). Thus, the mixture of intuition and reflection in AlphaGo makes it more powerful than any search based approach. But in AlphaGo, these networks help a faster and optimized tree search as per the intuition developed and reflection learnt.

The following figure is a neural network training pipeline and architecture:

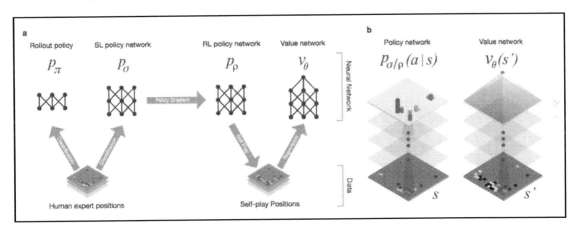

Neural network training pipeline and architecture of AlphaGo taken from Google DeepMind's publication on AlphaGo in Nature
(https://storage.googleapis.com/deepmind-media/alphago/AlphaGoNaturePaper.pdf) by Silver et. al.

Let's discuss the neural network architectural diagram of AlphaGo shown previously in detail:

- **a**: A fast rollout policy ϱ_π and supervised learning policy network ϱ_σ are trained on human experts playing dataset containing 30 million board positions to learn to predict the moves like human experts. A reinforcement learning policy network is initialized with the weights of the learnt supervised learning policy network, and its policy ϱ_ϱ is improved by using a policy gradient by maximizing the quality of the policy against previous versions of the policy network. A new dataset is generated from self-playing with this updated policy network. The dataset contains the image of the board position and its corresponding end result, that is win or lose. Finally, a value network v_θ is trained using this self-playing dataset by regression to output the probability of winning.

- **b:** The architectural flow of the process where policy network takes the image representation of the board position (game state) as the input, which propagates through convolution layers of parameters σ (if it is a supervised learning policy network) or ϱ (if it is a reinforcement learning policy network), and returns a probability distribution $p_\sigma(a|s)$ or $p_\rho(a|s)$ for all possible moves a as the output. The value network also uses many convolution layers of parameters θ returning a scalar value $v_\theta(s')$ that represents the probability of outcome (end result) that is winning or losing in given position s':

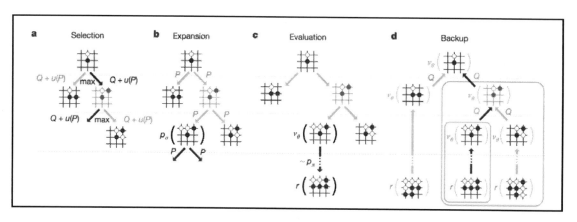

Monte Carlo Tree Search of AlphaGo taken from Google DeepMind's publication on AlphaGo in Nature (https://storage.googleapis.com/deepmind-media/alphago/AlphaGoNaturePaper.pdf) by Silver et. al.

Let's discuss the **Monte Carlo Tree Search (MCTS)** used in AlphaGo shown previously in detail:

- **a:** During each simulation while traversing the tree that edge is chosen, which has the maximum value for the sum of action value Q and the value $u(P)$, which is the function of the stored prior probability P for that edge.
- **b:** The leaf nodes are expanded, that is the new node is processed after the policy network p_σ and the output probabilities are stored as prior probabilities P for each action.
- **c:** Evaluation of the leaf node happens at the end of a simulation in two ways:
    - Using the value network v_θ
    - Using the learnt fast rollout policy p_π run a rollout till the end of the game and compute the winner with function r
- **d:** Action values Q are updated to track the mean value of all evaluations r $(\cdot)$ and $v_\theta(\cdot)$ in the subtree below that action.

A policy network was trained on 30 million game positions as mentioned previously. Without using tree search, AlphaGo won 85% of the games it played against Pachi (the strongest AI program of Go) where Pachi relied on 100,000 simulations based on Monte Carlo Tree Search. A value network was trained on 30 million game positions and learnt a model to predict the probability of winning. The policy network output acts a guide for the tree search. For a given game state, policy networks provide the probability for each possible move. This helps in reducing the action candidates during tree search.

Energy consumption analysis – Lee Sedol versus AlphaGo

The following table is an energy consumption analysis (Lee Sedol versus AlphaGo):

Lee Sedol (9-dan Go player)	Google DeepMind's AlphaGo
Calories per man per day ~ 2,500 kCal (average BMR)	Assuming : CPU ~ 100W, GPU ~ 300W 1,202 CPUs and 176 GPUs used
Assuming Lee Sedol consumed all the energy in one game. Therefore, 2,500 kCal * 4184 J/kCal $\cong$ 10M J	Therefore, [1,202*100+176*300] W = [1,202*100+176*300] J/s = 173,000 J/s Considering it to be atleast 4 hours game. Therefore, 173,000 J/s * 3 * 3,600 s $\cong$ 2,500M J

AlphaGo Zero

The first generation of AlphaGo was able to beat the professional Go players. In October 2017, Google DeepMind published the paper (https://www.nature.com/articles/nature24270) on AlphaGo Zero in Nature. AlphaGo Zero is the latest version of AlphaGo. Earlier versions of AlphaGo learnt to play the game after being trained on thousands of human games varying from amateur to professional games. But the final version of AlphaGo, that is AlphaGo Zero has learnt everything from scratch, that is from the first basic principle neither using any human data nor any human intervention and was able to achieve the highest level of performance. Thus, AlphaGo Zero learns to play the game of Go by playing against itself. One of the biggest feats was that in 19 hours AlphaGo Zero was able to learn the fundamentals of more advanced Go strategies, which include life and death, influence, and territory. In just three days AlphaGo Zero defeated all the previous versions of AlphaGo, and within 40 days surpassed a thousand years of human knowledge of Go.

The most important idea behind AlphaGo Zero is that it learns completely from a blank state, that is, a clear Go board, and figures out by itself through self play without any human knowledge, without any human game examples and data, and even without any human intervention. It discovers and develops the intuition to learn the game of Go from the first basic principles. This type of learning from scratch is called **tabula rasa learning** or **blank slate learning**.

Tabula rasa learning is highly important for any AI agent because if there is an agent that has achieved tabula rasa learning then it can be transplanted from the game of Go to other domain environments (maybe any other game). Tabula rasa learning unties the agent from the specifics of the domain it is in and it tries to develop an algorithm that is general enough to learn to achieve the objectives related to that environment and can be applied anywhere.

The goal behind the project of AlphaGo is not defeating the best human Go players but to discover what it means to learn and do science and for a computer program to learn the essence of knowledge and intuition itself. AlphaGo Zero not only rediscovered the common patterns and openings that humans tend to play, it learnt them by figuring them out on its own, it also discarded many of the known human moves in preference for better moves it discovered over millions of games it played against itself over days. These better moves were not even known to humans.

In a short span of time, AlphaGo Zero understood all Go knowledge that had been accumulated by humans over thousands of years of playing. AlphaGo Zero discovered most of this knowledge itself and discovered most of the moves yet to be discovered by human Go players. Thus, apart from adapting knowledge faster than humans it developed new pieces of knowledge, that is, knowledge creation and this achievement is thus regarded to be novel in many ways.

Thus, AlphaGo Zero being the first computer program that achieved a very high level of performance in a domain as complicated and challenging as Go has started a new journey where we can start tackling some of the more challenging problems that follow a sequence and are less or equally complicated such as the game of Go, to adversely affect the humanity.

Google DeepMind has already started using AlphaGo Zero to understand protein folding because misfolded proteins are responsible for many diseases such as Alzheimer's, Parkinson's, Type II Diabetes, and cystic fibrosis. Thus understanding protein folding, reducing energy consumption, discovering new elements or materials, and many more could be possible using the tabula rasa based approach of deep reinforcement learning.

Architecture and properties of AlphaGo Zero

There were five changes from the previous version of AlphaGo. They were as follows:

- Trains entirely from self play that is no human experts game play data and learning everything from scratch. Earlier versions had supervised learning policy networks, which was trained on expert game plays.
- No hand-crafted features.
- Replaced the normal convolution architecture with residual convolution architecture.
- Instead of a separate policy and value network, AlphaGo Zero has combined both of them into a single large network.
- Simplified the Monte Carlo Tree Search, which uses this large neural network for simulations.

The network input consists of:

- 19 x 19 matrix plane representing the board of Go
- One feature map for white stones (binary matrix having 1 in the positions having white stone and 0 elsewhere)
- One feature map for black stones (binary matrix having 1 in the positions having black stone and 0 elsewhere)
- Seven past feature maps for player using white stones (represents history as it captures the past seven moves)
- Seven past feature maps for player using black stones (represents history as it captures the past seven moves)
- One feature map for turn indication (turn can be represented by 1 bit but here it has been duplicated over the entire feature map)

Therefore, network input is represented by 19 x 19 x (1+1+7+7+1) = 19 x 19 x 17 tensor. The reason behind using feature maps of the past seven moves is that this history acts like a attention mechanism.

Why do we use residual architecture instead of normal convolution architecture? The reason behind this is that a residual architecture allows the gradient signal to pass straight through layers. Moreover, even during early stages of learning where convolution layers are not doing anything useful, then the important learning signals go into the convolution layers and go straight into further layers. Explaining residual architecture in detail is beyond the scope of this book.

Thus, we take an input of 19 x 19 x 17 tensor representation of the board and pass it through a residual convolution network, which generates a feature vector. This feature vector is passed through fully connected layers resulting in final feature extraction, which contains two things:

- **Value representation**: Probability of AlphaGo Zero winning the game in the current board position.
- **Policy vector**: Probability distribution over all the possible moves AlphaGo can play at the current position.

The goal therefore would be to obtain higher probability for good moves and lower probability for bad moves. In reinforcement learning, training a network by self playing a game of such higher complexity often leads to a network being highly unstable. Here, the simplified Monte Carlo Tree Search performs the task of stabilization of the network weights.

Training process in AlphaGo Zero

Input of the board representation is received, which is a 19 x 19 x 17 tensor. It is passed through a residual convolution network then fully connected layers finally output a policy vector and a value representation. Initially, the policy vector will contain random values since the networks start with random weights initially. Post obtaining the policy vector for all possible moves for the given state, it selects a set of possible moves having very high probabilities, assuming that the moves having the high probabilities are also potentially strong moves:

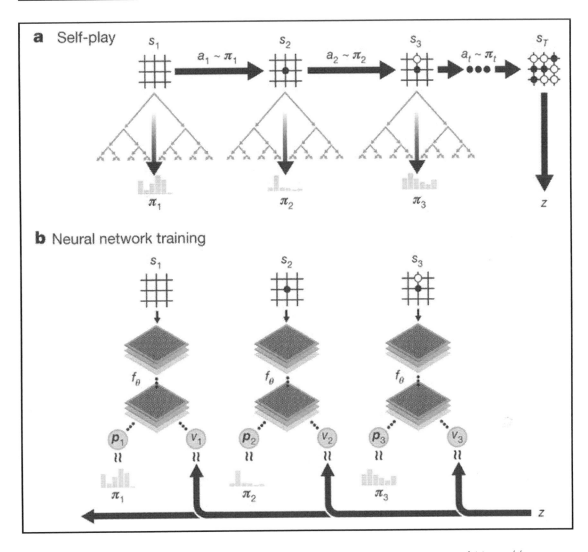

Self-play reinforcement learning architecture of AlphaGo Zero taken from Google DeepMind's publication on AlphaGo Zero in Nature (https://www.nature.com/articles/nature24270) by Silver et al

Based on those selected sets of moves, different games states are received each corresponding to their move. Since you simulate playing those moves on the previous state, this results in a bunch of different states. Now, for these next sets of state, repeat the preceding process by inputting the representation tensor for these game states and obtain their policy vectors.

Thus, for the current board position this repetitive process will explode into a giant tree. More simulations are run, and the tree will expand as the expansion is exponential. Thus, the idea would be to explode this search tree to a certain depth because owing to limited computation power further search wont be possible.

The AlphaGo team decided to play about 1600 simulations for every single board position evaluation. Therefore, for every single board state a Monte Carlo Tree Search is going to run until 1600 simulations are obtained. After which, a value network decides which of the resulting board positions is the best, that is, has the highest probability of winning. Then backup all those values to the top of the tree till the current game state (that is current board position which is being evaluated) and receive a very strong estimate for the moves that are genuinely strong and which are not:

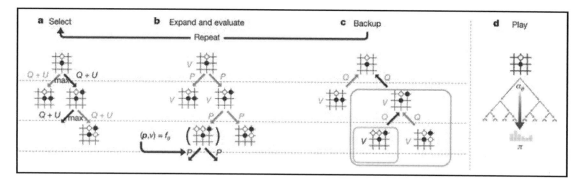

Monte Carlo tree search of AlphaGo Zero taken from Google DeepMind's publication on AlphaGo Zero in Nature (https://www.nature.com/articles/nature24270) by Silver et al

Summary

In this chapter, we studied the best reinforcement learning architecture at the moment, that is AlphaGo. We understood the reason behind choosing Go and its complexity with respect to chess. We also learnt how DeepBlue AI architecture works and how a different and better architecture and training process is needed for Go. We studied the architectures and training processes used in AlphaGo and AlphaGo Zero, and also understood the differences between the versions and how AlphaGo Zero surpassed its earlier versions.

In the next chapter, we will study how reinforcement learning can be used and implemented in autonomous and self-driving cars.

9
Reinforcement Learning in Autonomous Driving

In this chapter, we will cover different approaches researchers are working on to make end-to-end autonomous driving possible. We have seen many companies, such as Google, Tesla, Uber, Mercedes Benz, Audi, Volvo, Bosch, and many more enter the domain of self-driving cars. For the AI community, end-to-end autonomous driving will be the next milestone to achieve on the route to **artificial general intelligence (AGI)**.

Looking at the current trend in automotive industry, we witness the following:

- Environment and climate friendly electric cars are increasing
- Monetization through cab aggregator service and carpooling, that is, ride sharing
- Disruptive research on autonomous vehicles using AI and cloud power

Key Lego blocks of autonomous driving are as follows:

- Sensor fusion (sensors can be camera, LIDAR, RADAR, GPS, and so on)
- Object detection and classification
- Vehicular path planning—which action to take such as steer left or right, accelerate, or braking, and many more depending upon:
    - Different types of maneuvers
    - Complexity of the maneuvers

Machine learning for autonomous driving

Firstly, in order to develop an end-to-end self-driving car we must know the development process at a high-level before delving into the use of reinforcement learning in the whole process. The following is a diagram that depicts the development process:

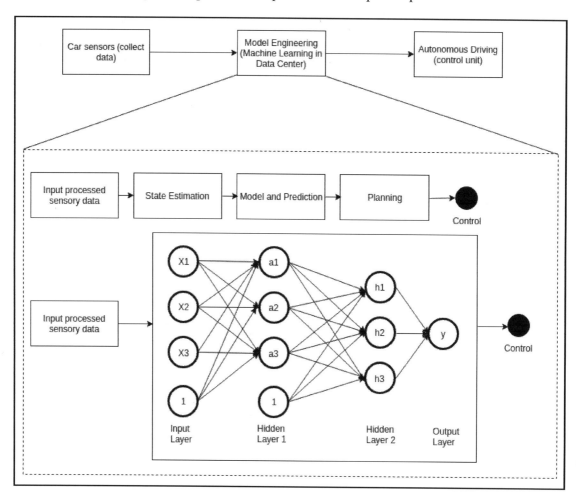

As shown in the preceding figure, the first step of the process is the collection of sensor data. Sensors comprise a camera, LIDAR, IMU, RADAR, GPS, CAN, and many more devices that can capture the state of the vehicle as well as the surrounding environment in the best possible way. After receiving these sensory signals, they are preprocessed, aggregated, and then prepared for sending to the next process, which includes **machine learning (ML)** and analysis in the data center. This step of implementing ML on the prepared sensory signals is a key part, which involves state estimation from the input data, thereby modeling it, predicting the possible future actions, and finally, the planning as per the predicted output, that is, which action to take so that the overall reward is maximized.

ML can be used in different tasks when it comes to autonomous driving. They are mainly the following:

- **Sensor fusion**: Clustering, pattern recognition, and segregation
- **Environment understanding**: Image processing, object detection, object classification, and motion detection
- **Trajectory planning**: Motion planning and control
- **Control strategy**: Reinforcement and supervised learning
- **Driver model**: Image processing and pattern recognition

Moreover, the biggest reason behind the use of reinforcement learning is that it's the best candidate to handle multiple vehicular maneuvers owing to their different types as follows:

- Overtaking while lane changing
- Traffic congestion
- Merging highways
- Diverging highways
- Narrowing lanes
- Stopping at red traffic light
- Stopping at stop sign
- Slowing down for speed limit signs
- Changing route or driving safely while driving near construction or accident sites
- Road intersections
- Roads merging into a roundabout (circular road)

Some of the previously mentioned vehicular maneuvers are shown as follows:

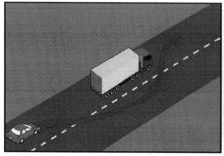

Overtaking while lane changing (left) and Merging highways (right)

Diverging highways (left) and Road intersection (right)

Road merging into a roundabout (circular road)

Reinforcement learning for autonomous driving

The challenge posed by autonomous driving cannot be solved by a full supervised learning approach owing to strong interactions with the environment and multiple obstacles and maneuvers (discussed previously) in the environment. The reward mechanism of reinforcement learning has to be highly effective so that the agent is very cautious about the safety of the individual inside and all the obstacles outside, whether it's humans, animals, or any ongoing construction.

One of the approaches to rewards could be:

- **Agent vehicle collides with the vehicle in front**: High negative reward
- **Agent vehicle maintains safer distance from both front and rear end**: Positive reward
- **Agent vehicle maintains unsafe distance**: Moderate negative reward
- **Agent vehicle is closing the distance**: Negative reward
- **Agent vehicle speeds up**: Decreasing the positive reward as the speed increases and negative when it crosses the speed limit

Incorporating **recurrent neural networks (RNNs)** to integrate the time series information will enable the car to handle partially observable scenarios. Moreover, using attention models to focus on relevant information also reduces computational complexity. As discussed previously, the next and certainly one of the biggest milestones for AI is creating end-to-end autonomous driving cars.

Creating autonomous driving agents

Driving a vehicle requires good skill, focus, and experience. Thus, being a highly-skilled task, the processes involved in creating an autonomous driving agent can be broadly classified into three categories, as shown in the following figure:

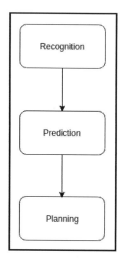

- Recognizing the components of the surrounding environment, which includes pavements, people, traffic signal, any construction, road boundaries, other vehicle, and so on. For AI, object detection and classification is relatively easy owing to the advancements in deep learning for computer vision using **Convolution Neural Networks (CNNs)** and **Generative Adversarial Networks (GANs)**. The success of CNNs and GANs can be used for this process of recognition of environmental components for autonomous driving.

- **Predicting** the future states of the environment. Recognizing the current components of the environment of the current environmental state is important but using that as the input and predicting the future environmental state is also necessary to plan the next action. One of the basic approaches to solving this problem would be to create an environmental map. Moreover, we can incorporate deep neural networks such as variants of Recurrent Neural Networks such as **Long-Short Term Memory Networks (LSTMs)** or **Gated Recurrent Units (GRUs)** to incorporate and integrate the data from past time steps along with the current time step and predicting the future. As we discussed in `Chapter 1`, *Deep Learning – Architectures and Frameworks*, there are issues surrounding the vanishing gradient problem owing to long-term dependency and how LSTMs cell were a solution to that in the case of RNNs. RNNs are the state of the art when it comes to integrating time series data and it has shown improvements in object tracking in DeepTracking (`https://arxiv.org/pdf/1602.00991.pdf`).

- **Planning** is the hardest part of the whole process. This task includes integrating the results of recognition and prediction together to plan out future action sequences and what would be the next set of driving actions (steer left or right, accelerate, and so on) such that the navigation is safe and successful. This is a painful task as the integration and planning requires handling unavoidable circumstances to reach the destination safely. Reinforcement learning is the best suited for this sort of control planning task. We have seen how reinforcement learning has been successfully deployed to control planning tasks in 50 Atari games and then the state of the art AlphaGo Zero by Google DeepMind. In these cases, we witnessed deep learning performing representation learning while reinforcement learning doing the planning.

Owing to the multiple types of sensors used, integration of all this information is critical for autonomous driving. It's difficult to integrate sensory inputs from different sources owing to the difference in dimensionality of the data. For example, camera inputs are high-dimensional while LIDAR inputs are low dimensional. Extracting relevant information and ignoring the irrelevant ones certainly improves the performance and accuracy. It reduces the utilization of computational and storage power. Thus for the sake of fetching relevant information, attention models are fit for the purpose since reinforcement learning with recurrent neural networks using attention mechanisms have been successfully applied to images to focus on the relevant parts only.

Why reinforcement learning ?

One big reason we have already discussed is the variability in vehicle maneuvers that cannot be learned in a supervised manner. In this section, we will go into the details of why reinforcement learning is the best suitable candidate for autonomous driving.

In terms of ML, driving is a multi-agent interaction problem. Consider human drivers driving in a lane without any other cars in proximity. This is way easier compared to changing lanes when there is heavy traffic. The reason why the second scenario is difficult is because it also includes the uncertain and unknown behavior of other drivers. Thus, the number of vehicles interacting with your vehicle, the type of vehicle (small or big), and the behavior of their corresponding drivers is vast and highly variable information. Due to this high variability, designing a supervised learning model on such data will not cover all different types of scenario. In supervised learning, the more training data there is the better it becomes, but variability and volume matters a lot. Thus, covering all scenarios wouldn't be possible if we go with supervised learning.

When we drive, we can understand the behavior of other drivers in proximity as it depends on the way their vehicle is moving on the road. Say, if the vehicle is moving very fast and passing other vehicles, this gives you an idea that the driver of the other vehicle is aggressive and experienced. Thus, the human brain performs this online learning, which understands the environment and its components.

This type of on-the-go learning and planning is required to understand variable scenarios ranging from when you are driving along without any traffic, to lane changing in heavy traffic. Thus, these are the cases where humans learn through experience but what about cases where humans also find it difficult? Thus, the potential challenges include those cases that are difficult for humans at present. These scenarios include driving in a disastrous situation, such as flooding, collapsing construction, or navigating in new surroundings without GPS connectivity, and many more.

Thus, all these explicit scenarios can't be fed into a learning model and require approaches such as reinforcement learning that can cover these scenarios and enhance its learning through rewards received from different actions performed.

We have discussed the different categories of tasks involved in the creation of an end-to-end autonomous driving vehicle. Currently, these tasks are decoupled and approached separately, and then combined using a post processing layer. A basic and very important drawback of this is that these isolated tasks might not combine properly.

Thus, reinforcement learning, owing to its action-reward mechanism, can model as per the driving actions taken and the corresponding rewards received, and then plan which action to take. Testing the reward mechanism for autonomous driving is very risky and expensive for real cars, as the reward values should be stable based on good driving and accidental scenarios. Therefore, it's better to test in a simulated environment such as TORCS or Unity.

Proposed frameworks for autonomous driving

In this section, we will discuss a proposed deep reinforcement learning framework for autonomous driving given by El Sallab et. al 2017 (`https://arxiv.org/pdf/1704.02532.pdf`).

The following is an architecture of end-to-end deep neural networks:

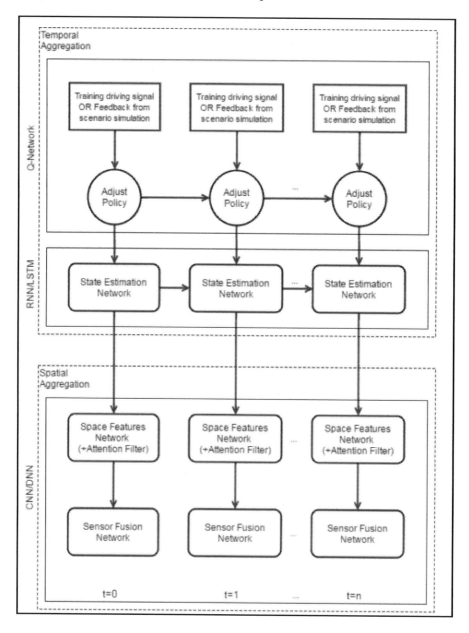

End to End training of Deep Neural Networks for Autonomous Driving by El Sallab et. al 2017 (https://arxiv.org/pdf/1704.02532.pdf)

Let's discuss the preceding architecture in detail. Inputs in this case are the aggregation of states of the environment over multiple timesteps.

Spatial aggregation

The first unit of the architecture is the spatial aggregation network. It consists of two networks, each for the the following sub-processes:

- Sensor fusion
- Spatial features

The overall state includes the state of the vehicle as well as the state of the surrounding environment. The state of the vehicle includes position, geometric orientation, velocity, acceleration, current fuel left, current steering direction, and many more. Environmental states include its components, that is, objects, living beings, obstacles, and their features, that is, their location, geometric orientation, whether in motion or not, and many more. The state of the surrounding objects is perceived through cameras, LIDAR, and so on. Thus, there are multiple sensory inputs that need to be combined together for the tasks of recognition, prediction, and planning.

Sensor fusion

This step includes fusing the inputs from different sensors and processes, and preparing them to feed into the deep neural network. Each sensor information captures the state of the environment in the form of a raw vector. Grouping all these raw vectors is done and fed into a deep neural network. Each sensory input will form a separate feature vector. Thus, as a result of learning, that is, cost minimization, optimization of the weights associated with each of those sensor features occurs. These learned weights quantify the relevancy of the corresponding sensor features. As far as the deep neural network is concerned, CNN is the best choice for the task.

Spatial features

Convolution Neural Networks are used to find hidden representations and is followed by applying attention mechanisms. Attention mechanisms direct the convolution layers of the network to focus on the relevant parts of the data. The advantage of using attention models is that it reduces the dimensionality of the dataset. As a result, a huge amount of computation, including convolution and so on, over the raw data is also reduced.

The best approach to applying attention models is to use action and glimpse networks (explaining which is beyond the scope of this book but for further details in action and glimpse networks please go to this research publication *"End-to-end Learning of Action Detection from Frame Glimpses in Videos"* at `https://arxiv.org/pdf/1511.06984.pdf`) and avoid using attention filters, because attention filters don't reduce the dimensionality of the computations, and convolution is applied to the whole data. But this is not the case for action and glimpse networks that comprise neural networks, which learn to attend the relevant parts of the data, thereby, directing the convolution layer to focus on those relevant parts of the data.

Recurrent temporal aggregation

Recurrent temporal aggregation involves aggregating environmental states across different time steps. Let's discuss the reason behind this in detail. First, fetching environmental states is not an easy task and sensor readings provide the best possible state representation of the environment. Therefore, state information of the current time step is not enough to get the full information of the environment. Therefore, integration of state information over multiple time steps captures the motion behavior, which is very important in the case of autonomous driving where the environmental state changes in split seconds.

Thus, by adding recurrence, handling of POMDP (partially observable Markov decision process) scenarios becomes possible, which is very common in driving since the whole environmental state isn't fully observable. Traditional algorithms such as Bayes filters were used to handle such scenarios, by integrating information over time but they are derived from the MDP framework (where environment state is fully observable).

Thus, by creating a time series format, we can use RNNs to model long-term dependencies using past state information along with the current state data. As we know, LSTMs are capable enough to handle long-term dependencies without facing any issues of vanishing gradients. This is because LSTM has cell state and hidden state where, for every new time step it updates its new hidden state as per the relevant information from both previous hidden state and the new incoming data at the current time step. Moreover, cell state stores relevant data across different timesteps and forgets irrelevant data from the stored information in cell state. Thus, LSTM has full control over what information to include in its cell and hidden state.

Planning

The preceding network forms part of a **Deep Q-Network (DQN)**, which takes state information as the input and stores the experiences in an experience buffer. Sample data from this experience buffer is used to train the deep neural network used in DQN, which in turn predicts state-action values. The state action values help in deriving the optimal policy, that is, plan out best actions for a given state.

The DQN-based approach is suitable for continuous state spaces but it requires the action spaces to be discrete. Therefore, in case of continuous action space, actor-critic algorithms are preferred. Recalling the actor-critic algorithm from Chapter 4, *Policy Gradients*, the following is a diagram of the actor-critic algorithm:

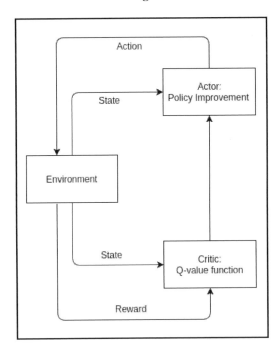

An actor-critic algorithm consists of:

- One network that acts as a critic updating the weight parameter vector of a function approximator of the state-action
- Another network acting as an actor updating the policy parameter vector as per the direction given by the critic

DeepTraffic – MIT simulator for autonomous driving

DeepTraffic (`https://selfdrivingcars.mit.edu/deeptraffic/`) was created for the course *MIT 6.S094: Deep Learning for Self-Driving Cars* at MIT taught by Lex Fridman. Course content and assignment is public. DeepTraffic gained a lot of popularity owing to its leaderboard. With over 13,000 submissions to date, DeepTraffic is highly competitive. The users have to write their neural networks in `convnet.js` (a framework created by Andrej Karpathy) in the coding ground present in the link mentioned at the start of the section. The agent with the maximum average speed tops the leaderboard.

Simulations such as DeepTraffic help train different approaches to make the car agent adapt to the simulated environment quickly. Moreover, the competitive element of it adds to better submissions over time, beating the past top scores. The competition makes it fun but in the real world a student can't test their deep reinforcement learning scripts. Therefore, DeepTraffic forms the best test bed for next generation AI developers to play with different approaches, which in the future certainly result in good AI developers creating self driving cars in the real world, with better approaches owing to the learning from such simulations.

As we know, in the real world, autonomous vehicles should plan the safest path. Thus, lots of pruning and better neural network architecture would be required to achieve that goal. DeepTraffic is the starting step in that direction so that interested folks in the AI community can play and create better learning architecture and approaches:

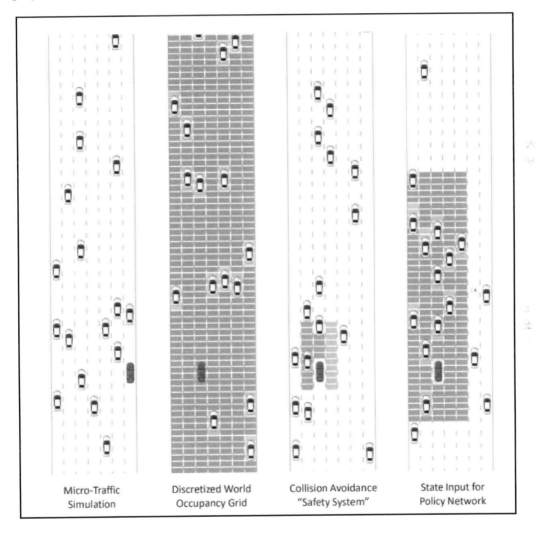

| Micro-Traffic | Discretized World | Collision Avoidance | State Input for |
| Simulation | Occupancy Grid | "Safety System" | Policy Network |

Four perspectives on the DeepTraffic environment: the simulation, the occupancy grid, the collision avoidance system, and the slice of the occupancy grid that represents the reinforcement learning *state* based on which the policy network learns to estimate the expected reward received by taking each of the five available actions.(DeepTraffic: Driving Fast through Dense Traffic with Deep Reinforcement Learning by Fridman et. al, https://arxiv.org/pdf/1801.02805.pdf)

DeepTraffic consists of a highway strip showing seven lanes and twenty cars driving at the same time (see first column of the preceding figure) with a speed limit of 80 mph (none of the cars are allowed to go beyond this limit). DeepTraffic is a simplified simulated representation of a real-world highway scenario. The focus of this simulation is only to learn efficient movement patterns in heavy traffic. All cars can choose from five actions which include:

- Lane changing towards left
- Lane changing towards right
- Accelerating
- Deaccelerating
- Do nothing

For other cars, actions are chosen at random following a realistic pattern, for example, not to change lanes too often because of random action selection. The car displayed in red (dark-gray) is controlled by the deep reinforcement learning agent. Competitors get a predefined neural network implemented in a DQN. The task is to configure different hyperparameters and achieve the best performance, that is, highest average speed.

Summary

In this chapter, we touched on the main concepts and challenges related to one of the biggest AI problems, that is, autonomous driving. We learned about the challenges posed by the problem and also learned the current approaches being used to make autonomous driving successful. Moreover, we went through an overview of different sub-tasks of the process, starting from receiving sensory inputs to planning. We also looked at a bit about the famous DeepTraffic simulation where you can test your neural networks to learn efficient movement patterns in heavy traffic. Autonomous driving is itself a vast evolving research topic and covering all of them is beyond the scope of this book.

In the next chapter, we will study another evolving research hotspot, using AI in finance, where we will learn how reinforcement can help in financial portfolio management.

10
Financial Portfolio Management

A financial portfolio is the process of distribution of funds into different financial products. The implementation of deep learning for portfolio management has been a research sector in the artificial intelligence community. With the advancements in reinforcement learning there has been active research in creating finance model free reinforcement learning frameworks to produce end to end finance portfolio managing agents.

Portfolio management is a continuous decision making process of reallocating funds into numerous different financial products with an objective of maximizing the returns.

Traditional state-of-the-art online portfolio management approaches include:

Approach	Important Algorithms
Benchmarks	• Buy and Hold • Best Stock • Constant Rebalanced Portfolios
Follow the winner	• Universal Portfolios • Exponential Gradient • Follow the Leader • Follow the Regularized Leader • Aggregating-type Algorithms
Follow the loser	• Anti Correlation • Passive Aggressive Mean Reversion • Confidence Weighted Mean Reversion • Online Moving Average Reversion • Robust Median Reversion

Pattern matching	• Nonparametric Histogram Log-optimal Strategy • Nonparametric Kernel-based Log-optimal Strategy • Nonparametric Nearest Neighbor Log-optimal Strategy • Correlation-driven Nonparametric Learning Strategy • Nonparametric Kernel-based Semi-Log-optimal Strategy • Nonparametric Kernel-based Markowitz-type Strategy • Nonparametric Kernel-based GV-type Strategy
Meta learning	• Aggregating Algorithm • Fast Universalization Algorithm • Online Gradient Updates • Online Newton Updates • Follow the Leading History

Follow the winner and Follow the loser are based on previously constructed financial models, which may or may not use machine learning techniques in their corresponding algorithms mentioned in the preceding table. The performance of these mentioned approaches is judged by their validity in different financial markets.

The pattern matching model takes a sample of historical data as the input, optimizes the portfolio according to the sample distribution, and predicts the market distribution for the next period. Meta learning aggregates multiple strategies of different categories to achieve a stable performance.

Currently, there are deep learning approaches for financial market trading, which predict price movements and trends but don't perform automatic fund allocation and reallocation across different financial products. Since we have the historical prices of all the assets, we can prepare input data comprising them into a recurrent neural network, which will predict the asset prices of the next period as the output. This is a supervised regression problem in machine learning.

The performance of these models depends totally on the prediction accuracy of the asset prices in future, not only in the next period. However, future market prices are extremely difficult to predict as they don't solely depend on the historical prices and can only capture the movement and flow, not include the sentiment factors that also drive the financial markets.

One more important point to notice is that predicting market prices doesn't mean predicting market actions. Thus, it requires domain knowledge and logic to convert the predicted prices to actions. Incorporation of deep reinforcement learning automates this logic conversion according to the goal of maximizing returns.

Many successful attempts of the finance model free and fully machine learning based approaches have been proposed for algorithmic trading. The major issues among them using reinforcement learning was that they weren't predicting future prices and they were applicable only to single asset trading. Therefore, they cannot be applied to portfolio management, which includes managing multiple assets simultaneously.

Moreover, portfolio management is a continuous action space problem and not a discrete action space. Most of the established state-of-the-art deep reinforcement learning algorithms work very well with discrete action spaces. However, though we have developed the process of discretization of continuous action spaces for the portfolio management problem, if we adopt the process of discretization then we lose many, possible, important market actions. This leads to a bigger risk of information loss and unavailability.

The algorithms that are needed for portfolio management, and even for any devised trading algorithm, should be scalable across different markets. Traditional algorithms used to fail because of the inability to scale across different markets, as a market is governed by factors such as type of assets and total number of assets, which vary from market to market. This is because the pattern and behavior of assets differ from market to market and traditional algorithms were not generalized. Machine learning here comes with an advantage of generalization across different verticals, that is, different financial markets.

Moreover, as discussed previously, applications of reinforcement learning in financial portfolio management are important among researchers in the artificial intelligence community. In this chapter, we will discuss one: the latest paper on *A Deep Reinforcement Learning Framework for the Financial Portfolio Management Problem* (https://arxiv.org/pdf/1706.10059.pdf) published by the researchers from *Xi'an Jiaotong-Liverpool University*. We will cover the approach taken by them and its performance relative to the current online portfolio management approaches, as follows:

- Introduction
- Problem definition
- Data preparation
- Reinforcement learning
- Further improvements

Introduction

The core of the proposed reinforcement learning framework is the **Ensemble of Identical Independent Evaluators (EIIE)** topology. Here, EIIE is a neural network that takes the asset history as the input and evaluates the potential growth of the asset in future. The evaluation score of each asset is used to calculate the portfolio weights for the next trading period.

The portfolio weights (which we will discuss later) are actually the market actions of the portfolio managing agent powered by reinforcement learning. An asset whose target weight is increased will be bought, while the assets with decreased target weights will be sold. Thus, the portfolio weights from the last period of trading are also fed as an input to EIIE. Therefore, the portfolio weights of each period are stored in **portfolio vector memory (PVM)**.

The EIIE is trained in by **Online Stochastic Batch Learning (OSBL)** where the reward functions of the reinforcement learning framework are the average logarithmic returns of the period. Since, the reward function is dynamic, therefore, as the training happens through gradient ascent, the EIIE evolves. As mentioned, EIIE consists of a neural network, therefore, for the current framework three different types of EIIEs are tested each with a different type of neural network, namely **convolutional neural networks(CNNs)**, **recurrent neural networks (RNNs)**, and **Long Short Term Memory neworks (LSTMs)**, which is a better variant of the RNN cell. This type of framework is easily scalable to different markets and not restricted to one.

The test bed for this proposed framework is a cryptocurrency exchange market named Poloniex. Before the experiment, the coins were selected by their ranking in trading volume over a time interval. The experiments were performed in a trading period of 30 minutes and the performance of EIIE was compared with the previously mentioned online portfolio selection methods. The EIIE was able to beat all those methods.

Since the framework is not tested in a real-world financial market but in a cryptocurrency market, we must know the differences between cryptocurrencies and traditional financial assets, and why the cryptocurrency market is a better test bed for algorithmic portfolio management experimentation beforehand. They are as follows:

- Decentralization in cryptocurrencies (not central authority controlling the protocols)
- Openness of cryptocurrency market (more accessible market)
- Abundance of small volume currencies in cryptocurrencies
- Crytocurrency market is open all of the time, therefore very good for a learning agent to learn over time unlike the real world, which is restricted by time-frame.

Problem definition

As we already know, portfolio management is the continuous reallocation of funds across different multiple financial products (assets). In this work, the time is divided into equal length periods, where each period $T = 30$ minutes. At the beginning of each period, the trading agent reallocates the fund across different assets. The price of an asset fluctuates within a period, but four important price metrics are taken into consideration, which are good enough to characterize the price movement of an asset in the period. These price metrics are as follows:

- Opening price
- Highest price
- Lowest price
- Closing price

For a continuous market (such as our test case), the opening price of an asset in a period t is its closing price in the previous period t-1. The portfolio consists of m assets. For a time period t, the closing prices of all the m assets create the price vector v_t. Thus, i^{th} element of v_t that is $v_{i,t}$ is the closing price of the ith asset in that t^{th} time period.

Similarly, we have vector $v_t^{(hi)}$ and $v_t^{(lo)}$, where:

- $v_t^{(hi)}$: Vector consisting of highest prices of all the m assets in time period t
- $v_t^{(lo)}$: Vector consisting of lowest prices of all the m assets in time period t

The first asset in the portfolio is special and will be referred to as cash from now onward. The reason it is regarded as special is because prices of all the assets are quoted in cash denominations. Since the first asset defines the base currency, the first element v_t $v_t^{(hi)}$ of , and $v_t^{(lo)}$ will always be 1, that is:

$$v_{0,t}^{(hi)} = v_{0,t}^{(lo)} = v_{0,t} = 1 \ \forall \ t$$

Here, Bitcoin is considered to be cash. Therefore, all the asset pricing would be done in terms of Bitcoin. As we have already discussed that this is a continuous market, opening prices for the period *t+1* will be equal to closing prices for the period *t*. The **price relative vector** of the period *t* is denoted as y_t, which is element-wise division of v_t and v_{t-1}, as follows:

$$y_t = (1, \frac{v_{1,t}}{v_{1,t-1}}, \frac{v_{2,t}}{v_{2,t-1}}, \ldots, \frac{v_{m,t}}{v_{m,t-1}})^T$$

This is element-wise division of the closing price of the assets at time period *t* and closing price of the assets at time period *t-1*, in other words, element-wise division of the closing and opening price of the assets at time period *t*. Thus, elements of y_t are the ratio of closing and opening prices of the individual assets at time period *t*. The **price relative vector** is used to calculate the change in total portfolio value in a period.

Let the portfolio value at the beginning of the time period *t* be p_t. Therefore, ignoring the transaction costs:

$$p_t = p_{t-1} \cdot y_t \cdot w_{t-1}$$

Here, w_{t-1} is the **portfolio weight vector** also known as the **portfolio vector** at the start of the time period *t*, whose i^{th} element, that is, $w_{i,t-1}$ is the proportion of asset *i* in the current portfolio. Since, w_t being a vector of weights (proportions), by definition the sum of elements of w_t will always sum up to one, that is, $\sum_i w_{t,i} = 1, \forall t$.

The **rate of return** for the time period *t* is given by:

$$\rho_t = \frac{p_t}{p_{t-1}} - 1 = y_t \cdot w_{t-1} - 1$$

The **logarithmic rate of return** is given by:

$$r_t = ln(\frac{p_t}{p_{t-1}}) = ln(y_t \cdot w_{t-1})$$

The initial portfolio weight vector, that is w_0, indicates that the amount is in the trading currency (which is called **cash**, and here cash is Bitcoin) before entering the market because the initial investment amount will be in the trading currency. Since the amount is in trading currency and the first asset of the portfolio vector refers to the trading currency asset therefore:

$$w_0 = (1, 0, 0, \ldots, 0)^T$$

Therefore, if there's no transaction cost, then the final portfolio value would be given by:

$$p_f = p_o e^{(\sum_{t=1}^{t_f+1} r_t)} = p_o \prod_{t=1}^{t_f+1} y_t \cdot w_{t-1}$$

Here, p_o is the initial investment amount. Thus, the objective of the portfolio manager is to maximize p_f for a given time frame. Two assumptions imposed for the experiment are:

- **Zero slippage**: Each order is carried out at the last price when the order is placed, there's no lag and trading happens immediately

- **Zero market impact**: The amount invested by the trading agent in the market is insignificant enough not to influence the market

Data preparation

The trading experiment is tested in a cryptocurrency exchange called Poloniex. In order to test the current approach, $m = 11$ non-cash assets having the highest volume are pre-selected for the portfolio. Since the first base asset is cash, that is Bitcoin, the size of the portfolio is $m+1 = 12$. If we had tested in a market with larger volumes, such as foreign exchange market, there m would be as large as the total number of assets in the market.

Historical data of the assets is fed into a neural network, which outputs a portfolio weight vector. Input to a neural network at the end of period t is a tensor X_t, of rank 3 with shape (f, n, m), where:

- m is the number of pre-selected non-cash assets
- n is the number of input periods before t (here $n = 50$)
- $f=3$ is the feature number

Since $n = 50$, that is, number of input periods is 50 and each period is of 30 minutes, the total time *frame* = 30*50 *minutes* = 1500 *minutes* = 25 *hours*. Features of the asset i on time period t are its closing, highest and lowest prices in the time period t. The price matrices are not input directly to the neural networks. Price changes determine the performance of the portfolio management. All prices in the input tensor will be normalized by the latest closing prices as follows:

$$V_t = \left[v_{t-n+1} \oslash v_t \middle| v_{t-n+2} \oslash v_t \middle| \dots\dots \middle| v_{t-1} \oslash v_t \middle| 1 \right]$$

$$V_t^{(hi)} = \left[v_{t-n+1}^{(hi)} \oslash v_t \middle| v_{t-n+2}^{(hi)} \oslash v_t \middle| \dots\dots \middle| v_{t-1}^{(hi)} \oslash v_t \middle| 1 \right]$$

$$V_t^{(lo)} = \left[v_{t-n+1}^{(lo)} \oslash v_t \middle| v_{t-n+2}^{(lo)} \oslash v_t \middle| \dots\dots \middle| v_{t-1}^{(lo)} \oslash v_t \middle| 1 \right]$$

Here:

- V_t, $V_t^{(hi)}$ and $V_t^{(lo)}$ are the normalized price matrices
- $1 = (1,1,1,\dots,1)^T$ and $\oslash$ is the element-wise division operator

Therefore, X_t is a stack of the three normalized price matrices:

$$X_t = \begin{bmatrix} V_t^{(lo)} \\ V_t^{(hi)} \\ V_t \end{bmatrix}$$

The portfolio managing agent uses the input tensor X_t and last time period's (that is *t-1*) portfolio weight vector w_{t-1} outputs the portfolio weight vector w_t for the time period t as per the policy π.

Therefore:

$$w_t = \pi(X_t, w_{t-1})$$

and since(as shown in the preceding *Problem Definition* section):

$$r_t = ln(\frac{p_t}{p_{t-1}}) = ln(y_t . w_{t-1})$$

Therefore, by framing the preceding statements in terms of reinforcement learning we can say that the previous weight vector w_{t-1} being the action at time period *t-1* received the immediate reward r_t.

Reinforcement learning

In this experiment of algorithmic portfolio management, the portfolio managing agent performs the trading actions in the financial market environment powered by reinforcement learning. The environment comprises all the available assets of the given market. Since the environment is large and complex, it's impossible for the agent to fully observe the state, that is, to get all the information of the state. Moreover, since the full order history of the market is too huge to process, sub-sampling from the order history data simplifies the processing of state representation of the environment. These sub-sampling methods include:

- **Periodic feature extraction**: Discretizes the time into many periods and then extracts the opening, highest, lowest, and closing prices for each of those periods
- **Data slicing**: Consider only the data from recent time periods and avoid the older historical data in order to do current state representation of the environment

The agent made some buying and selling transactions at the end of period *t*, that is, at the beginning of period *t+1* as per the output portfolio weight vector w_t output by the neural network. Thus, the agent's action at time *t* is represented only by the portfolio weight vector w_t. Thus, in the current framework, w_{t-1} is considered part of the environment and fed into the agent as input to output the agent's action policy for the next time period, that is w_t. Thus, the state at period *t*, that is, s_t is represented by the price tensor X_t and the portfolio weight vector from the previous period w_{t-1}:

$$s_t = (X_t, w_{t-1})$$

and,

$$w_o = (1, 0, \ldots, 0)^T$$

As discussed earlier, the objective of the portfolio managing agent is to maximize the final portfolio value, that is p_f, where:

$$p_f = p_o e^{(\sum_{t=1}^{t_f+1} r_t)}$$

Therefore, the overall return over t_f time periods is $\frac{p_f}{p_o}$. Therefore, the average of the logarithmic of overall return is given by:

$$\frac{1}{t_f} ln(\frac{p_f}{p_o})$$

Thus, maximizing the final portfolio value can be converted as maximizing the average of the logarithm of the overall return given by:

$$R(s_1, a_1, \ldots, s_t, a_t, s_{t+1}) = \frac{1}{t_f} ln(\frac{p_f}{p_o})$$

$$= \frac{1}{t_f} ln(e^{\sum_{t=1}^{t_f+1} r_t})$$

$$= \frac{1}{t_f} \sum_{t=1}^{t_f+1} r_t$$

Three policy networks are created having three different variants of deep neural networks, which are CNNs, RNNs, and LSTMs. The output from the previous time period is the input to the networks in the current time period. Therefore, using the idea of experience replay in policy gradients and deep Q-networks, a PVM is created that stores the network output, that is, it will contain the portfolio weights vectors from each time step.

PVM is the collection of portfolio vectors in time step order, that is, chronological order. At each time step t of the training epoch, the policy network takes in the portfolio weight vector w_{t-1} of the last time period from the memory location at $t-1$, and overwrites the memory at t with the output portfolio weight vector w_t. The values in the PVM converge with increase in training epochs owing to the convergence of the policy network parameters.

A single memory stack such as PVM, also helps in parallelism of the training process using mini-batches, thereby increasing the efficiency of the training process.

For supervised learning, the ordering of the data is in mini-batches but here the data needs to be ordered as per time steps in each batch passed for the training process. Now, since the data is in time-series format, the mini-batches starting with different time periods are preferred as they cover distinctive data for the training process. The ongoing nature of the financial markets results in continuous input of new data to the agent network leading to data explosion in the training data.

Thus, OSBL is proposed, where at the end of the period *t*, the price movement of the period will be added to the training set. After the order for the period *t+1* is completed the policy network is trained using the randomly chosen mini-batches from this set. A full detailed study of OSBL is beyond the scope of this book but in order to explore further in please go through section 5.3 in the "*A Deep Reinforcement Learning Framework for the Financial Portfolio Management Problem*" publication at `https://arxiv.org/pdf/1706.10059.pdf`.

This framework is tested using all three different policy networks, that is CNNs, RNNs, and LSTMs, on the cryptocurrency exchange Poloniex. The financial metrics of the portfolio used to check the performance of the framework are:

- **Portfolio value**: The worth of the final portfolio
- **Maximum drawdown**: Maximum loss from one peak (highest point) to the trough (lowest point), before a new peak is attained
- **Sharpe ratio**: The return to the risk (variability) ratio

The performance of the proposed framework is compared with the existing online portfolio management methods on the basis of the previously mentioned metrics and it was able to successfully defeat the existing online portfolio management methods. Thus, the proposed reinforcement learning framework was able to solve the general financial portfolio management problem.

Key features of the proposed framework were:

- Multi-channel, multi-market input
- Market actions in form of portfolio weight vectors are directly provided by the policy networks
- Here, only three variants of deep neural networks were used but other variants can also be applied
- Linearly scalable with increase in portfolio size

- PVM adds the feature of parallelism in training using minibatches
- OSBL helps in online consumption of the live incoming data

Further improvements

There are further improvements that can be made to the previous framework, and also better approaches to creating end to end financial portfolio managing agents using deep reinforcement learning. They are as follows:

- Current framework assumptions, which are zero slippage and zero market impact. Thus, considering market impact and slippage will provide real-world trading samples, which will improve the training dataset.
- Use of an actor-critic type of framework will help more in long-term market reactions.
- Preferring LSTMs and GRUs over basic RNNs overcomes the issue of the vanishing gradient problem.

Summary

In this chapter, we looked at one of the recently published approaches to using deep reinforcement learning in financial portfolio management. We looked at a problem statement in financial portfolio management, the objectives of a portfolio manager, and mapped the problem statement to a reinforcement learning task. We also learned about different financial metrics for benchmarking performance and different existing online portfolio management approaches. This research topic of automating financial portfolio using deep reinforcement learning is among the most challenging tasks to solve in the AI community. Therefore, apart from the approach covered in this chapter do try to study other traditional machine learning approaches in algorithmic trading.

In the next chapter, we will study the use of reinforcement learning in robotics, the current challenges, and their proposed solutions.

11
Reinforcement Learning in Robotics

So far, we have seen the advancements of reinforcement learning in AlphaGo, autonomous driving, portfolio management, and a lot more. Studies and research say that reinforcement learning can provide features of cognition such as animal behavior.

A close comparison with cognitive science would be the many successful implementations of reinforcement learning in dynamic robotic systems and autonomous driving. They have proved the theory behind applying reinforcement learning algorithms for real-time control of physical systems.

The use of neural networks in deep Q-networks and policy gradients removes the use of hand engineered policy and state representations. The direct implementation of CNNs in deep reinforcement learning and using image pixels as states instead of hand engineered features, became a widely accepted practice. The concept of mini batch training and separate primary and target networks brought success to deep reinforcement learning algorithms. The success of DeepMind and deep reinforcement learning in 50 of the Atari 2600 games with pixels as inputs achieved super human levels of performance and was the turning point in the research of reinforcement learning.

Researchers have tried to implement deep Q-network in robotics but haven't achieved significant success. The main reason behind this is the high dimensional continuous action spaces in the domain of robotics. In order to implement DQN in continuous action spaces one has to discretize them, but this discretization causes loss of information, which can be very risky for a domain such as robotics.

The algorithms dealing with discrete action space domains are grouped under the **discrete action space** (**DAS**) algorithm. Further approaches, such as policy gradients, directly connect the state space with the action space by taking state space as input and returns optimal policy as output, that is, which feasible actions to take. The advantage of the policy-based approach over value-based approaches, such as Q-learning, is that they solve the handling of continuous action spaces as the output policy is a stochastic distribution across different possible actions for a given state input.

Algorithms such as policy gradients dealing with continuous action space domains are grouped under the **continuous action space** (**CAS**) algorithm. Thus, the policy-based approach giving stochastic representation over the action space solves the issue instead of discretization in DAS algorithms. CAS algorithms were initially developed and used on low dimensional state spaces, later scaling to high dimensional state spaces using CNN-based architecture. The CAS algorithms are segregated into two subcategories, which are: **stochastic continuous action space** (**SCAS**) and **deterministic continuous action space** (**DCAS**) algorithms. The key difference between them being the complexity, as SCAS algorithms provide better coverage, large training samples to learn better policies were needed. Getting large training samples in real-world robotic applications is quite infeasible, therefore, simulations must represent the real world in the best possible manner, otherwise generating real-world data would be highly expensive.

The discovery of deterministic policy gradients surpassed stochastic policy algorithms as shown by Silver et al (`http://proceedings.mlr.press/v32/silver14.pdf`) covered in `Appendix A`, *Further topics in Reinforcement Learning*). In this chapter, we will cover the challenges behind robot reinforcement learning and how robot reinforcement learning is being implemented currently.

The topics that we will be covering in this chapter include:

- Reinforcement learning in robotics
- Challenges in robot reinforcement learning
- Open questions and practical challenges
- Key takeaways

Reinforcement learning in robotics

Robotics is associated with a high level of complexity in terms of behavior, which is difficult to hand engineer nor exhaustive enough to approach a task using supervised learning. Thus, reinforcement learning provides the kind of framework to capture such complex behavior.

Any task related to robotics is represented by high dimensional, continuous state, and action spaces. The environmental state is not fully observable. Learning in simulation alone is not enough to say the reinforcement learning agent is ready for the real world. In the case of robotics, a reinforcement learning agent should experience uncertainty in the real-world scenario but it's difficult and expensive to obtain and reproduce.

Robustness is the highest priority for robotics. In normal analytics or traditional machine learning problems, minor errors in data, pre-processing, or algorithms result in a significant change in behavior, especially for dynamic tasks. Thus, robust algorithms are required that can capture the real-world details. The next challenge for robot reinforcement learning is the reward function. Since the reward function plays the most important role in optimized learning, generating a domain specific reward function is needed that helps the learning agent to adapt better to the real world as quickly as possible. Thus, domain knowledge is the key behind devising a good reward function, which is again a hard task in robot machine learning.

Here, were will discuss the types of tasks in the field of robotics that can be achieved by the reinforcement learning algorithms we have studied in this book, and try connect them together to build a promising approach.

Evolution of reinforcement learning

In this book, we have covered most of the algorithms in the area of reinforcement learning from basic to advanced. Therefore, those chapters are prerequisites to understand applications and challenges faced by different algorithms in the domain of robotics. Early reinforcement learning algorithms dealt in obtaining optimal policies by first obtaining state action values and then deriving the policy from them. Then, policy iteration methods came into the picture, which are directly used to output the optimized policy. The exploration-exploitation techniques helped in refining existing policies, exploring new actions, and updating the existing policies. Reinforcement learning approaches, such as MDP (in Chapter 3, *Markov Decision Process*) where value iteration methods needed a transition model are called **model based learners**. On the other hand, algorithms such as Q-learning (in Chapter 5, *Q-Learning and Deep Q-Networks*) don't need such a transition model nor any predefined policy therefore, they are called **model free land off-policy learner**.

In the domain of deep reinforcement learning, action-value function approximators and policy function approximators play a key role in making state of the art sets of learning algorithms. Policy search algorithms, such as policy gradients aim at finding the optimal policy by maximizing the expected sum of rewards, while algorithms using action-value function approximators such as deep Q-networks aim at finding action values for a given state by maximizing the expected sum of rewards. However, the difference comes in the performance while dealing with the environment constituted of high dimensional and continuous state-action spaces, which best describes a real-world environment where the robot operates. In such cases, policy search algorithms perform way better because of their feasibility to work better in the continuous state action spaces domain:

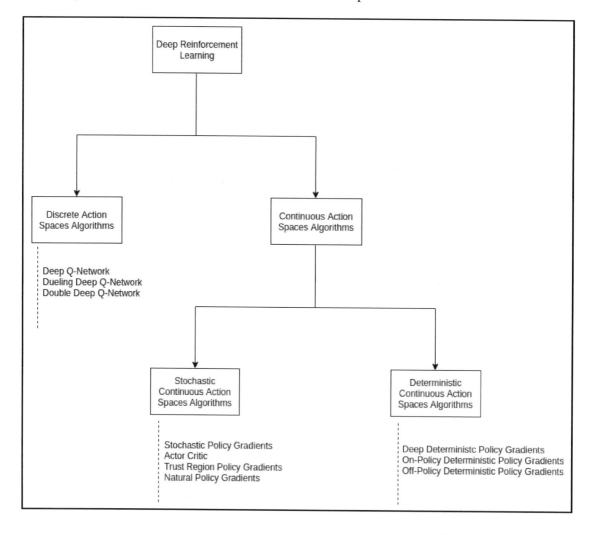

The preceding diagram shows the categories of different deep reinforcement learning algorithms. Mapping continuous and high dimensional state spaces was solved by the use of neural networks in deep Q-networks and policy gradient approaches. Various DAS and CAS algorithms use neural networks to perform the task of continuous state space mapping efficiently. But the major issue is mapping that input state space to high dimensional and continuous action spaces. In order to achieve better results in the task of mapping to continuous action spaces CAS algorithms were derived.

Challenges in robot reinforcement learning

Applications of reinforcement learning in robotics include:

- Locomotion
- Manipulation
- Autonomous machine control

As discussed previously, in order for a reinforcement learning agent to perform better in a real-world task it should have a well-defined, domain-specific reward function, which is hard to implement. This problem is being tackled by using techniques such as apprenticeship learning. Another approach to solve the uncertainty in reward is to continuously update the reward functions as per the state so that the most optimized policy is generated. This approach is called inverse reinforcement learning.

Robot reinforcement learning is a hard problem to solve owing to many challenges. The first being continuous state-action spaces. The decision is, as per the problem statement, whether to go for DAS algorithms or CAS algorithms. This means at what granular level the robot control should be. One big challenge is the complexity of the real-world systems leading to an increase in execution time, manual interventions, and maintenance. Thus, there's a need for an algorithm that can run in real time and cope with the real-world complexities.

Therefore, the algorithm must deal with the complexity of the real-world systems and run in real time with the objective of maximizing the expected sum of rewards by designing a good, domain specific, knowledge-derived reward function. Thus, there are many challenges faced by robot reinforcement learning discussed in the following sections and shown in the following diagram:

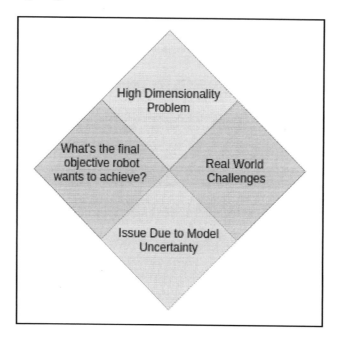

High dimensionality problem

With the increase in the number of dimensions, data increases. As a result, there is more computation covering the complete state-action spaces.

Let's take an example:

- For each dimension, state-space is discretized in 10 different states
- Therefore, a three-dimensional state space will have *10x10x10 = 1000* states
- Thus with increase in dimensionality, the state will increase 10 fold

Thus, with an increase in dimensions, evaluation becomes difficult. Function approximators such as neural networks handle this problem effectively. The issues with robotic systems are high dimensional states and actions because of anthropomorphic (human-like) robots. Classical reinforcement learning approaches consider a grid-world kind of environment with discrete state action space. In a grid-world environment, navigation tasks will involve many discrete actions covering the direction to move, accelerate up, accelerate down, starting, stopping, and many more with high precision.

Using discretization to reduce the dimensionality results in loss of information, especially in the domain of robotics. This hampers the dynamic capabilities because of the continuous action space. Reducing the action space to discrete values masks many important actions. Function approximation is a judicious approach when deal with mapping to continuous action spaces.

Real-world challenges

Robots interact with the real physical world. Thus, a genuine problem with robot reinforcement learning is to deal with these real-world problems. This is because of regular wear and tear in the real world of robot components, which are expensive. The continuous maintenance and repair comes at a great cost in terms of labor and loss of time in maintenance and repair. Thus, safe exploration is the key issue during the learning process in robot reinforcement learning.

Perkins and Barto (2002) came up with a method for constructing reinforcement learning agents based on Lyapunov functions (Appendix A, *Further topics in Reinforcement Learning*). The challenges posed by the real world include changes of environmental factors, that is, climate, temperature, light, and so on. As a result, the dynamics of the robot will be affected owing to the extremes of temperature and climate, and will avoid the convergence of the learning process. The real-world environment is uncertain; as a result, a past learning period cannot be produced because of the external factors of climate, temperature, light, and so on. Thus, state is not certain and therefore, simulation of the exact real-world scenario is difficult. Thus, most of the simulators don't consider the elements of climate, temperature, and light. Therefore, this poses a serious challenge for the algorithms to solve. Apart from these, uncertainty in noise measurement from sensors causes an inability to observe all states directly with sensors.

The majority of real-world robot learning tasks need human supervision, and getting real-world samples is very expensive in terms of time, labor, and money. In robot reinforcement learning, episodic setups such as a simulator are not possible, as they cost a lot in terms time, repairs, and money. A robot needs to interact with the real world under strict constraints to avoid significant damage.

Moreover, since these reinforcement learning algorithms are implemented in a computing machine, discretization of time cannot be avoided leading to the inability to replicate the continuous time system in case of real-world scenarios. The state representation of the real world may lag compared to the real-world state due to the following processes:

- Delay in communication of signal
- Processing of the signal information
- Creating a learning model in real time to output the optimal action to take
- Delay in receiving the action signal and actuation causing machine movements in the robot

As a result of these delays, actions don't get implemented instantaneously causing delayed effects. In reinforcement learning algorithms such as **markov decision processes (MDP)** assume that actions instantaneously effect the environment neglecting the real-world associated delays. This issue can be tackled by aggregating some of the recent actions and providing them to the state but this will also lead to an increase in dimensionality (a challenge in robot reinforcement learning discussed in the preceding section). Another approach of resolving the issue is increasing the duration of time steps, but this comes with two disadvantages, one being hampering the robot control and second being, adversely affecting the dynamics of the system owing to changes in duration.

Thus, we sum up the real-world challenges discussed as follows:

- Wear and tear in the real world
- Expensive hardware
- Environmental factors such as climate, temperature, light, noise, and many more
- Delay between environmental signal reception and effect of the action implemented
- Includes significant investment in terms of time, labor, and money for maintenance

Issues due to model uncertainty

In order to avoid the cost associated with real-world interactions, simulators are used. The catch is that the simulating model should be close to a real-world scenario. For an ideal setting, the approach is to perform the learning tasks in the simulation and transfer the knowledge model to the robot. Creating a good accurate learning model for the robot and the simulating environment model of the real-world scenario is highly challenging as it requires a huge amount of real-world data samples.

Small models learned on small sets of data leads to under-modeling, causing the robot to diverge easily from the real-world system. The issue with the simulators is that they can't replicate the real-world complexities associated with physical interactions such as friction and touch, so they get neglected. As a result, in the real world, the energy of the robot and control of it is also lost because of the challenges related to physical interactions. Thus, neglecting these features has made the robot reinforcement learning model difficult to train accurately according to the real-world scenario. Thus, learning in the real world helps in capturing these intrinsic features of the environment.

Thus, model uncertainty owing to the incomplete state representation of the real world is a huge challenge for robot reinforcement learning to overcome.

What's the final objective a robot wants to achieve?

Reward function is of key importance in specifying the objective of the learning agent in robot reinforcement learning. As we have learned, for reinforcement learning algorithms, the ultimate objective is to maximize the expected sum of rewards from the start state till the goal state is reached.

In a real-world scenario, devising a good reward function is a big challenge. Therefore, representing or specifying a goal is a challenge in real-world scenarios. The real-world environment is full of uncertainty therefore, the reward function should be able to capture the positive state associated with such uncertainty.

Some domains receive rewards after task completion, where uncertainty is less but in some cases each action leading to better end result is associated with different rewards. This is due to the importance of each state resulted because of the actions taken like in case of real world scenarios. Thus, the post task completion reward mechanism can't be implemented in a real-world system as it would not capture the uncertainty and never lead to convergence in learning, leading to performance failure.

In the majority of existing simulations we have come across, we see a binary reward mechanism, which only captures the success and failure of the learning agent. Including the intermediate rewards as a part of the reward function will work better than a binary reward approach, thereby leading to a better solution. Including intermediate rewards will capture the uncertainty from state to state transition in a real-world system.

Thus, reward function is generally represented as a function of a state action pair. As discussed previously, the simulation doesn't represent the real-world state accurately owing to the real world challenges discussed previously. But apart from the environmental factors and time lag, the robot reinforcement agent is able to learn to optimize time and manage risks owing to a good reward function and avoid the cost of real-world system setup and maintenance.

Recently, further research developments have been done to build complex policies on top of simple models to achieve this goal by exploring those complex policies using better parameterized reward functions. In their research, Sorg et al., 2010, and Zucker and Bagnell, 2012, derived complex policies by adapting a reward function for simple optimal control through policy search techniques.

Open questions and practical challenges

As per the different challenges in reinforcement learning algorithms, they cannot be directly implemented to robotics compared to supervised learning where large scale significant progress has already been done in terms of research and better deployment.

Reinforcement learning can be introduced for various physical systems and control tasks in robotics where risk isn't very high. The reason behind this is the question of stability of a reinforcement learning model in the real-world system. All learning processes require implemented domain knowledge for better state representations and devising accurate reward functions. This requires further research and development.

Let's discuss some of the open questions for reinforcement learning algorithms that require more attention in ongoing and future research in the space of robot reinforcement learning.

Open questions

Following is a list of open, non-exhaustive questions that demand special care to deliver better reinforcement learning models in the field of robotics:

- How do we automate the process of state-action space representation?
    - State-action spaces in robotics is continuous and multi-dimensional. The high-dimensionality and continuous nature of the state and action space makes the process of representation selection difficult to automate.

- State approximation is also an open question to deal with and is under intense study.
- How do we generate a reward function from the data received?
    - The success of a reinforcement learning algorithm is highly dependent on the quality of the reward function, its coverage of different state representation, and the uncertainty associated with them
- What's the importance of prior domain knowledge?
    - Prior knowledge is better for accuracy of the reinforcement learning agent.
    - The amount of prior knowledge required for better learning in the least possible number of episodes is not certain and an open question to deal with. Therefore, a significant amount of iterations are repeated to assure better learning.
    - There are cases where prior knowledge might not help owing to a huge amount of uncertainty associated with the environment.
- How do we learn closely according to the perception data?
    - Heavy pre-processing and constraints abstract away most of the key information perceived
    - This abstraction is due to the limitations associated with handling incomplete, ambiguous, and noisy sensor data
    - Learning on the go simultaneously when the data signals are received is an active area of research
- How do we deal with the errors and uncertainty associated with the model?
    - In order to reduce needed real-world interactions, use a model-based approach
    - The policies learned only in simulation should not be transferred directly to the robot
    - This problem looks to be inevitable because of the uncertainty associated with the real-world systems
    - Creating algorithms robust enough to deal with the uncertainty associated with real-world systems is an active area of research

Practical challenges for robotic reinforcement learning

Apart from the basic challenges discussed previously, there are bigger problems and practical challenges in robot reinforcement learning. This is because practical challenges are important to overcome to make the robot work efficiently with a minimized error rate. In order to avoid the practical challenges, one must do the following tasks:

- Better exploitation of the datasets:
    - Humans are able to enhance their learning on top of the already learned knowledge and new interactions.
    - For example, a child touches a hot pot and quickly learns to stay away from it. Similarly, when walking or doing any task, human performance gets better, which in turn enhances the learning.
    - Transferring previously learned knowledge and enhancing it on the go with robots is highly challenging.
    - For simple tasks, convergence can be achieved in learning but for complex tasks, learning might never converge owing to a lack of adequate data to enhance the learning.
    - Better exploitation of data leads to better handling of noise.
    - Creating datasets dealing with the variance of the environment for better state representation is an active area of research in robot reinforcement learning.
- Performing better experiments and constantly evaluating them for further improvement.
    - Performing a large-scale, real world experiment is a challenging task in robot reinforcement learning
    - Standard setups for experimenting with robot reinforcement learning are being made by researchers in the AI community

Key takeaways

In this chapter, we have gone through the major challenges faced by reinforcement learning algorithms in the field of robotics. Therefore, the key takeaways for students who want to enter this great research domain of robot reinforcement learning are shown in the following diagram:

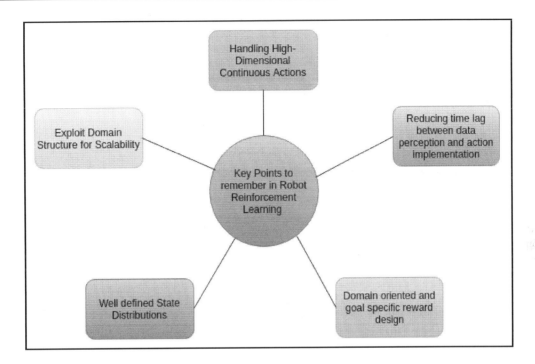

Summary

In this chapter, we covered the current state of reinforcement learning algorithms and the challenges in the field of robotics. We also tried to take a look at each of the challenges in detail. We also learned about the practical challenges and its proposed solutions. Cracking the solution for end-to-end robotics will be the biggest milestone for the AI community. At present, there are challenges with continuous improvements in algorithms and data processing units; however, the day we see robots doing general human tasks is not far off. In case, you want to follow-up some of the researches done in robot reinforcement learning then you would like to start with the options below:

- *"Deep Reinforcement Learning for Robotic Manipulation with Asynchronous Off-Policy Updates"* by Shixiang Gu et al. 2016 (`https://arxiv.org/pdf/1610.00633.pdf`)

- *"Collective Robot Reinforcement Learning with Distributed Asynchronous Guided Policy Search"* by Yahya et al. 2016 (https://arxiv.org/pdf/1610.00673.pdf)

In the next chapter, we will try to cover another interesting domain, that is advertisement technology and how deep reinforcement learning can be used to disrupt it.

12
Deep Reinforcement Learning in Ad Tech

So far in this unit of discussing reinforcement learning application research domains, we saw how reinforcement learning is disrupting the field of robotics, autonomous driving, financial portfolio management, and solving games of extremely high complexity, such as Go. Another important domain which is likely to be disrupted by reinforcement learning is advertisement technology.

Before getting into the details of the problem statement and it's solution based on reinforcement learning, let's understand the challenges, business models, and bidding strategies involved, which will work as a basic prerequisite in understanding the problem that we will try to solve using a reinforcement learning framework. The topics that we will be covering in this chapter are as follows:

- Computational advertising challenges and bidding strategies

- Real-time bidding by reinforcement learning in display advertising

Computational advertising challenges and bidding strategies

Advertising is a mode of conveying information. The core task of computational advertising is to find the best match between a given user in a given context and an advertisement, where the following factors apply:

- **Context/Auctioneer**: A platform visited by a user and that is deemed fit for advertisements, for example:
    - A user using a search engine. Therefore, sponsored advertisements in such a scenario form a good plan.
    - A user reading a web page. Therefore, display advertisements fit such cases.
    - A user watching any video (movie, clips, short videos, and so on). Therefore, short video advertisements are good.
- **Constraints**: The biggest constraint of all for the advertiser is limited budget and limited time period.

The core challenges to meet regarding the preceding goals are as follows:

- Designing markets and exchanges that can facilitate the task and maximize value for all the participating stake holders, which are users, advertisers, and publishers.
- Building infrastructure for this complete end-to-end process:

The relationship between these elements is shown here:

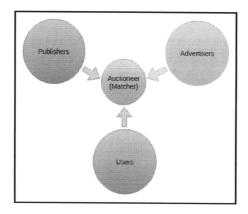

Business models used in advertising

Business models for the advertising platforms consist of different models that govern the metrics of the payable amount that the advertiser has to pay for using the advertising platform. There are different metrics in the computational advertising domain, which are as follows:

- **CPM**: Cost Per Thousand Impressions
  - In this type of model, the advertiser pays a fixed amount per thousand impressions, where impressions can be clicks, views, and so on
- **CPC**: Cost Per Click, **Pay Per Click (PPC)**
  - In this type of online advertising model, the advertiser pays the platform owner for each click action a user makes on the advertisement link
- **CPA**: Cost Per Action / Cost Per Acquisition / **Pay Per Acquisition (PPA)** / Cost Per Conversion
  - In this type of model, the platform owner (for instance, the publisher running the advertisement) takes all the risk and the advertiser pays only for those amount of users whole have been acquired, in other words, who have completed the desired action that can be completed, a sign-up subscription, or made a purchase transaction

Sponsored-search advertisements

Sponsored search plays an important role in online advertising, especially in search engines such as Google, Yahoo, Bing, and so on. These search platforms are some of the biggest platforms for advertisements owing to the enormous size of the audience accessing them daily.

Search-advertisement management

The advertisers place bids for rate per click on certain search queries, which are received by the search engine. Then, the advertisements are displayed as a part of those search query results, and if the user clicks on the advertisement, the advertiser has to pay the amount of the bid.

Adwords

Once all the advertisers place their bids for rate per click on certain search queries, the platforms receive the data, which comprises the set of bids by different advertisers along with the total budget for each advertiser, and the historical data of **click-through-rate (CTR)** for each of those search queries.

The main objective is to select a set of advertisements in response to each query such that the revenue made by the search engine (that is, the auctioneer) is maximized. Just like the revenue maximization of the auctioneer, profit maximization of the advertiser is also important and includes various bidding strategies.

Bidding strategies of advertisers

Bidding strategies for advertisers mainly include budget optimization for the different keywords while making a bid. The key points are discussed as follows:

- Better splitting of budget among different keywords by the advertiser
- Better bidding strategy for profit maximization

Moreover, in this world of online advertisements, the bidding happens in real time. How do you achieve a better real-time bidding strategy leading to profit maximization?

- Autonomous bidding agents
    - These agents will use the historical market data and also interact with the market participants directly, and they model their behavior according to this data and, thereby, help in different decision strategies
- Machine-learning approaches using reinforcement learning
    - A framework of the **Markov Decision Process (MDP)** seen in `Chapter 3`, *Markov Decision Process* where we maximize the expected utility of each state from which the path to the goal state is most optimized by maximizing the expected sum of rewards

Real-time bidding by reinforcement learning in display advertising

Online displays are majorly served through real-time bidding where each impression of the display advertisement is auctioned in real time simultaneously when generated from a user visit. Placing a bid automatically, and in real time, is highly critical for advertisers to maximize their profits. Thus, a learning algorithm needs to be devised that can devise an optimal learning strategy in real time based on historical data, so that dynamic allocation of the budget takes place across different impressions according to immediate and future returns. Here, we will discuss formulating a bid-decision process in terms of a reinforcement learning framework published in *Real-Time Bidding by Reinforcement Learning in Display Advertising* by Cai et. al. 2017.

In this research by Cai et. al., the machine bidding in the context of display advertising is considered, where real-time bidding is a highly challenging task because, in the case of online display advertising, the bidding for the ad impression starts as soon as it is generated by a user visit. Calculating an optimal bid for each ad auction after considering the remaining budget, availability of relevant ad impressions in the future, result of the auction and feedback received, all helps the advertiser to refine the bidding strategy, thereby resulting in better allocation.

Here, researchers have tried to obtain an optimal bidding function that maximizes the key performance indicators of the advertisement campaign, which are mainly total clicks or total revenue. However, this approach mainly works in static bidding cases, where bidding happens where the advertiser is paying a fixed average rate for each of the impressions. In the case of real-time bidding, it's dynamic at impression level, which means that in a platform depending upon the demand of the impression generated the bid value varies.

This research tries to solve the real-time bidding challenge as a sequential decision by using a reinforcement learning framework, where:

- The learning agent will learn from an advertiser's point of view
- The whole advertisement market and all internet users form the environment
- The state space comprises auction information and real-time campaign parameters
- The action is the bid price to be set

Therefore, at each step, the agent representing a bidder for the advertiser observes the state consisting of current campaign parameters, such as budget and time remaining, and the bid request for that particular ad impression. Then, it posts an action; for instance, the bid price is made, the winning results and user feedback will together as as a reward for the action taken and will be used to reinforce the model. The MDP framework has been used along with a Q-network based approach owing to large volume in real-world auctions, which uses neural network as a state-action value function approximator. A basic reinforcement learning framework for bidding is shown as follows:

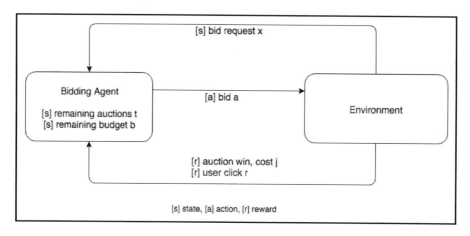

Initially, **budget b** is provided to the agent, and the target here is to acquire as many clicks as possible during the following **auctions t**. The following is the important information considered by the agent:

- The remaining auctions, that is, the remaining auction number $t \in \{0, \cdots, T\}$
- The remaining amount left from the initial allocated budget, namely, the unspent budget $b \in \{0, \cdots, B\}$
- Feature vector x, which represents the bid request

At each episode, each auction is sent to the agent in a sequential manner, and for each of them the agent decides the bid price according to the current information t, b, and x. Thus, the agent decides the appropriate action on the basis of all the key information which is remaining time of the auction, the remaining amount left from the initial allocated budget, and the bid request made.

As shown in the preceding diagram, the agent maintains the remaining auctions *t* and the **remaining budget b**. At each time step, the agent receives a bid request along with the auction $x \in X$ (the feature vector space), and it has to determine the bidding price a.

The market price probability distribution function for a given feature vector *x* is $m(\delta, x)$, where δ is the market price and *m* is its probability. So, if the agent bids at price $a \geq \delta$, then it wins the auction and pays δ, and the remaining budget changes to $b - \delta$. The agent gets nothing from the auction in case it loses. Here, the **predicted CTR (pCTR)** is denoted by $\theta(x)$ if winning the auction is considered as the expected reward. After each auction, the remaining number of auctions is reduced by 1. When $t=0$, that is, there are no remaining auctions left, then the episode ends. As the current episode ends, both the remaining auction number and budget are reset to *T* and *B* respectively.

The following is the pseudo-code of implementation for the preceding reinforcement-learning framework to bid:

```
(In this part of the process: approximation of the optimal value function
V(t, b) is done)

Inputs: probability distribution function of market price that is m(δ),
            average click through rate (CTR) θavg,
            episode length that is number of auctions in an episode T,
            budget B

Output: value function V(t, b)

Steps:
initialize V(0, b) = 0
for t = 1, 2, · · · , T - 1 do
    for b = 0, 1, · · · , B do
        enumerate at,b from 0 to min(δmax, b) and set V (t, b) as per the
following equation:
```

$$V(t,b) \approx max_{0 \leq a < b} \left[\sum_{\delta=0}^{a} m(\delta)\theta_{avg} + \sum_{\delta=0}^{a} m(\delta)V(t-1, b-\delta) + \sum_{\delta=a+1}^{\infty} m(\delta)V(t-1, b) \right]$$

```
    end for
end for

(In this part of the process: as per the converged optimal value function
V(t, b) obtained from the above part, using that value function the action
to bid price is performed)

Input: CTR estimator θ(x),
value function V(t, b),
```

```
current state ($t_c, b_c, x_c$)

Output: optimal bid price $a_c$ in current state

Steps:
calculate the pCTR for the current bid request: $\theta_c = \theta(x_c)$
for δ = 0, 1, · · · , min($\delta_{max}$, $b_c$) do
    if θc + V ($t_c$ − 1, $b_c$ − δ) − V ($t_c$ − 1, $b_c$) ≥ 0 then
        $a_c$ ← δ
    end if
end for
```

Summary

In this chapter, we understood the basic concepts and challenges in the domain of advertising technology. We also learned about the relevant business models, such as CPC, CPM, and CPA, and real-time strategy bidding and why there's a need for an autonomous agent to automate the process. Moreover, we discussed a basic approach to converting the problem state of real-time bidding in online advertising into a reinforcement-learning framework. This is a totally new domain for reinforcement learning to disrupt. Many more exploratory works utilizing reinforcement learning for advertising technology, and their results, are yet to be published.

In the next chapter, we will study how reinforcement learning is being used in the field of computer vision, especially for object detection.

13
Reinforcement Learning in Image Processing

In this chapter, we will cover one of the most famous application domains in the **artificial intelligence** (**AI**) community, computer vision. Applying AI to images and videos has been going on for over two decades now. With better computational power, algorithms such as **convolutional neural networks** (**CNNs**) and its variants have worked fairly well in object detection tasks. Advanced steps have been taken towards automated image captioning, diabetic retinopathy, video object detection, captioning, and a lot more.

Due to its promising results and more generalized approach, applying reinforcement learning to computer vision successfully forms challenging tasks for researchers. We have seen how AlphaGo and AlphaGo Zero have outperformed professional human Go players, where the deep reinforcement learning approach is applied to the image of the game board at each step.

Therefore, here in this chapter we will be covering the most famous domain in computer vision, **object detection**, and how reinforcement learning is trying to do it.

Hierarchical object detection with deep reinforcement learning

In this section, we will try to understand how deep reinforcement learning can be applied for hierarchical object detection as per the framework suggested in *Hierarchical Object Detection with Deep Reinforcement Learning* by Bellver et. al. (2016)(https://arxiv.org/pdf/1611.03718.pdf). This experiment showcases a method to perform hierarchical object detection in images using deep reinforcement learning with the main focus on important parts of the image carrying richer information. The objective here was to train a deep reinforcement learning agent to which an image window is given and the image gets further segregated into five smaller windows and the agent is successfully able to focus its attention on one of the smaller windows.

Now let's consider how we humans look at an image. We always extract information in a sequential manner to understand the content of the image:

- First, we focus on the most important part of the image
- The information provided by the most important part guides us to the next part of the image to focus on
- The preceding steps continue as long as different parts of the image provide some relevant information

In computer vision, images are analyzed at the local scale where we take a small window of some pixel size and we slide the window to scan the whole image. This is how we traditionally approach the tasks of processing and analyzing an image. With this window sliding approach different parts of the image are analyzed independently without relating them to each other. Relating the different image parts can be achieved by hierarchical representation of the image.

In order to obtain a hierarchical representation of the image, firstly, top-down scanning of the image is done sequentially, as before, to focus on different local parts of the image containing relevant information. Using reinforcement learning, the agent is made capable enough to detect an object in the image. The agent firstly analyzes the whole image and then decides upon which part to focus and the agent finally stops after finding the object in the image. In this experiment, an image window is divided into five predefined smaller parts, where four parts represent the four quadrants and one being the central region.

Reinforcement learning is used because the agent can explore the hierarchical representation in a different order and still achieve the goal. This is because its objective would be to maximize the expected sum of rewards with the goal state being finding that part of the image that contains the object.

Related works

Most of the traditional solutions in object detection include window size selection and then sliding the window over the image focusing on different regions. The relationship between the regions was never captured and all the regions were used for computation. Here we will briefly discuss some of the other research done in the field of object detection. A detailed explanation of the following researches in this section is out of the scope of this book but this will give you the basic knowledge of advancements made in the field of object detection.

Region-based convolution neural networks

In earlier models of object classification, CNNs were very slow and computationally expensive. Moreover, being a classification problem success totally depended on the amount of accuracy. Running convolutions in a CNN is done by sliding the window across all the regions at each layer. Thus, more bounding boxes (total number of different regions analyzed by sliding the window) means higher cost of computation.

Region-based convolution neural networks (R-CNN) were the first take on applying selective search approaches to reduce the number of bounding boxes being fed to the classifier. Moreover, selective searches use features of texture, intensity, color, and so on to create possible box locations of the object. Now these boxes can be fed to the CNN model.

Thus, key components of R-CNN include the following:

- Generate probable box regions containing the objects (creating regions of interest)
- Feed these generated box regions to CNN
- Representation output from the CNN is then fed in to a SVM layer to predict the class of each box region
- Separately optimize these box regions by bounding box regression for better localization

Spatial pyramid pooling networks

By removing the focus on unnecessary regions of the image R-CNN was faster than normal CNN but still R-CNN was practically very slow, since the number of regions R-CNN was focusing on was high enough for the overall computation to be still expensive.

Spatial Pooling Pyramid networks (SPP-net) were the first attempt to fix this issue. In SSP-net, the CNN representation for the entire image is calculated only once and that is further used to calculate the CNN representation for each of the box regions generated by the selective search approach. This is done by pooling on that section of the convolution representation corresponding to the box region. The section of convolution representation corresponding to a box region is calculated by projecting the box region on a convolution layer by taking into account the downsampling in intermediate layers.

Spatial pooling is done after the last convolution layer in SPP-net unlike the max pooling in a traditional CNN approach. This spatial pooling layer divides a box region of any size into a fixed number of bins and max pooling is done on each of the bins.

One big disadvantage with SPP-net is that only the fully connected layers of the network can be fine tuned and not the spatial pooling layer where backpropragation doesn't happen.

Fast R-CNN

Firstly, it was Fast R-CNN (proposed by Ross Girshick of Microsoft Research in 2015) that suggested the idea of sharing the convolution outputs among different regions of the image:

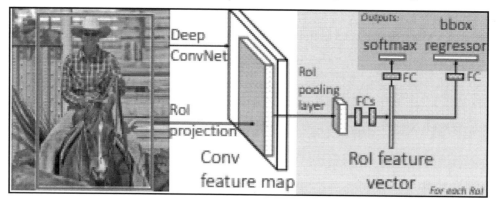

Fast R-CNN(https://arxiv.org/pdf/1504.08083.pdf) by Ross Girshick

In Fast R-CNN, an input image and multiple regions of interest are given as an input to a CNNs. Pooling of RoI is done to obtain a fixed-size feature map and then sent through **fully connected layers (FCs)** to obtain a feature vector. The R-CNN has two output vectors per regions of interest which are as follows:

- Softmax probabilities
- Per-class bounding-box regression offsets

Fast R-CNN fixed the key problem that was associated with SPP-net; the spatial pooling layer not being fine-tuned, therefore, Fast R-CNN provided an end-to-end learning network. Fast R-CNN used simple back-propagation similar to max pooling gradient calculation with the exception of overlapping of pooling regions.

Moreover, Fast R-CNN incorporated the bounding box regression along with the neural network training unlike R-CNN where this box region optimization using bounding box regression was performed separately, which helps in better localization. Therefore, in Fast R-CNNs no separate networks were required for classification and localization. As a result, the overall training time is significantly reduced relative to any other object detection models developed before and better accuracy compared to SPP-net because of end-to-end learning.

Faster R-CNN

Faster R-CNN goes by its name. It's faster than previous Fast R-CNNs. This was achieved by replacing the slowest part of Fast R-CNN, selective search for generation box regions (of interest) with a very small convolution network called **Regional Proposal Network** to perform the same task, generating box regions that are highly probable to contain the object (regions of interest).

Faster R-CNN implements the idea of anchor boxes to handle the variations in aspect ratio and scale of objects. For each region there are three anchor boxes for scale and three aspect ratios. Therefore, for each location we have nine boxes fed to the **Regional Proposal Network (RPN)** predicting the probability of the region being a background or a foreground. The bounding box regression is used to improve the anchor boxes for each such regions. Therefore, RPN outputs the bounding boxes of variable sizes and their class probabilities.

So, RPN gives out bounding boxes of various sizes with the corresponding probabilities of each class with the remaining network being similar to Fast-RCNN. Faster-RCNN is 10 times faster than Fast-RCNN with similar accuracy thereby, making it one of the most accurate object detection models available. The speed analysis of the different variants of R-CNN is shown in the following table:

Type	Test time per image (in seconds)	Speed up
R-CNN	50	1x
Fast R-CNN	2	25x
Faster R-CNN	0.2	250x

You Look Only Once

YOLO learns the class probabilities and the size of bounding boxes by performing regression and thus performs object detection on the input image. YOLO divides an image into SxS grids and each grid predicts N bounding boxes and confidence. This confidence value quantifies the accuracy of the bounding box and the occurrence of the object in the bounding box.

YOLO also predicts the class score of each box for all the classes in training. Thus, the summation of class scores over all boxes in the image also helps in calculating the class probability of the whole image and thus helping to predict the object. Since an image is divided in SxS grids and for each output N bounding boxes are predicted, therefore, $SxSxN$ boxes are being predicted. But since we have confidence scores for boxes and by using a significant threshold, all boxes with low confidence (which don't contain the object) can be removed.

Moreover, YOLO scans the whole image at once without going through the steps of generating regions of interest first and then feeding those regions into CNN in earlier methods. Thus, in YOLO running the image needs to go through a CNN once and results are generated in real time.

Single Shot Detector

A **single shot detector** (SSD) is known for its balance between speed and accuracy. SSD just like YOLO runs a CNN on the input image only once to learn the representations. A small 3x3 convolution kernel is run on this representation to predict the bounding boxes and class probability. In order to handle the scale, SSD predicts bounding boxes after multiple convolutional layers. Since each convolutional layer operates at a different scale, it is able to detect objects of various scales.

The performance metric for Fast R-CNN, Faster R-CNN, YOLO, and SSD are shown in the following graph:

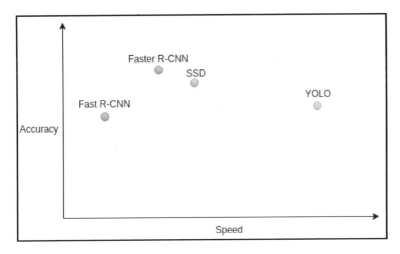

Hierarchical object detection model

Here, we will try to implement the object detection problem in terms of a reinforcement learning framework where a reinforcement learning agent will interact with the image of the environment and with every time step the agent will decide which region to focus attention on with the goal of finding the object in minimal time steps. The problem statement is represented as a **Markov Decision Processes** (**MDP**) framework and its different parameters are discussed as follows:

State

The first part of the state of the agent is defined by the visual features extracted by using two models, which are:

- Image-Zooms model
- Pool45-Crops model

These two variations are explained in the *Model and Training* section that will follow.

The second part of the state of the agent is the memory vector, which captures the actions of the past four time steps the agent took in order to search for the object. At each time step, there are six possible actions (described in the section to follow). Therefore, the memory vector has $4*6 = 24$ dimensions. This memory vector has been found useful to stabilize the search trajectories.

Actions

There are two categories of possible actions as follows:

- Movement actions implying a change in the current observed region
- Terminal action to indicate that the object is detected and that the search has ended

Each movement action can only transfer the attention top-down between regions from a predefined hierarchy. The image gets further segregated into five smaller sub-regions to focus upon. Hence, a hierarchy is built in the five sub-regions (in the following figure) created as:

- Four quarters
- One central overlapping region

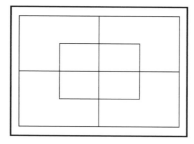

Thus, there are five movement actions, each associated with sub-regions and one terminal action, which is selected to indicate the ending of the search with the object being detected successfully.

Reward

The reward function for the movement actions is represented by the following equation:

$$R_m(s, s') = sign(IoU(b', g) - IoU(b, g))$$

The reward function for the terminal action in represented by the following equation:

$$R_t(s, s') = \begin{cases} +\eta & if IoU(b, g) \geq \tau \\ -\eta & otherwise \end{cases}$$

Here, g is the ground truth, b is the region in the current step, b' is the new region in the next step, and IoU is the intersection over union between the ground truth.

Intersection **over Union (IoU)** is a metric in object detection where you have two overlapping bounding boxes. Firstly, intersection of the boxes is computed, that is, the area of the overlap. Secondly, union of the overlapping boxes is computed, the sum of the areas of the entire boxes minus the area of the overlap. Then dividing the intersection by the union gives you the IoU.

For the movement actions, for a certain state s, a better reward is received by those actions that move towards a region b' with a greater IoU with the ground truth g than the IoU of g with the region b considered at the previous step. Otherwise, the actions are negatively rewarded.

For the terminal action, the reward is positive if the IoU of the current region b with the ground truth is greater than a certain threshold τ, and negative otherwise.

Model and training

Here, a deep Q-network is trained for which two models are used to create a part of state representation of the agent. The two models are as follows:

- ImageZooms model
- Pool45-Crops model

For the Image-Zooms model, each region is resized to 224x224 and fed into VGG-16 through the Pool5 layer to obtain a feature map. For the Pool45-Crops model, the image at full-resolution is fed into VGG-16 through the Pool5 layer. The feature maps extracted from the whole image for all the **regions of interest (ROI)** is pooled.

The two models for feature extraction outputs a feature map of *7x7*, which is fed into the common block (as shown in the following architecture). These feature maps and the memory vector (discussed previously) are fed into the deep Q-network consisting of two fully connected layers of 1024 neurons each. Each fully connected layer has ReLU activation function and is trained with dropout:

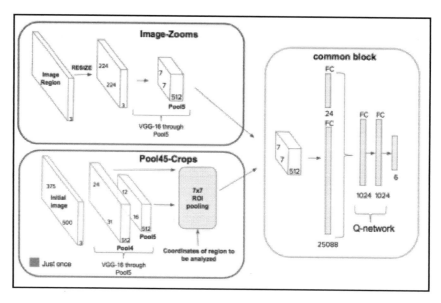

Hierarchical Object Detection Model (architecture) from Hierarchical Object Detection with Deep Reinforcement Learning(https://arxiv.org/pdf/1611.03718.pdf) Bellver et. al. 2016

Training specifics

A deep Q-network is learnt with ϵ-greedy approach, starting with ϵ=1 (full 100% exploration) and decreases until =0.1 (only 10% exploration, 90% exploitation) in steps of 0.1. During exploration random actions are chosen, this is because with better exploration local minima can be avoided and the unknown optimized path to goal state can also be unveiled. Moreover, in order to help the agent learn the terminal action, the agent is forced to take that action each time the current region has a $IoU > \tau$ which in turn accelerates the learning process.

One fact that we detected while training was that we should not impose which object of the image to look at first. At each time step, the agent will focus on the object in the current region with the highest overlap with its ground-truth. This way, it is possible that the target object changes during the top-down exploration.

The weights and bias parameters for the deep Q-network are initialized from a normal distribution and Adam optimizer for loss minimization. A high gamma (discount factor) is used to balance the immediate and future rewards.

This approach of using deep reinforcement learning for object detection showed an approach of top-down exploration of a hierarchy of regions by a learning agent. Thus with appropriate hierarchy the objects can be detected properly in fewer time steps as shown in the results shared in the following diagram:

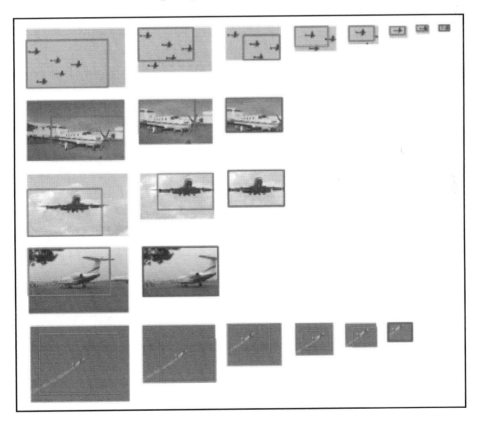

Summary

In this chapter, we went through different state of the art approaches in object detection such as R-CNN, Fast R-CNN, Faster R-CNN, YOLO, SSD, and others. Furthermore, we explored an approach given by *Hierarchical Object Detection with Deep Reinforcement Learning* by Bellver et. al. (2016). As per this approach we learnt how to create an MDP framework for object detection and hierarchically detect objects in a top-bottom exploration approach in minimal time steps. Object detection in an image is one application in computer vision. There are other domains such as object detection in videos, video tagging, and many more where reinforcement learning can create state of the art learning agents.

In the next chapter, we will learn how reinforcement learning can be applied in the domain of NLP (natural language processing).

14
Deep Reinforcement Learning in NLP

Reinforcement learning in **natural language processing** (**NLP**) became a hot topic of research in the artificial intelligence community no more than a year ago. Most of the research publications catering to the use of reinforcement learning in NLP were published in the latter half of 2017.

The biggest reason behind the use of a reinforcement learning framework in any domain is the representation of the environment in the form of state, an exhaustive list of all possible actions in the environment, and a domain-specific reward function to achieve the goal through the most optimized path of actions. Thus, if a system has many possible actions but the correct set of actions is not given, and the objective highly depends on different options (actions) of the system then reinforcement learning framework can model the system better than existing supervised or unsupervised models.

Why use reinforcement learning in NLP ?

- NLP-oriented systems, such as text summarization, dialog generation, question answering, machine translation, and many more, do have a typical reinforcement learning scenario. For example, a dialog system has a reinforcement learning agent that generates responses as per the query received, where the query received can be the signal representing the current state, and it can take a certain action to generate a response for which the agent receives feedback in the form of the reward.
- There are many hidden variables in the form of hidden states and many more; deciding which latent variable to include can also represented as an action associated with some reward.

- Currently, for sequence-to-sequence models, we have a BLEU score (see `Appendix A`, *Further topics in Reinforcement Learning*) that evaluates the error score between the generated language and the actual output, but the BLEU score can only evaluate after the whole predicted language for the input is generated. It cannot evaluate while the generation is going on; therefore, it cannot enhance the process on the go.

As per the active research done till now, reinforcement learning finds an opportunity to disrupt and enhance the results of the following domains in NLP:

- Text summarization
- Question answering
- Dialog generation
- Dialog system
- Knowledge-based QA
- Machine translation
- Text generation

Here we will cover the use of reinforcement learning in text summarization and question answering, which will give you a basic idea of how researchers are reaping the benefits of reinforcement learning in these domains.

Text summarization

Text summarization is the process of automatically generating summarized text of the document test fed as an input by retaining the important information of the document. Text summarization condenses a big set of information in a concise manner; therefore, summaries play an important role in applications related to news/articles, text search, and report generation.

There are two types of summarization algorithms:

- **Extractive summarization**: Creates summaries by copying parts of the text from the input text
- **Abstractive summarization**: Generates new text by rephrasing the text or using new words that were not in the input text

The attention-based encoder decoder model created for machine translation (Bahdanau et al., 2014) is a sequence-to-sequence model and was able to generate abstractive summaries with good performance by achieving good ROUGE score (see `Appendix A`, *Further topics in Reinforcement Learning*). The performance was good on short input sequences and it deteriorated with increase in the length of input text sequence.

On the bigger input sequence and output summary dataset of the CNN/Daily Mail dataset (Hermann et al., 2015), the abstractive summarization model proposed by Nallapati et al. (2016) were applied, where input sequences were up to 800 tokens and summaries were up to 100 tokens. The analysis of this experiment illustrates the problem associated with attention-based encoder-decoder models for larger input sequences was that they often generate abnormal summaries, mostly comprised of repeated phrases. This is because encoder decoder models trained only via a supervised learning approach often suffer from exposure bias, that is, the assumption of ground truth (actual text) being provided at each time step during the training process.

Here, we will discuss the research publication *A Deep Reinforced Model for Abstractive Summarization* by Paulus et. al. (November 2017), which introduces us to a new model for abstractive summarization that achieves powerful results on the CNN/Daily Mail dataset and also on the **New York Times (NYT)** dataset (Sandhaus, 2008).

The proposed model achieves these state-of-the-art results by using a **neural intra-attention model** and a **hybrid learning objective** to tackle the previously mentioned issue of repeating phrases:

- **Neural intra-attention model**: This consists of **intra-temporal attention** in the encoder to record attention weights for each of the input tokens and a **sequential intra-attention model** in the decoder to record the words that have already been generated by the decoder.
- **Hybrid learning objective**: This is a combination of the maximum-likelihood cross-entropy loss (generally used in supervised deep learning frameworks) and rewards obtained from policy gradient reinforcement learning in order to reduce exposure bias. Thus, when standard word prediction using supervised learning combines with the global sequence prediction training of reinforcement learning, the resulting summaries become more readable rather than repeating phrases.

The proposed approach was tested on the CNN/Daily Mail dataset and achieved a 41.16 ROUGE-1 score, which is a significant improvement relative to previous abstractive summarization approaches. Moreover, human evaluation also showed that the resulting summaries were more readable compared to the earlier approaches.

In the next section, we briefly go through the approach to understand how reinforcement learning was used to create the state-of-the-art abstractive summarization model.

Deep reinforced model for Abstractive Summarization

As discussed previously, this approach consists of two important approaches:

- Neural intra-attention model
- Hybrid learning objective

Neural intra-attention model

This section explains the neural intra-attention model on the encoder-decoder network. Here, $x = [x_1, x_2, \ldots \ldots x_n]$ represents the sequence of input (article) tokens, and $y = [y_1, y_2, \ldots \ldots y_m]$ represents the sequence of output (summary) tokens. The encoder part of the network consists of bi-directional LSTM (see `Appendix A`, *Further topics in Reinforcement Learning*). Thus, the input sequence x is read using a bi-directional LSTM which computes the hidden states $h_i^e = [h_i^{e_{fwd}} || h_i^{e_{bwd}}]$ from the embedding vectors of x_i, where $||$ represents concatenation of the vectors.

In the decoder part of the framework, single LSTM is used, which computes the hidden state h_t^d from the embedding vectors of y_t. The initial hidden state at time step zero, that is, h_0^d, is initialized with the last hidden state of the encoder, that is, h_n^e. Therefore, $h_0^d = h_n^e$.

Intra-temporal attention on input sequence while decoding

While decoding, at each time step t, an intra-temporal attention function is used to attend over important parts of the encoded input sequence along with the hidden state of the decoder and previously generated words (during decoding in earlier time steps before t). This approach of attention is used to prevent attending the same parts of the input sequence during decoding at different time steps.

The attention score of the hidden input state h_i^e at the decoding time step t is given by e_{ti}. Therefore, $e_{ti} = f(h_t^d, h_i^e)$, where f is any function returning a scalar value for e_{ti}.

Attention weights are further normalized (shown in the following) in order to penalize those input tokens that have received high attention scores in previous decoding steps. This gives us the new temporal attention score e'_{ti}:

$$e'_{ti} = \begin{cases} e^{e_{ti}} & t = 1 \\ \dfrac{e^{e_{ti}}}{\sum_{j=1}^{t-1} e^{e_{ji}}} & otherwise \end{cases}$$

Finally, the normalized attention score α_{ti}^e is computed across the inputs, which in turn is used to compute the input context vector c_t^e:

$$\alpha_{ti}^e = \frac{e'_{ti}}{\sum_{j=1}^{n} e'_{tj}}$$

$$c_t^e = \sum_{i=1}^{n} \alpha_{ti}^e h_i^e$$

Intra-decoder attention

Even an intra-temporal attention function ensures that, during each decoding step, different parts of the encoded input are attended but the decoder can still generate repeated phrases during long sequences. In order to prevent that, information from the previously decoded sequence can also be fed into the decoder. Information from the previous decoding steps will help the model to avoid repetition of the same information and lead to structured prediction.

In order to accomplish this approach to incorporate the information from previous decoding steps, an intra-decoder attention is applied. This approach is not used in current encoder-decoder models for abstractive summarization. For each time step t while decoding, new decoder context vector c_t^d is computed. Since the generated sequence for the first time step while decoding would be empty, therefore the initial decoder context vector for time step 1, that is, c_1^d is set to a vector of zeros.

For $t>1$, the temporal attention score $e_{tt'}^d$, the normalized attention score $\alpha_{tt'}^e$, and the decoder context vector c_t^d are computed as follows:

$$e_{tt'}^d = f(h_t^d, h_{t'}^d)$$

$$\alpha_{tt'}^d = \frac{e^{e_{tt'}^d}}{\sum_{j=1}^{t-1} e^{e_{tj}^d}}$$

$$c_t^e = \sum_{i=1}^{n} \alpha_{ti}^e h_i^e$$

The following figure shows the use of two context vectors C (the green one being the context encoder vector and the blue one being the context decoder vector) and the current hidden state H of the decoder to generate a new word of the output sequence:

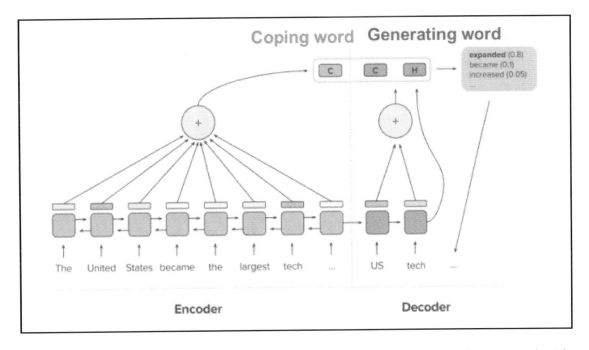

Intra-temporal attention and intra-decoder attention, published in A Deep Reinforced Model for Abstractive Summarization (https://arxiv.org/pdf/1705.04304.pdf) by Paulus et. al. 2017

Token generation and pointer

While deciding the output sequence token, the decoder decides either to use a softmax layer for token generation or to use a pointer mechanism to point at the rare important token in the input and copy that as an output sequence token. At each decoding step, a switch function is used to decide whether to use token generation or to use point to copy an input token. u_t is defined as a binary value, which is equal to 1 if the pointer mechanism is used, otherwise 0. Therefore, the probability of y_t as an output token is given by the following:

$$p(y_t) = p(u_t = 1)p(y_t | u_t = 1) + p(u_t = 0)p(y_t | u_t = 0)$$

Here, the token generation layer creates the following probability distribution:

$$p(y_t | u_t = 0) = softmax(W_{out}[h_t^d][c_t^e][c_t^d] + b_{out}),$$

Here, W_{out} and b_{out} are the weight and bias parameter of the decoder network connecting to the output node, and the pointer mechanism generates the following probability distribution to copy the input token x_i:

$$p(y_t = x_i | u_t = 1) = \alpha_{ti}^e$$

The probability of using a pointer mechanism, that is, $p(u_t = 1)$, is given by the following:

$$p(u_t = 1) = \sigma(W_u[h_t^d][c_t^e][c_t^d] + b_u)$$

Here, σ is the sigmoid activation function.

Hybrid learning objective

In this section, the previously proposed framework of a neural intra-attention model on an encoder decoder network is trained using the combination of supervised learning and reinforcement learning.

Supervised learning with teacher forcing

The teacher forcing algorithm (by Williams et. al., 1989) is the most widely used method to train a decoder RNN for sequence generation. At each time step during decoding, the teacher forcing algorithm minimizes the maximum-likelihood loss. $y^* = [y_1^*, y_2^*, \ldots \ldots y_m^*]$ is defined as the ground truth output sequence for a given input sequence x. Then, the maximum likelihood objective of supervised learning using the teacher forcing algorithm would be to minimize the loss function, given by the following:

$$L_{ml} = -\sum_{t=1}^{n'} log\ p(y_t^* | y_1^*, y_2^*, \ldots, y_{t-1}^*, x)$$

But such an objective of minimizing L_{ml} doesn't always generate the best results. The two main reasons behind this issue are as follows:

- **Exposure bias**: While training, the neural network has knowledge of the ground truth sequence up to the next token, but that's not the case while testing.
- **Multiple output candidates (that is, multiple potentially valid summaries)**: There are more ways to arrange tokens to generate multiple summaries. The maximum likelihood objective does not take this possibility into account.

Policy learning

The idea here is to learn a policy which maximizes a metric instead of minimizing the loss obtained from maximum likelihood objective. For this, a reinforcement learning approach is used, where a self-critical policy gradient algorithm is used for training. For this training, two separate output sequences are generated at each training iteration:

- y^s is obtained by sampling from the probability distribution of $p(y_t^s | y_1^s, y_2^s, \ldots, y_{t-1}^s, x)$ at each decoding time step
- $\hat{y}$ is the baseline output obtained by maximizing the output probability distribution at each time step

Thus, the reward function r can be any evaluation metric of our choice and the objective is to minimize the following loss:

$$L_{rl} = (r(\hat{y}) - r(y^s)) \sum_{t=1}^{n'} \log p(y_t^s | y_1^s, y_2^s, \ldots, y_{t-1}^s, x)$$

Minimizing L_{rl} is equivalent to minimizing L_{ml} of the sampled sequence y^s. Therefore, to minimize L_{rl}, $r(y^s)$, the reward of the output sequence needs to be increased and become higher than the reward of baseline $\hat{y}$, thereby increasing the expected reward.

Thus, a reinforcement learning framework is used to learn a policy that maximizes a specific discrete metric. The reinforcement learning framework is summarized as follows:

- **Action**: $u_t \in$ [generate(0), copy(1)] and word y_t^s
- **State**: Hidden states of encoder and previous outputs
- **Reward**: ROUGE score or any other evaluation metric

Mixed training objective function

Since the maximum likelihood objective computes the probability of the next token based on the previously generated token and a reward metric such as ROUGE helps in the measurement of human readability through perplexity, both are used to derive a mixed learning objective function as follows:

$$L_{mixed} = \gamma L_{rl} + (1 - \gamma)L_{ml}$$

Here, γ is the scaling factor to balance the difference in magnitude of L_{rl} and L_{ml}.

Text question answering

Question answering is the task where a document context is provided along with a question whose answer is present within the given document context. Existing models for question answering used to optimize the cross-entropy loss, which used to encourage the exact answers and penalize other probable answers that are equally accurate as the exact answer. These existing question answering models (state of the art dynamic coattention network by Xiong et. al. 2017) are trained to output exact answer spans from the document context for the question asked. The start and end position of the actual ground truth answer is used as the target for this supervised learning approach. Thus, this supervised model uses cross-entropy loss over both the positions and the objective is to minimize this overall loss over both the positions.

As we can see, the optimization is done by using the positions and evaluation is done by using the textual content of the answer. Thus, there is a disconnect between the optimization and evaluation approaches. Due to this disconnect, many of the textually similar answers get penalized as if they are incorrect answers because of their presence in other positions, unlike the position of the ground truth answer.

In order to address this issue, Xiong et. al. published their research *DCN+: Mixed Objective and Deep Residual Coattention for Question Answering,* where they proposed to use a mixed objective function which is a combination of cross-entropy loss and self-critical policy learning. This mixed objective uses a reward obtained from the overlapping of words to solve the issue of disconnect between the evaluation and optimization in existing models.

The proposed new framework performs better for long questions that require capturing long-term dependencies and was able to achieve a powerful result of 75.1% of exact match accuracy and 83.1% of F1-score while the ensemble model obtains 78.9% exact match accuracy and 86.0% F1-score.

Thus the approach of mixed objective provides two benefits:

- The reinforcement learning objective also encourages textually similar answers
- Cross-entropy helps policy learning by encouraging more correct roll-out trajectories

Apart from the mixed training objective, improvements in the existing dynamic coattention network (by Xiong et al. 2017) were done by using a deep residual coattention encoder to build better representations of the input.

Some examples from the **Stanford Question Answering Dataset (SQuAD)** (by Rajpurkar et al.) are as follows:

```
Context/Passage 1:
Nikola Tesla (Serbian Cyrillic: Никола Тесла; 10 July 1856 — 7 January 1943)
was a Serbian American inventor, electrical engineer, mechanical engineer,
physicist, and futurist best known for his contributions to the design of
the modern alternating current (AC) electricity supply system.
```

Questions and Answers:
In what year was Nikola Tesla born?
Ground Truth Answer: 1856

What was Nikola Tesla's ethnicity?
Ground Truth Answer: Serbian

What does AC stand for?
Ground Truth Answer: alternating current

Context/Passage 2:
Tesla went on to pursue his ideas of wireless lighting and electricity distribution in his high-voltage, high-frequency power experiments in New York and Colorado Springs, and made early (1893) pronouncements on the possibility of wireless communication with his devices. He tried to put these ideas to practical use in an ill-fated attempt at intercontinental wireless transmission, his unfinished Wardenclyffe Tower project. In his lab he also conducted a range of experiments with mechanical oscillators/generators, electrical discharge tubes, and early X-ray imaging. He also built a wireless controlled boat, one of the first ever exhibited.

Questions and Answers:
What were some of Tesla's experiments?
Ground Truth Answer: mechanical oscillators/generators, electrical discharge tubes, and early X-ray imaging

Other than New York where did Tesla conduct experiments?
Ground Truth Answer: Colorado Springs

The existing state-of-the-art **dynamic coattention network (DCN)** takes in the context/passage and the question as two different input sequences and outputs the start and end positions of the answer span in the context fed as input. A brief overview of DCN is given in the following diagram:

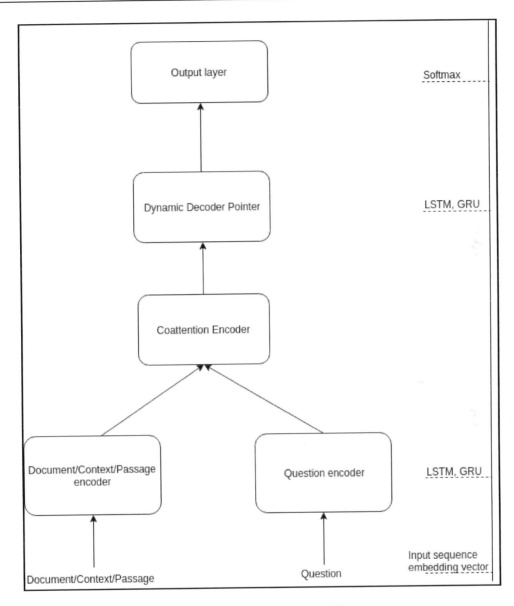

Dynamic coattention network (by Xiong et al. 2017)

In the next section, we will briefly go through the approach to understand how reinforcement learning was used to create the state-of-the-art question answering model.

Mixed objective and deep residual coattention for Question Answering

The framework proposed in this research is based on the DCN model (see the preceding diagram), which consists of a coattention encoder and dynamic decoder pointer. The encoder encodes the question and document context separately and then forms a collaborative representation of the both through coattention followed by the decoder outputting the start and end position estimate as per the coattention.

In the new framework of DCN+, two new changes are introduced to the original DCN framework. They are as follows:

- Adding a deep residual coattention encoder
- Mixed training objective function which is the combination of the maximum likelihood cross-entropy loss function and reward function from reinforcement learning

Deep residual coattention encoder

Since the original DCN has only one single-layer coattention encoder, the ability to form complex representations of the input sequence is also limited. Thus, two modifications are done to the coattention encoder. They are as follows:

- Modifying the coattention encoder by stacking many coattention layers so that the network is able to create better complex representation
- Merging all the coattnetion outputs from each layer to reduce the signal path length:

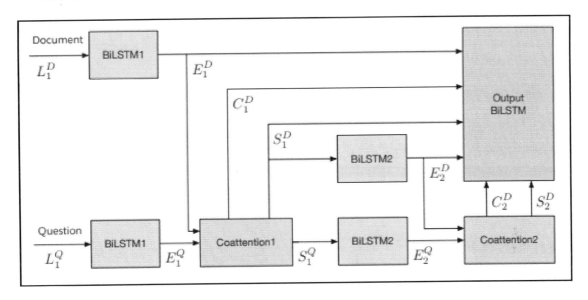

Deep residual coattention encoder, published in DCN+: Mixed Objective and Deep Residual Coattention for Question Answering(https://arxiv.org/pdf/1711.00106.pdf) by Xiong et. al

Mixed objective using self-critical policy learning

A DCN creates a probability distribution on the start position of the answer and a separate probability distribution on the end position of the answer. At each decoding time step, the model aggregates the cross-entropy loss for each position. The question answering task comprises of two evaluation metrics. They are as follows:

- **Exact match**: A binary value indicating that the answer span output by the model has an exact string match with the ground truth answer span
- **F1-score**: A value quantifying the degree of overlapping of words between the predicted answer span by the model and the ground truth answer span

As per the original DCN framework, the objective function and evaluation metric are disconnected, owing to which heavy encouragement is given to the exact matches. Say, for example, there are two answer spans A and B, and neither of them match the ground truth answer spans but A has an exact string match while B has no string match. Then, in this case, the old objective approach of only cross-entropy loss will penalize both A and B equally, despite A being a correct output as per the previous metrics of exact match and F1-score.

If we examine the F1-score, then the metric of A shows the word overlapping in span A with the ground truth answer span but that's not the case with answer B. Therefore, the F1-score is used as a reward function with a self-critical policy gradient algorithm for training.

Summary

In this chapter, we learned how reinforcement learning can disrupt the domain of NLP. We studied the reasons behind the use of reinforcement learning in NLP. We covered two big application domains in NLP, that is, text summarization and question answering, and understood the basics of how a reinforcement learning framework was implemented in the existing models to obtain state-of-the-art results. There are other application domains in NLP where reinforcement learning has been implemented, such as dialog generation and machine translation (discussing them is out of the scope of this book).

This brings us to the end of this amazing journey of deep reinforcement learning. We started with the basics by understanding the concepts, then implemented those concepts using TensorFlow and OpenAI Gym, and went through cool research areas where deep reinforcement learning is being implemented at the core level. I hope the journey was interesting and we were able to build the best foundation possible.

Further topics in Reinforcement Learning

In this appendix, we will cover an introductory overview of some of the topics which were out of the scope of this book. But we will mention them in brief and end these topics with external links for you to explore further. This book as has already covered most of the advanced topics in deep reinforcement learning theory as well as active research domains.

Continuous action space algorithms

There are many continuous action space algorithms in deep reinforcement learning topology. Some of them, which we covered earlier in Chapter 4, *Policy Gradients*, were mainly stochastic policy gradients and stochastic actor-critic algorithms. Stochastic policy gradients were associated with many problems such as difficulty in choosing step size owing to the non-stationary data due to continuous change in observation and reward distribution, where a bad step would adversely affect the learning of the policy network parameters. Therefore, there was a need for an approach that can restrict this policy search space and avoid bad steps while training the policy network parameters.

Here, we will try to cover some of the advanced continuous action space algorithms:

- Trust region policy optimization
- Deterministic policy gradients

Trust region policy optimization

Trust region policy optimization (TRPO) is an iterative approach for optimizing policies. TRPO optimizes large nonlinear policies. TRPO restricts the policy search space by applying constraints on the output policy distributions. In order to do this, KL divergence loss function ($D_{KL}^{max}(\theta_{old}, \theta)$) is used on the policy network parameters to penalize these parameters. This KL divergence constraint between the new and the old policy is called the trust region constraint. As a result of this constraint large scale changes don't occur in the policy distribution, thereby resulting in early convergence of the policy network.

TRPO was published by Schulman et. al. 2017 in the research publication named *Trust Region Policy Optimization* (https://arxiv.org/pdf/1502.05477.pdf). Here they have mention the experiments demonstrating the robust performance of TRPO on different tasks such as learning simulated robotic swimming, playing Atari games, and many more. In order to study TRPO in detail, please follow the arXiv link of the publication: https://arxiv.org/pdf/1502.05477.pdf.

Deterministic policy gradients

Deterministic policy gradients was proposed by Silver et. al. in the publication named *Deterministic Policy Gradient Algorithms* (http://proceedings.mlr.press/v32/silver14.pdf). In continuous action spaces, policy improvement with greedy approach becomes difficult and requires global optimization. Therefore, it is better and tractable to update the policy network parameters in the direction of the gradient of the Q function, as follows:

$$\theta^{k+1} = \theta^k + \alpha E[\nabla_\theta Q(s, \mu_\theta(s))]$$

where, $\mu_\theta(s)$ is the deterministic policy, α is the learning rate and θ representing the policy network parameters. By applying the chain rule, the policy improvement can be shown as follows:

$$\theta^{k+1} = \theta^k + \alpha E[\nabla_\theta \mu_\theta(s) \nabla_a Q(s, \mu_\theta(s))]$$

The preceding update rule can be incorporated into a policy networks where the parameters are updated using stochastic gradient ascent. This can be realized as a deterministic actor-critic method where the critic estimates the action-value function while the actor derives its gradients from the critic to update its parameters. As mentioned in *Deterministic Policy Gradient Algorithms* (`http://proceedings.mlr.press/v32/silver14.pdf`) by Silver et. al., post experimentation, they were able to successfully conclude that the deterministic policy gradients are more efficient than their stochastic counterparts. Moreover, deterministic actor-critic outperformed its stochastic counterpart by a significant margin. A detailed explanation of this topic is out of the scope of this book. So please go to the research publication link mentioned previously.

Scoring mechanism in sequential models in NLP

Two scoring mechanisms were used to evaluate the approaches mentioned in `Chapter 14`, *Deep Reinforcement Learning in NLP*, as follows:

BLEU

One of the biggest challenges in sequential models in NLP used in machine translation, text summarization, image captioning, and much more is an adequate metric for evaluation.

Suppose your use case is machine translation; you have a German phrase and there are multiple English translations of it. All of them look equally good. So, how do you evaluate a machine translation system if there are multiple equally good answers? This is unlike image recognition, where the target has only one right answer and not multiple, equally good right answers.

For example:

- **German sentence**: *Die Katze ist auf der Matte*

A multiple reference human-generated translation of the preceding German sentence is as follows:

- *The cat is on the mat*
- *There is a cat on the mat*

If the target is just one right answer, the accuracy measurement is easy, but if there are multiple equally correct possibilities, then how is the accuracy in such a case measured? In this section, we will study BLEU score, which is an evaluation metric to measure accuracy in such cases of multiple equally correct answers.

What is BLEU score and what does it do?

BLEU score was published by Papineni et. al. 2002 in their research publication named *BLEU: a Method for Automatic Evaluation of Machine Translation* (https://www.aclweb.org/anthology/P02-1040.pdf). BLEU stands for Bi-Lingual Evaluation Understudy. For a given machine-generated output (say translation in the case of machine translation or summary in the case of text summarization), the score measures the goodness of the output, that is, how much close the machine-generated output is to any of the possible human-generated references (possible actual outputs). Thus, the closer the output text is to any human-generated reference, the higher will be the BLEU score.

The motivation behind BLEU score was to devise a metric that can evaluate machine-generated text with respect to human-generated references just like human evaluators. The intuition behind BLEU score is that it considers the machine-generated output and explores if these words exist in at least one of the multiple human-generated references.

Let's consider the following example:

- **Input German text**: *Der Hund ist unter der Decke*

Say we have two human-generated references which are as follows:

- **Reference 1**: *The dog is under the blanket*
- **Reference 2**: *There is a dog under the blanket*

And say our machine translation generated a terrible output, which is *"the the the the the the"*

Thus, the precision is given by the following formula:

$$Precision = \frac{total\ number\ of\ overlapping\ words}{total\ number\ of\ words\ in\ the\ machine\ generated\ output}$$

As such, the following applies:

$$precision = \frac{6}{6} = 1.0$$

Since *the* appears six times in the output and each *the* appears in at least one of the reference texts, precision is 1.0. The issue arises because of the basic definition of precision, which is defined as the fraction of the predicted output that appears in the actual output (reference). Thus, *the* occurring in the predicted output is the only text, and since it appears in the references, the resulting precision is 1.0.

Therefore, the definition of precision is modified to get a modified formula where a clip count is put. Here, clip count is the maximum number of times a word appears in any of the references. Thus, modified precision is defined as the maximum number of times a word appears in any of the references divided by the total number of appearances of that word in the machine-generated output.

For the preceding example, the modified precision would be given as:

$$modified\ precision = \frac{2}{6} = 0.33$$

Till now, we have considered each word in isolated form, that is, in the form of a unigram. In BLEU score, you also want to look at words in pairs and not just in isolation. Let's try to calculate the BLEU score with the bi-gram approach, where bi-gram means a pair of words appearing next to each other.

Let's consider the following example:

- **Input German text**: *Der Hund ist unter der Decke*

Say we have two human-generated references, which are as follows:

- **Reference 1**: *The dog is under the blanket*
- **Reference 2**: *There is a dog under the blanket*

Machine-generated output: *The dog the dog the dog under the blanket*

Bi-grams in the machine-generated output	Count	Count$_{clip}$ (maximum occurrences of the bi-gram in any one of the references)
the dog	3	1
dog the	2	0
dog under	1	0
under the	1	1
the blanket	1	1

Therefore, the modified bi-gram precision would be the ratio of the sum of bi-gram *count$_{clips}$* and the sum of bi-gram counts, that is:

$$modified\ precision = \frac{3}{8} = 0.375$$

Thus, we can create the following precision formulae for uni-grams, bi-grams, and n-grams as follows:

- p_1 = precision for uni-grams, where:

$$p_1 = \frac{\sum_{unigram\ \epsilon\ \hat{y}} Count_{clip}(unigram)}{\sum_{unigram\ \epsilon\ \hat{y}} Count(unigram)}$$

- p_2 = precision for bi-grams, where:

$$p_2 = \frac{\sum_{bigram\ \epsilon\ \hat{y}} Count_{clip}(bigram)}{\sum_{bigram\ \epsilon\ \hat{y}} Count(bigram)}$$

- p_n = precision for n-grams, where:

$$p_n = \frac{\sum_{n-gram\ \epsilon\ \hat{y}} Count_{clip}(n-gram)}{\sum_{n-gram\ \epsilon\ \hat{y}} Count(n-gram)}$$

The modified precisions calculated on uni-grams, bi-grams, or even any n-grams allow you to measure the degree to which the machine-generated output text is similar to the human-generated references. If the machine-generated text is exactly similar to any one of the human-generated references then:

$$p_1 = p_2 = \ldots\ldots = p_n = 1.0$$

Let's put all the p_i scores together to calculate the final BLEU score for the machine-generated output. Since, p_n is the BLEU score on n-grams only (that is, modified precision on n-grams), the combined BLEU score where $n_{max} = N$ is given by the following:

$$BP \times e^{\left[\frac{1}{N} \sum_1^N p_n\right]}$$

BP is called brevity penalty. This penalty comes into the picture if the machine-generated output is very short. This is because in case of short output sequence most of the words occurring in that have a very high chance of appearing in the human-generated references. Thus, brevity penalty acts as an adjustment factor which penalises the machine-generated text when it's shorter than the shortest human-generated output reference for that input.

Brevity penalty (BP) is given by the following formula:

$$BP = \begin{cases} 1 & if, len(MO) > s_{len}(REF) \\ e^{\left(1 - \frac{len(MO)}{s_{len}(REF)}\right)} & otherwise \end{cases}$$

where:

len(MO) = length of the machine-generated output

s_{len}*(REF)* = length of the shortest human-generated reference output

For more details, please check the publication on BLEU score by Papineni et. al. 2002 (https://www.aclweb.org/anthology/P02-1040.pdf).

ROUGE

ROUGE stands for Recall Oriented Understudy for Gisting Evaluation. It is also a metric for evaluating sequential models in NLP especially automatic text summarization and machine translation. ROUGE was proposed by CY Lin in the research publication named *ROUGE: A Package for Automatic Evaluation of Summaries* (`http://www.aclweb.org/anthology/W04-1013`) in 2004.

ROUGE also works by comparing the machine-generated output(automatic summaries or translation) against a set of human-generated references.

Let's consider the following example:

- **Machine-generated output**: *the dog was found under the bed*
- **Human-generated reference**: *the dog was under the bed*

Therefore, precision and recall in the context of ROUGE is shown as follows:

$$Recall = \frac{Total\ overlapping\ words}{Total\ words\ in\ human\ generated\ reference}$$

Thus, recall = 6/6 = 1.0.

If recall is 1.0, it means that all the words in the human-generated reference is captured by the machine-generated output. There can be a case that machine-generated output might be extremely long. Therefore, while calculating recall, the long machine-generated output has a high chance to cover most of the human-generated reference words. As a result, precision comes to the rescue, which is computed as shown as follows:

$$Precision = \frac{Total\ overlapping\ words}{Total\ words\ in\ machine\ generated\ output}$$

Thus, precision (for the preceding example) = 6/7 = 0.86

Now, if the machine-generated output had been *the big black dog was found under the big round bed*, then,

$$Recall = \frac{6}{6} = 1.0 \quad Precision = \frac{6}{11}$$

This shows that the machine-generated output isn't appropriate since it contains a good amount of unnecessary words. Therefore, we can easily figure out that only recall isn't sufficient, and as a result both recall and precision should be used together for evaluation. Thus, F1-score which is calculated as the harmonic mean of recall and precision, as shown as follows is a good evaluation metric in such cases:

$$F1 - score = \frac{2}{\frac{1}{Recall} + \frac{1}{Precision}}$$

- ROUGE-1 refers to the overlap of unigrams between the machine-generated output and human-generated references
- ROUGE-2 refers to the overlap of bi-grams between the machine-generated output and human-generated references

Let's understand more about ROUGE-2 with the following example:

- **Machine-generated output**: *the dog was found under the bed*
- **Human-generated reference**: *the dog was under the bed*

Bigrams of the machine-generated output that is *the dog was found under the bed*:

"the cat"

"cat was"

"was found"

"found under"

"under the"

"the bed"

Bigrams of the human-generated reference that is *the dog was under the bed*:

"the dog"

"dog was"

"was under"

"under the"

"the bed"

Therefore:

$$ROUGE-2_{Recall} = \frac{Total\ number\ of\ overlapping\ bi-grams}{total\ number\ of\ bi-grams\ in\ human\ generated\ reference} = \frac{4}{5} = 0.8$$

$$ROUGE-2_{Precision} = \frac{Total\ number\ of\ overlapping\ bi-grams}{total\ number\ of\ bi-grams\ in\ machine\ generated\ output} = \frac{4}{6} = 0.67$$

Thus, ROUGE-2$_{Precision}$ shows that 67% of the bi-grams generated by the machine overlap with the human-generated reference.

This appendix covered the basic overview of ROUGE scoring in sequential models in NLP. For further details on ROUGE-N, ROUGE-L and ROUGE-S please go through the research publication of *ROUGE: A Package for Automatic Evaluation of Summaries* (http://www.aclweb.org/anthology/W04-1013) by CY Lin.

Summary

As a part of appendix, we covered a basic overview of continuous action space algorithms of the deep reinforcement learning topology, where we covered trust region policy optimization and deterministic policy gradients in brief. We also learned about the BLEU and ROUGE scores being actively used for evaluation in NLP-based sequential models.

Finally, I would like to say that deep reinforcement learning is still a new topic as tons of more algorithms will be developed. But the most important thing that will help you to understand and explore those yet-to-be-discovered future algorithms will be the strong hold on the basics that this book has covered.

Other Books You May Enjoy

If you enjoyed this book, you may be interested in these other books by Packt:

Deep Learning with TensorFlow - Second Edition
Giancarlo Zaccone, Md. Rezaul Karim

ISBN: 978-1-78883-110-9

- Apply deep machine intelligence and GPU computing with TensorFlow v1.7
- Access public datasets and use TensorFlow to load, process, and transform the data
- Discover how to use the high-level TensorFlow API to build more powerful applications
- Use deep learning for scalable object detection and mobile computing
- Train machines quickly to learn from data by exploring reinforcement learning techniques
- Explore active areas of deep learning research and applications

Predictive Analytics with TensorFlow
Md. Rezaul Karim

ISBN: 978-1-78839-892-3

- Get a solid and theoretical understanding of linear algebra, statistics, and probability for predictive modeling
- Develop predictive models using classification, regression, and clustering algorithms
- Develop predictive models for NLP
- Learn how to use reinforcement learning for predictive analytics
- Factorization Machines for advanced recommendation systems
- Get a hands-on understanding of deep learning architectures for advanced predictive analytics
- Learn how to use deep Neural Networks for predictive analytics
- See how to use recurrent Neural Networks for predictive analytics
- Convolutional Neural Networks for emotion recognition, image classification, and sentiment analysis

Leave a review - let other readers know what you think

Please share your thoughts on this book with others by leaving a review on the site that you bought it from. If you purchased the book from Amazon, please leave us an honest review on this book's Amazon page. This is vital so that other potential readers can see and use your unbiased opinion to make purchasing decisions, we can understand what our customers think about our products, and our authors can see your feedback on the title that they have worked with Packt to create. It will only take a few minutes of your time, but is valuable to other potential customers, our authors, and Packt. Thank you!

Index

Monte Carlo Tree Search (MCTS) 168, 213, 216
Monte Carlo tree search algorithm
   about 168, 170
   game tree 168
   minimax algorithm 168
mountain car 134

N

neural intra-attention model
   about 287, 288
   intra-decoder attention 289, 290
   intra-temporal attention, on input sequence 288
   mixed training objective function 294
   pointer 291, 292
   token generation 291, 292
neural network model
   about 29, 30, 31, 32
   convolutional neural network (CNN) 39, 40, 42, 43
   recurrent neural networks (RNNs) 33, 34, 35, 36
neural networks, AlphaGo
   policy network 212
   value network 212
next state 141

O

off-policy learning 132
on-policy learning 132
online case-based planning
   about 197
   execution 199
   expansion 199
OpenAI Gym environment
   about 65, 66
   reference 64
   used, for programming agent 67
OpenAI Gym service 59
OpenAI Gym
   about 53, 58
   downloading 64
   gym open-source library 59
   installing 64
   reference 59
optimality criteria, reinforcement learning

policy model 51
value function 50

P

Partially observable Markov decision processes
   about 94
   state estimation 95
   value iteration 96
Pay Per Acquisition (PPA) 267
Pay Per Click (PPC) 267
policy gradient theorem 109, 110
policy gradients
   about 114
   actor-critic algorithms 115
   agent learning pong 118, 119
   Monte Carlo policy gradient 114
   vanilla policy gradient 117
policy iteration 94
policy objective functions 108
policy optimization method
   about 104
   advantages 105
   components 104
   disadvantages 105
pooling layer 42
proposed framework, for autonomous driving
   about 231, 233
   planning 235, 236
   recurrent temporal aggregation 234
   spatial aggregation 233

Q

Q-learning
   about 132
   approach, to reinforcement learning 51, 52
   exploitation dilemma 134
   exploration dilemma 134
   mountain car issues, in OpenAI gym 134, 136, 139
   reinforcement learning agent, programming 67
Q-Network
   using, for real-world applications 73, 77
question answering task 294, 295

R

real-time bidding, by reinforcement learning
 in display advertising 269, 271
real-time strategy (RTS) gaming
 about 195
 drawbacks 199
Recall Oriented Understudy for Gisting Evaluation
 (ROUGE) 308
receptive field 39
rectified linear unit function 17, 18
recurrent neural networks (RNNs) 33, 34, 35, 36,
 227
recurrent temporal aggregation 234
Region-based convolution neural networks (R-
 CNN) 275
Regional Proposal Network 277
reinforcement learning, in robotics
 about 252, 253
 applications 255
 challenges 255, 256
 high dimensionality problem 256
 model uncertainty issue 258
 open questions 260, 261
 practical challenges 262
 real-world challenges 257, 258
reinforcement learning
 about 7, 47, 48, 127, 130, 197, 200, 202
 actions 49
 agent 49
 consideration 230, 231
 environment 49
 episode 49
 evolution 253, 254, 255
 for autonomous driving 227
 in RTS gaming 200
 online case-based planning 197
 optimality criteria 50
 pioneers 59, 60
 rewards 49
 SAR triple 49
 state 49
reward 141

S

same padding 42
SARSA algorithm
 about 171
 for mountain car issues, in OpenAI gym 172,
  173, 175
scoring mechanisms, NLP
 BLEU 303
 ROUGE 308
search-advertisement management 267
sensor fusion 233
sequence of rewards, Markov decision process
 infinite horizons 84
 utility of sequences 85, 86
sequential intra-attention model 287
sigmoid function 13, 14, 15
single shot detector (SSD) 279
softmax function 16
spatial aggregation
 about 233
 sensor fusion 233
 spatial features 233, 234
spatial features 233, 234
Spatial Pooling Pyramid networks (SPP-net) 276
sponsored-search advertisements 267
Stanford Question Answering Dataset (SQuAD)
 295
state 141
State–Action–Reward–State–Action (SARSA) 171
stochastic environment 129
stochastic policy
 example 106
 need for 105
stride 42
summarization algorithms
 abstractive summarization 286
 extractive summarization 286
Supervised learning 128
supervised learning
 about 9
 in neural networks 8

Made in the USA
San Bernardino, CA
30 July 2018